KILL SHAKESPEARE
The Tide of Blood

CREATED AND WRITTEN BY
Conor McCreery
and
Anthony Del Col

ART BY
Andy Belanger

COLORS BY
Shari Chankhamma

LETTERING BY
Chris Mowry

ORIGINAL SERIES EDITS BY
Tom Waltz

COLLECTION COVER BY
Simon Davis

COLLECTION DESIGN BY
Chris Mowry

COLLECTION EDITS BY
Justin Eisinger
& Alonzo Simon

The Story So Far:

It is three months since the armies of Richard III and Lady Macbeth were defeated on the fields of Shrewsbury by Juliet Capulet's Prodigal rebellion and the appearance of the Wizard-God William Shakespeare.

The Prodigal rebels have begun the process of building a new nation led by a newly-formed Council of Thirty-Seven but find themselves facing threats from Titus' army massing at their border.

With Shakespeare still missing Hamlet, Juliet, Othello, Romeo, and the rest of the people of Delphos find their position as precarious as ever...

The Cast:

HAMLET
The Shadow King of prophesy, Hamlet succeeded in bringing Shakespeare back from his self-imposed exile. Now in love with Juliet, he seeks to build a new life for himself away from his bloody past in Denmark.

JULIET
The leader of the Prodigal movement, Juliet spearheaded the victory over Lady Macbeth and Richard III's forces at the battle of Shrewsbury. Having reclaimed the heart that once belonged to Romeo she has found love again in the arms of Hamlet.

ROMEO
A former member of the Shadow Hunters, Romeo had sworn to kill the Shadow King in Shakespeare's name, but Romeo's life was forever altered when Hamlet returned Shakespeare to the people. A new recruit of the Prodigals, Romeo stoically suffers to see his former love, Juliet, with another man.

FALSTAFF
DECEASED. A lovable pain-in-the-ass, Falstaff served as a true friend to Hamlet and believer in Shakespeare. He met his end at Shrewsbury at the hand of Richard III.

OTHELLO
The Prodigal's General, Othello's tactics were instrumental to securing victory at Shrewsbury. While Othello ultimately gained revenge on Iago, the man responsible for his wife's death, the Moor is still haunted by his past.

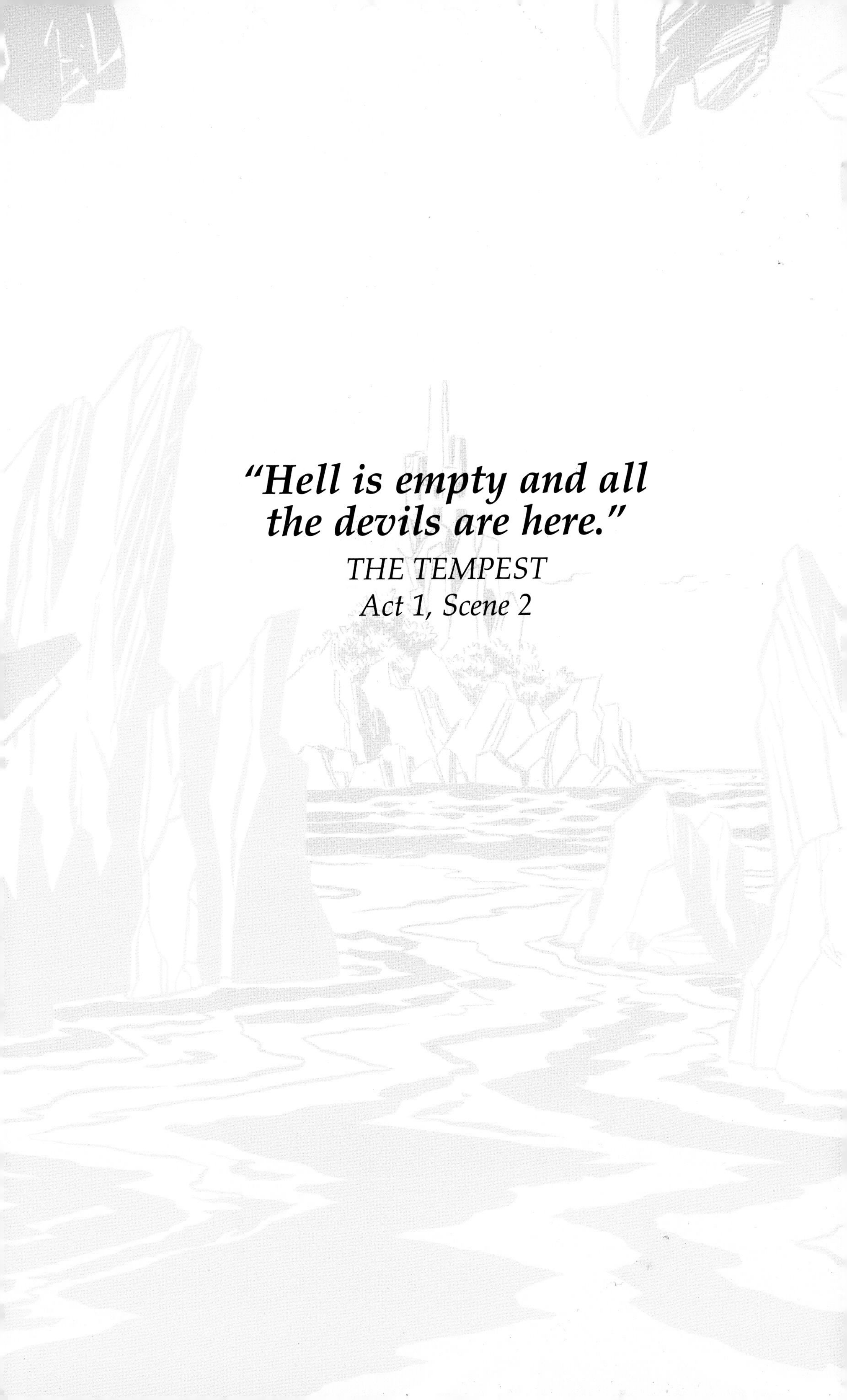

"Hell is empty and all the devils are here."

THE TEMPEST

Act 1, Scene 2

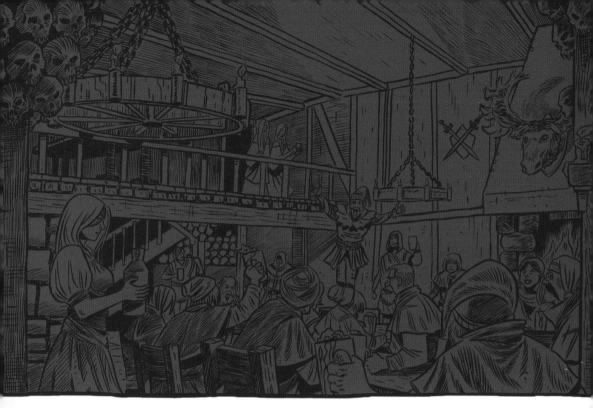

Many thanks to the following,
who have released us from our bands
with the help of their good hands...

Crystal Luxmore, Owen and Elizabeth McCreery, Brian McCreery, Anna Del Col, Jim and Marianne Del Col, Becky Cloonan, Bonnie Belanger, Paul Belanger, Jennifer Heath, Lisa Newal.

Everyone at IDW Publishing and Diamond Books — they continue to assist us in so many ways.

Keith Morris, Kelsie Yoshida, Vanlop "Pie" Chankhamma (flatter extraordinaire), Karl Kerschl, Serge LaPointe, Dr. Toby Malone, Martha Comog, Dr. Amy Scott-Douglass, Alex Franklin, Samara Nicholson, Beata Shih, Vanessa King, Michael Ball, Kevin Cox, Tony Kramreither, Jethro Bushenbaum, Dawn Douglas, Dahlia Thompson, Geoff Moore, Chris Smith, Sharon Fleming, Ted Fleming, Frank Galea, Andrew Apangu, Al Bugeja, Rob Chiasson, Steve Lawlor, Carrie Cole, Vivianne Ng, Bill Willingham, Brian Kelley, Katie Musgrave, Anderson Lawfer, D. Jeremy Smith, Gautam Goenka, Arafaat Ali Khan, Ben Caddy, Mike Rooth, Gibson Quarter.

And finally, the original mad wizard himself, Mr. W. Shakespeare.

IDW founded by Ted Adams, Alex Garner, Kris Oprisko, and Robbie Robbins

ISBN: 978-1-61377-732-9

18 17 16 15 2 3 4 5

IDW

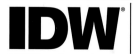

Ted Adams, CEO & Publisher
Greg Goldstein, President & COO
Robbie Robbins, EVP/Sr. Graphic Artist
Chris Ryall, Chief Creative Officer/Editor-in-Chief
Matthew Ruzicka, CPA, Chief Financial Officer
Alan Payne, VP of Sales
Dirk Wood, VP of Marketing
Lorelei Bunjes, VP of Digital Services

Become our fan on Facebook **facebook.com/idwpublishing**
Follow us on Twitter **@idwpublishing**
Check us out on YouTube **youtube.com/idwpublishing**
www.IDWPUBLISHING.com

Originally published as KILL SHAKESPEARE: THE TIDE OF BLOOD issues #1–5.

LYSANDER

An exuberant young swordsman, Lysander found glory at the battle of Shrewsbury but lost an eye – and his best friend Demetrius – on the field of battle.

NERISSA

A staunch supporter of the Prodigal cause, the wise and patient Nerissa has become the head of the Prodigal's Council of Thirty-Seven.

GHOST OF KING HAMLET

The former King of Denmark pushed his son Hamlet to kill Shakespeare and seize the quill in order to return him from hell. Still trapped between this world and the next the ghost has not yet given up hope of returning to the land of the living.

FESTE

The mysterious fool who knows the unknowable, Feste helped push Hamlet towards his destiny, but his motives remain shrouded in mystery.

SHAKESPEARE

The controller of the quill and creator of the world, Shakespeare has proven himself to be neither the evil wizard his detractors claimed, nor the benevolent God his followers believed him to be. The Bard still struggles with his place in the world and how to best use the power of the quill.

LADY MACBETH

The mistress of dark magic, Lady Macbeth hungers for the power of the quill and seeks revenge on Shakespeare for the tragedies that befell her in her past.

RICHARD III

DECEASED. The King of Delphos, Richard sought the quill to expand his dominion over other realms. Richard briefly possessed the quill but was ultimately defeated by Shakespeare and Lady Macbeth and died at Shrewsbury.

THE WEIRD SISTERS

Loyal to Lady Macbeth and as adept in black magic as their master, the two Weird Sisters seek to bring the quill to Lady Macbeth. Their power was diminished after the third member of their coven died at Shrewsbury.

IAGO

DECEASED. Iago pledged loyalty to all, but was trusted by none. He betrayed Richard and then Hamlet before being betrayed in turn by Lady Macbeth. He ultimately met his death at the hands of his great rival, Othello.

The eyes of the Father shine in the night.

His fury, a tempest, raging in the bloody light,

carrying a Shadowed King from beyond the seas.

What he seeks he shall not seize

The Father's gates shall open swing,

a welcome only, to this Shadowed King.

The two shall clash and blood will pour,

and things that were shall be no more.

The Wizard shall return to all;

The unjust Lord will flee and fall;

Humbled will the Lady be;

And a man once bound will be set free.

King and Father shall meet their ends,

to make way for true King's rise

where Shadow did bend.

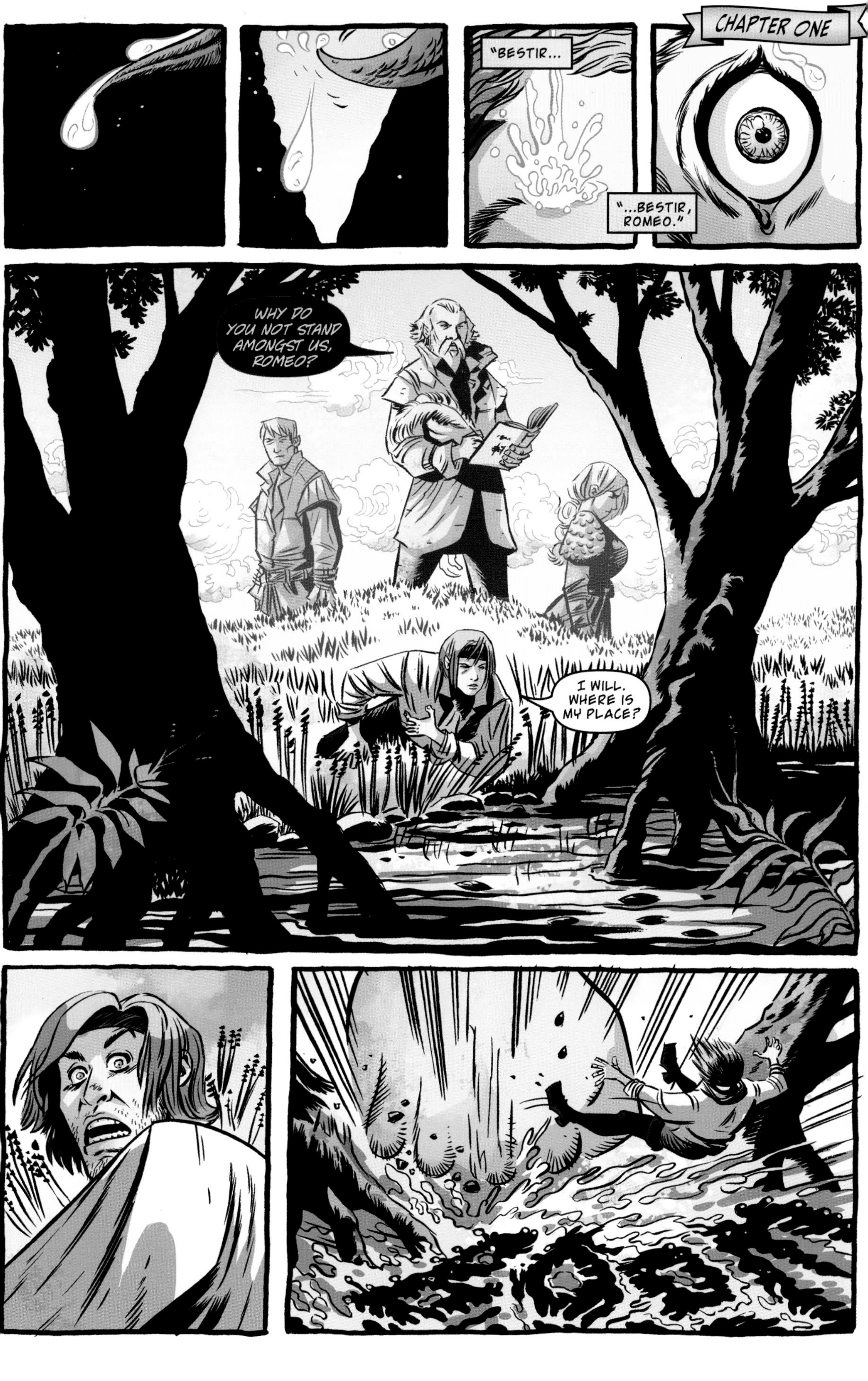
CHAPTER ONE
"BESTIR...
"...BESTIR, ROMEO."
WHY DO YOU NOT STAND AMONGST US, ROMEO?
I WILL. WHERE IS MY PLACE?

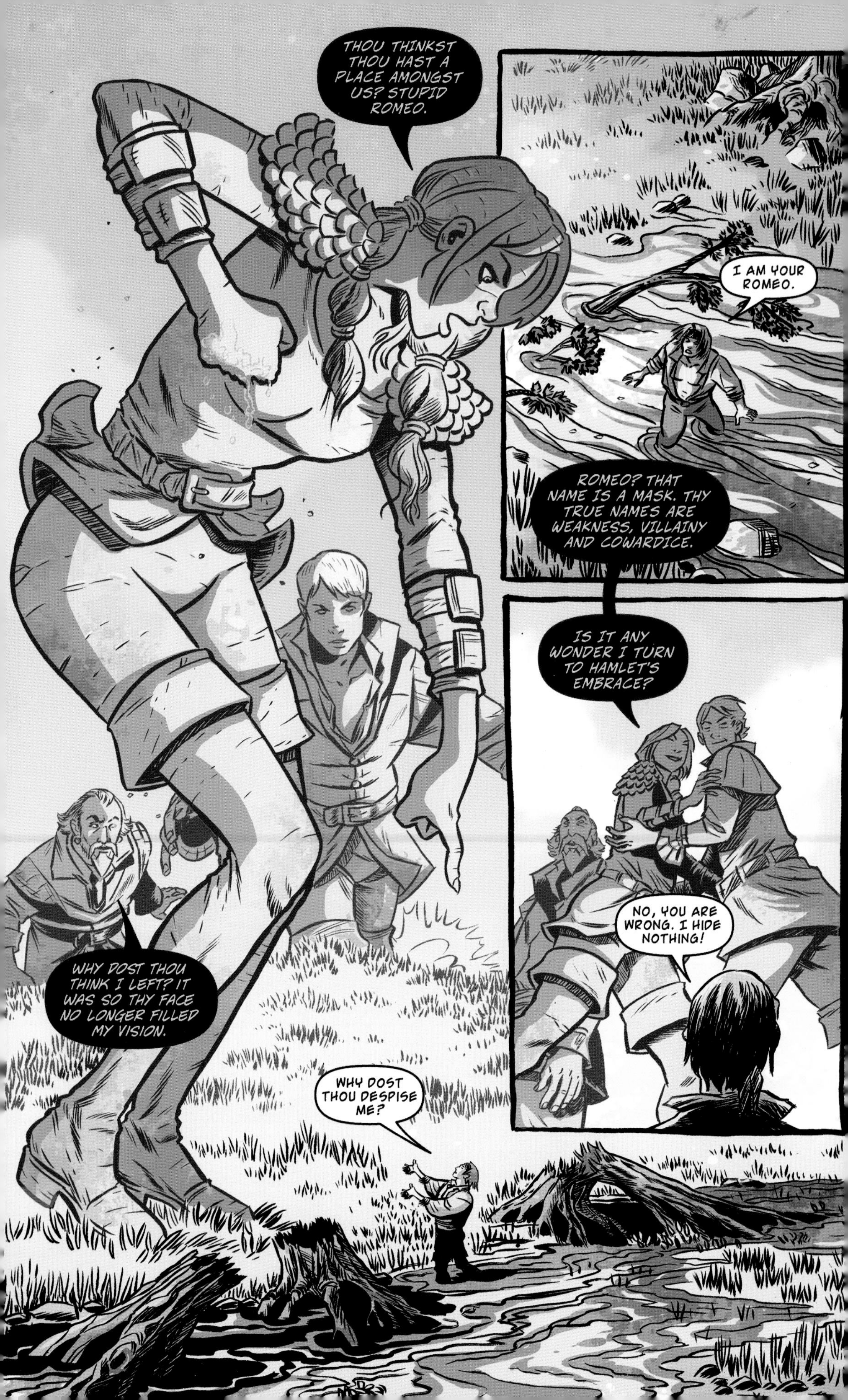
THOU THINKST THOU HAST A PLACE AMONGST US? STUPID ROMEO.
I AM YOUR ROMEO.
ROMEO? THAT NAME IS A MASK. THY TRUE NAMES ARE WEAKNESS, VILLAINY AND COWARDICE.
IS IT ANY WONDER I TURN TO HAMLET'S EMBRACE?
NO, YOU ARE WRONG. I HIDE NOTHING!
WHY DOST THOU THINK I LEFT? IT WAS SO THY FACE NO LONGER FILLED MY VISION.
WHY DOST THOU DESPISE ME?

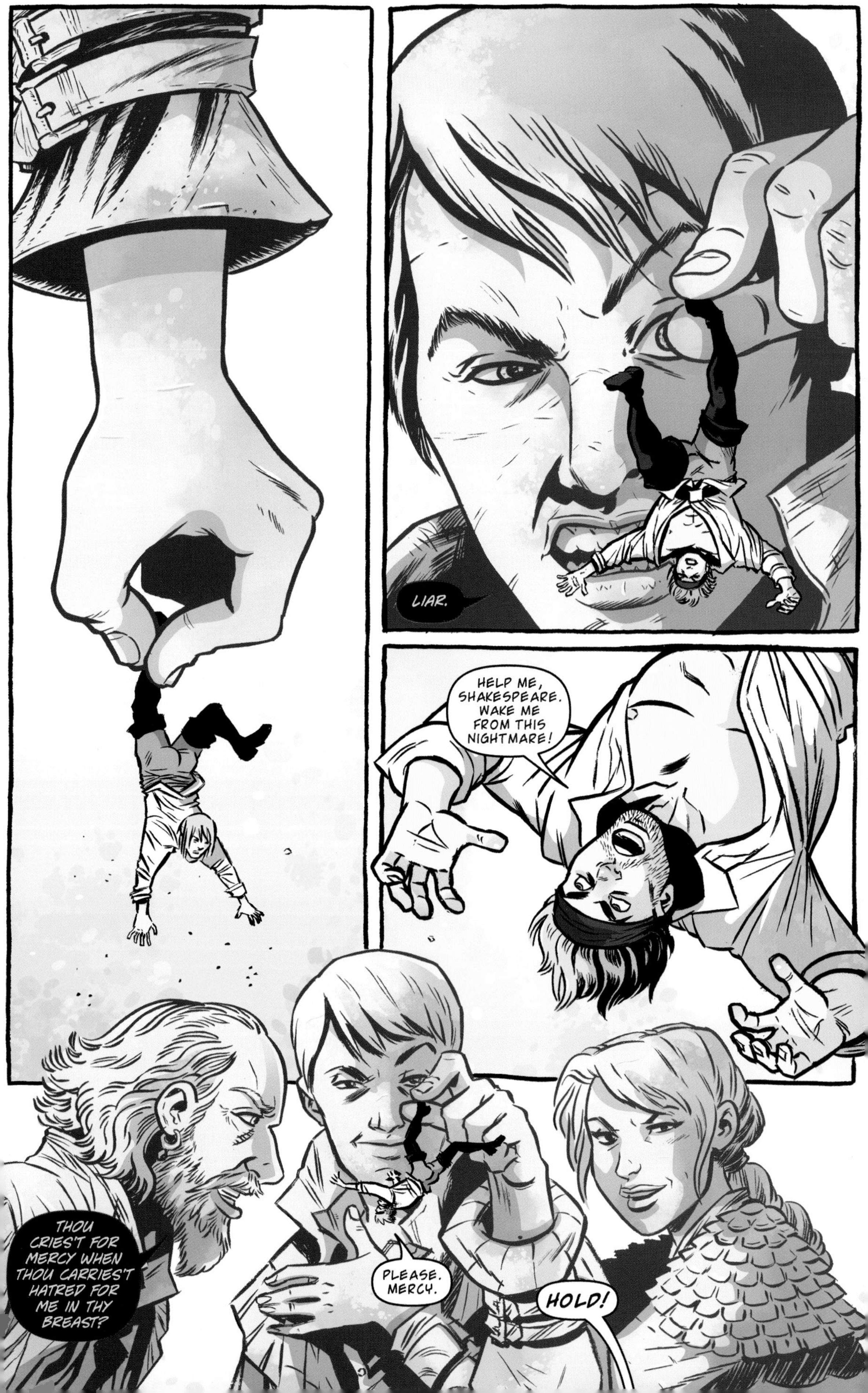
LIAR.
HELP ME, SHAKESPEARE. WAKE ME FROM THIS NIGHTMARE!
THOU CRIES'T FOR MERCY WHEN THOU CARRIES'T HATRED FOR ME IN THY BREAST?
PLEASE. MERCY.
HOLD!

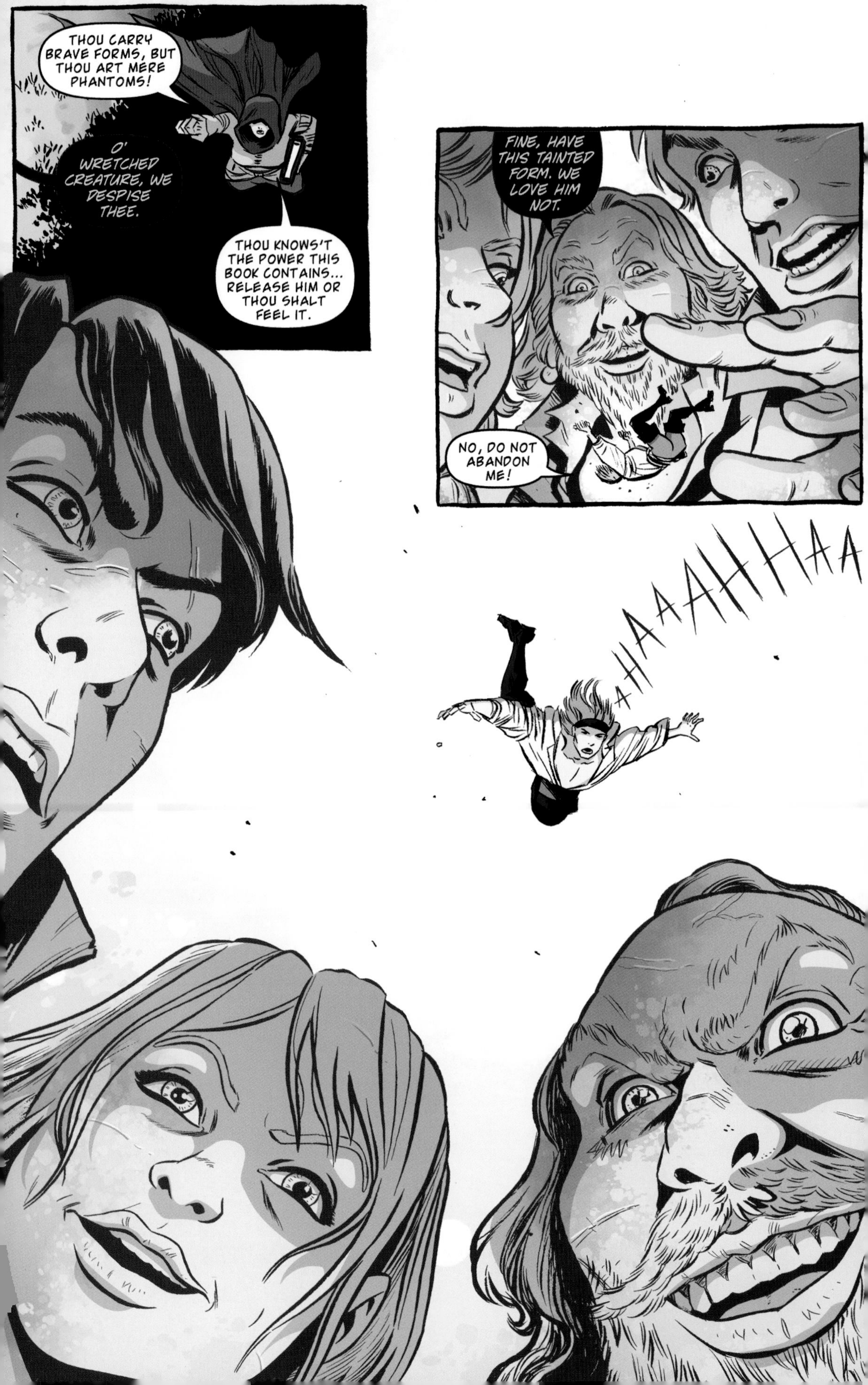
THOU CARRY BRAVE FORMS, BUT THOU ART MERE PHANTOMS!
O' WRETCHED CREATURE, WE DESPISE THEE.
THOU KNOWS'T THE POWER THIS BOOK CONTAINS... RELEASE HIM OR THOU SHALT FEEL IT.
FINE, HAVE THIS TAINTED FORM. WE LOVE HIM NOT.
NO, DO NOT ABANDON ME!
AHAAAAHHHAA

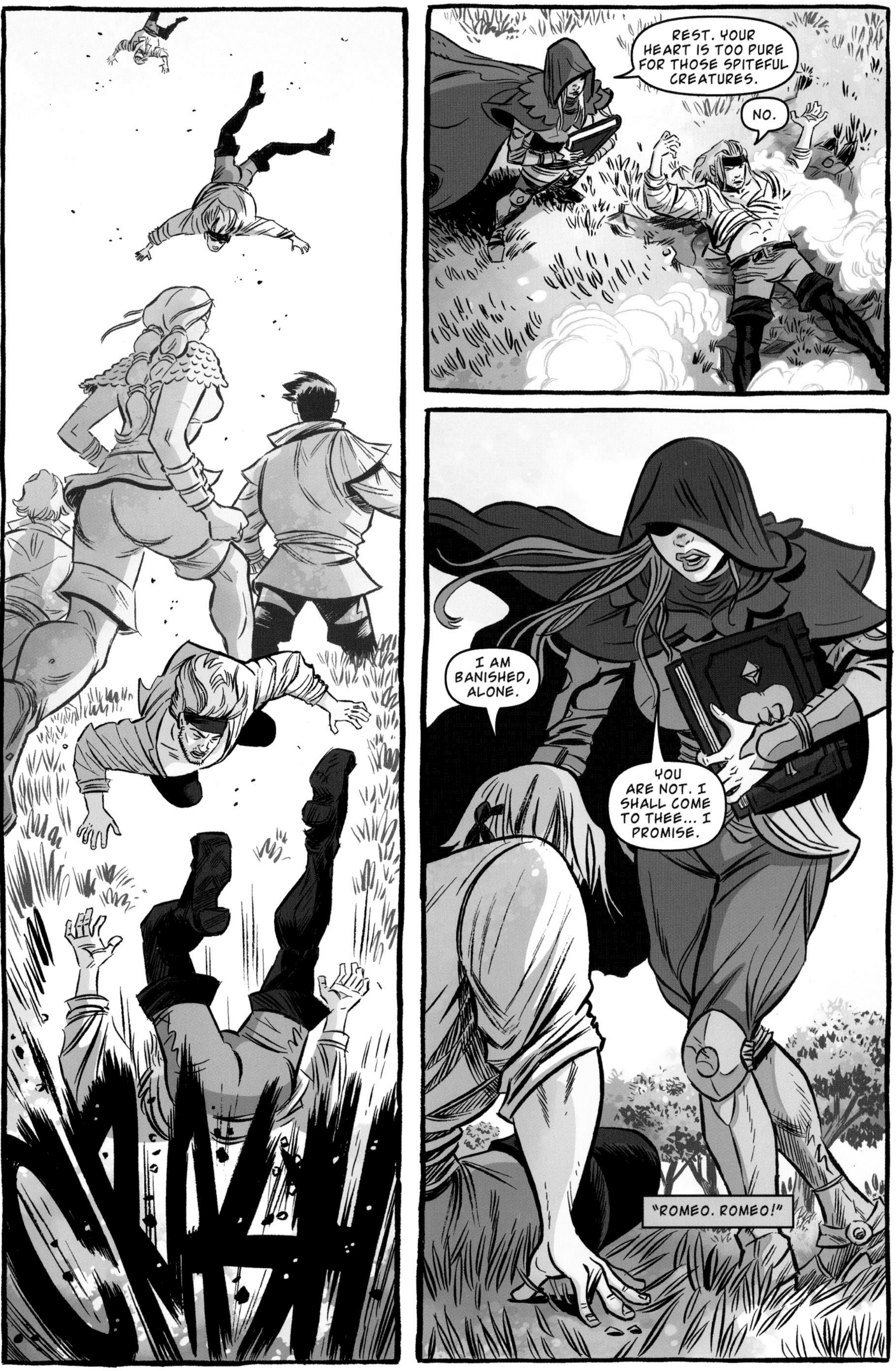
REST. YOUR HEART IS TOO PURE FOR THOSE SPITEFUL CREATURES.
NO.
I AM BANISHED, ALONE.
YOU ARE NOT. I SHALL COME TO THEE... I PROMISE.
"ROMEO. ROMEO!"

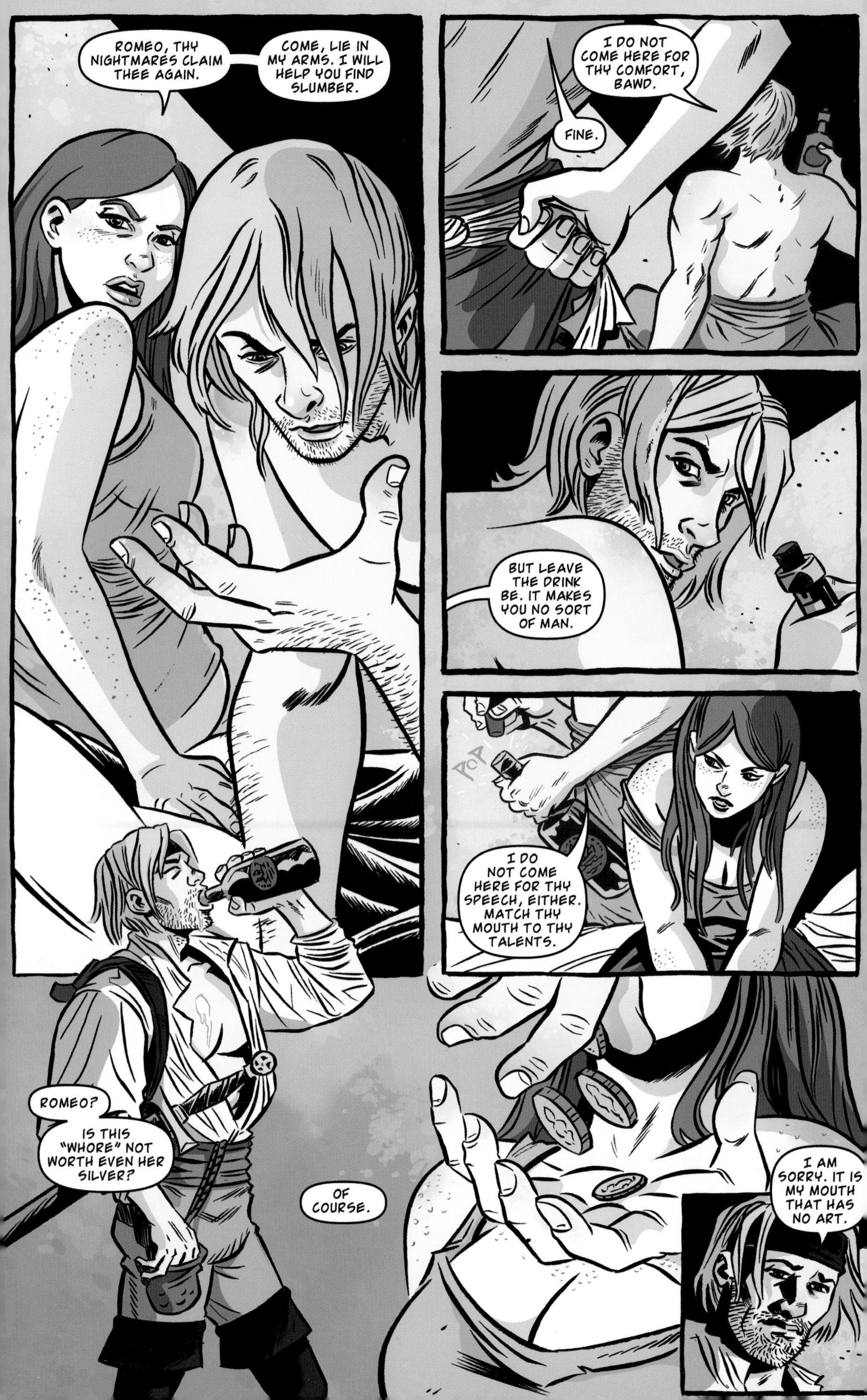
ROMEO, THY NIGHTMARES CLAIM THEE AGAIN.
COME, LIE IN MY ARMS. I WILL HELP YOU FIND SLUMBER.
I DO NOT COME HERE FOR THY COMFORT, BAWD.
FINE.
BUT LEAVE THE DRINK BE. IT MAKES YOU NO SORT OF MAN.
POP
I DO NOT COME HERE FOR THY SPEECH, EITHER. MATCH THY MOUTH TO THY TALENTS.
ROMEO?
IS THIS "WHORE" NOT WORTH EVEN HER SILVER?
OF COURSE.
I AM SORRY. IT IS MY MOUTH THAT HAS NO ART.

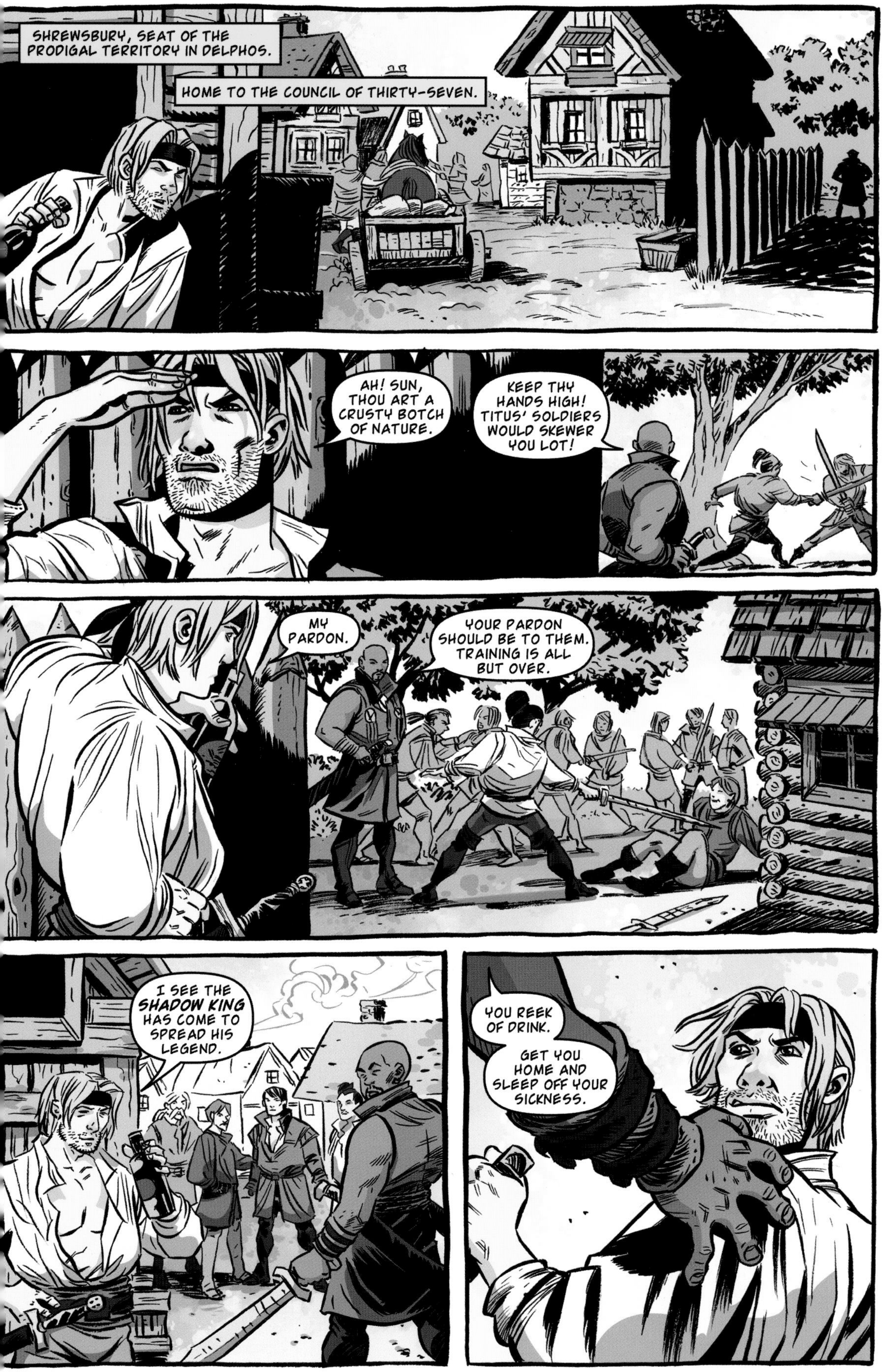
SHREWSBURY, SEAT OF THE PRODIGAL TERRITORY IN DELPHOS.
HOME TO THE COUNCIL OF THIRTY-SEVEN.
AH! SUN, THOU ART A CRUSTY BOTCH OF NATURE.
KEEP THY HANDS HIGH! TITUS' SOLDIERS WOULD SKEWER YOU LOT!
MY PARDON.
YOUR PARDON SHOULD BE TO THEM. TRAINING IS ALL BUT OVER.
I SEE THE *SHADOW KING* HAS COME TO SPREAD HIS LEGEND.
YOU REEK OF DRINK.
GET YOU HOME AND SLEEP OFF YOUR SICKNESS.

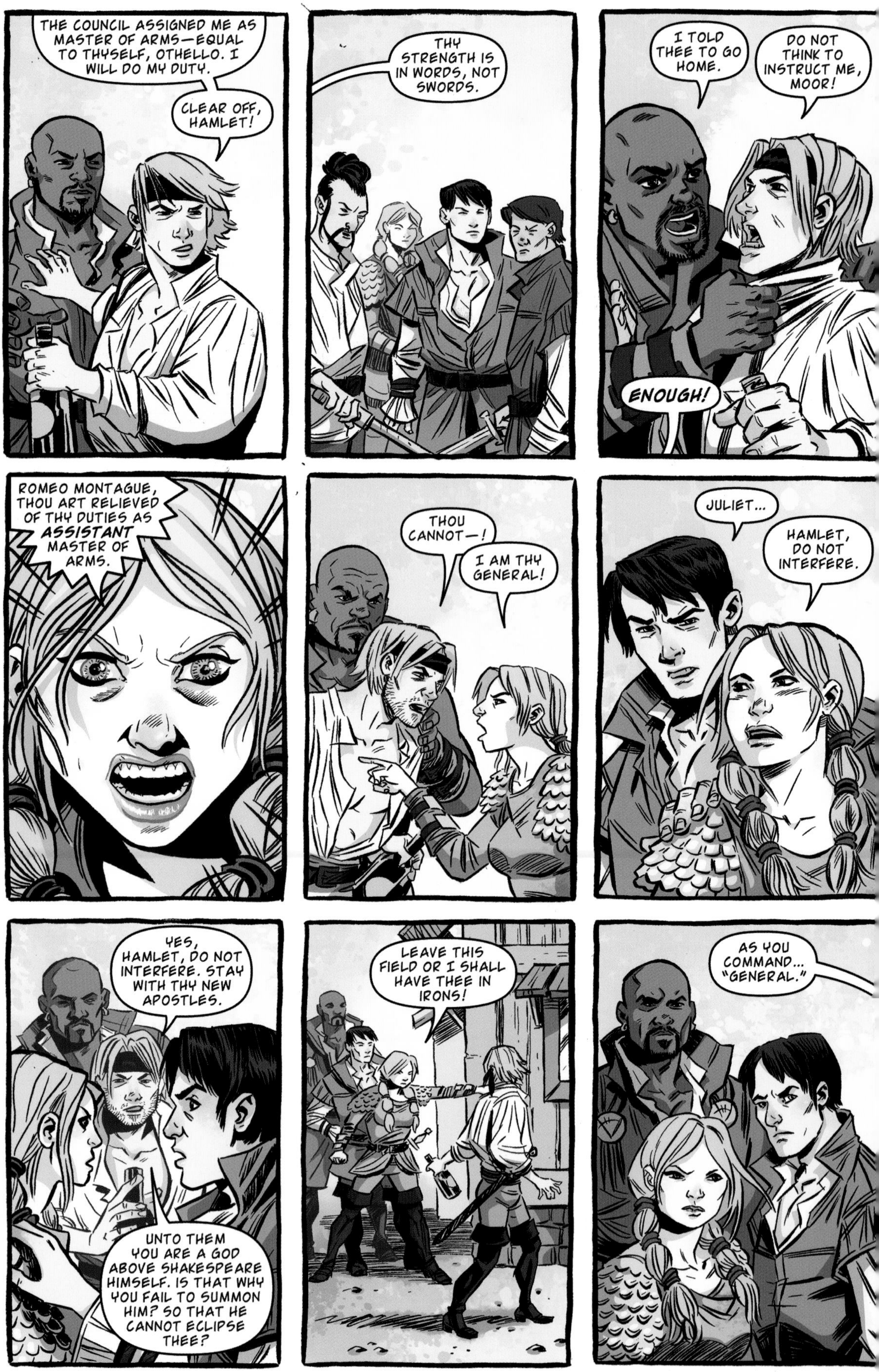
THE COUNCIL ASSIGNED ME AS MASTER OF ARMS—EQUAL TO THYSELF, OTHELLO. I WILL DO MY DUTY.
CLEAR OFF, HAMLET!
THY STRENGTH IS IN WORDS, NOT SWORDS.
I TOLD THEE TO GO HOME.
DO NOT THINK TO INSTRUCT ME, MOOR!
ENOUGH!
ROMEO MONTAGUE, THOU ART RELIEVED OF THY DUTIES AS ASSISTANT MASTER OF ARMS.
THOU CANNOT—!
I AM THY GENERAL!
JULIET...
HAMLET, DO NOT INTERFERE.
YES, HAMLET, DO NOT INTERFERE. STAY WITH THY NEW APOSTLES.
UNTO THEM YOU ARE A GOD ABOVE SHAKESPEARE HIMSELF. IS THAT WHY YOU FAIL TO SUMMON HIM? SO THAT HE CANNOT ECLIPSE THEE?
LEAVE THIS FIELD OR I SHALL HAVE THEE IN IRONS!
AS YOU COMMAND... "GENERAL."

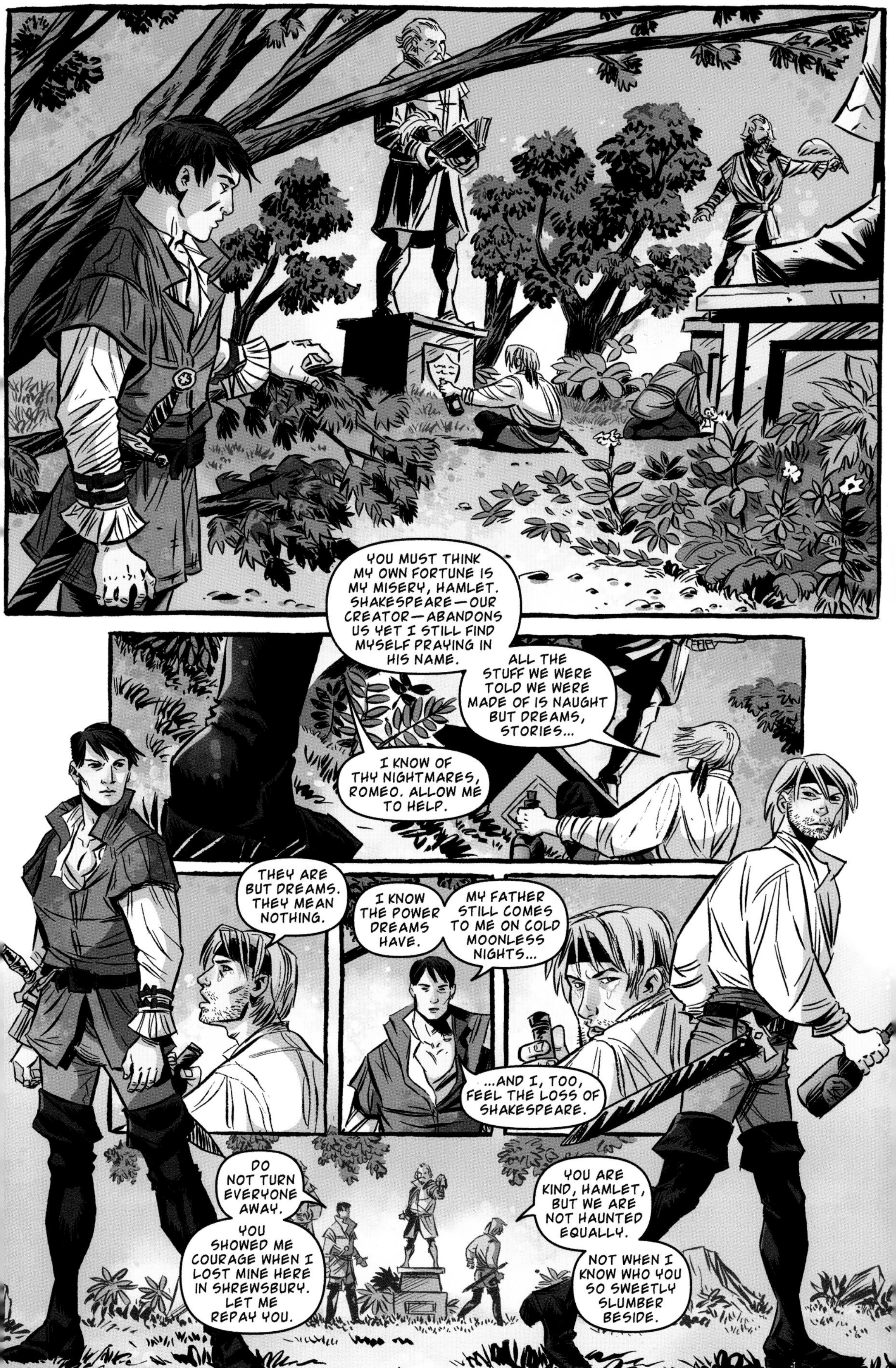
YOU MUST THINK MY OWN FORTUNE IS MY MISERY, HAMLET. SHAKESPEARE—OUR CREATOR—ABANDONS US YET I STILL FIND MYSELF PRAYING IN HIS NAME.
ALL THE STUFF WE WERE TOLD WE WERE MADE OF IS NAUGHT BUT DREAMS, STORIES...
I KNOW OF THY NIGHTMARES, ROMEO. ALLOW ME TO HELP.
THEY ARE BUT DREAMS. THEY MEAN NOTHING.
I KNOW THE POWER DREAMS HAVE.
MY FATHER STILL COMES TO ME ON COLD MOONLESS NIGHTS...
...AND I, TOO, FEEL THE LOSS OF SHAKESPEARE.
DO NOT TURN EVERYONE AWAY.
YOU SHOWED ME COURAGE WHEN I LOST MINE HERE IN SHREWSBURY. LET ME REPAY YOU.
YOU ARE KIND, HAMLET, BUT WE ARE NOT HAUNTED EQUALLY.
NOT WHEN I KNOW WHO YOU SO SWEETLY SLUMBER BESIDE.

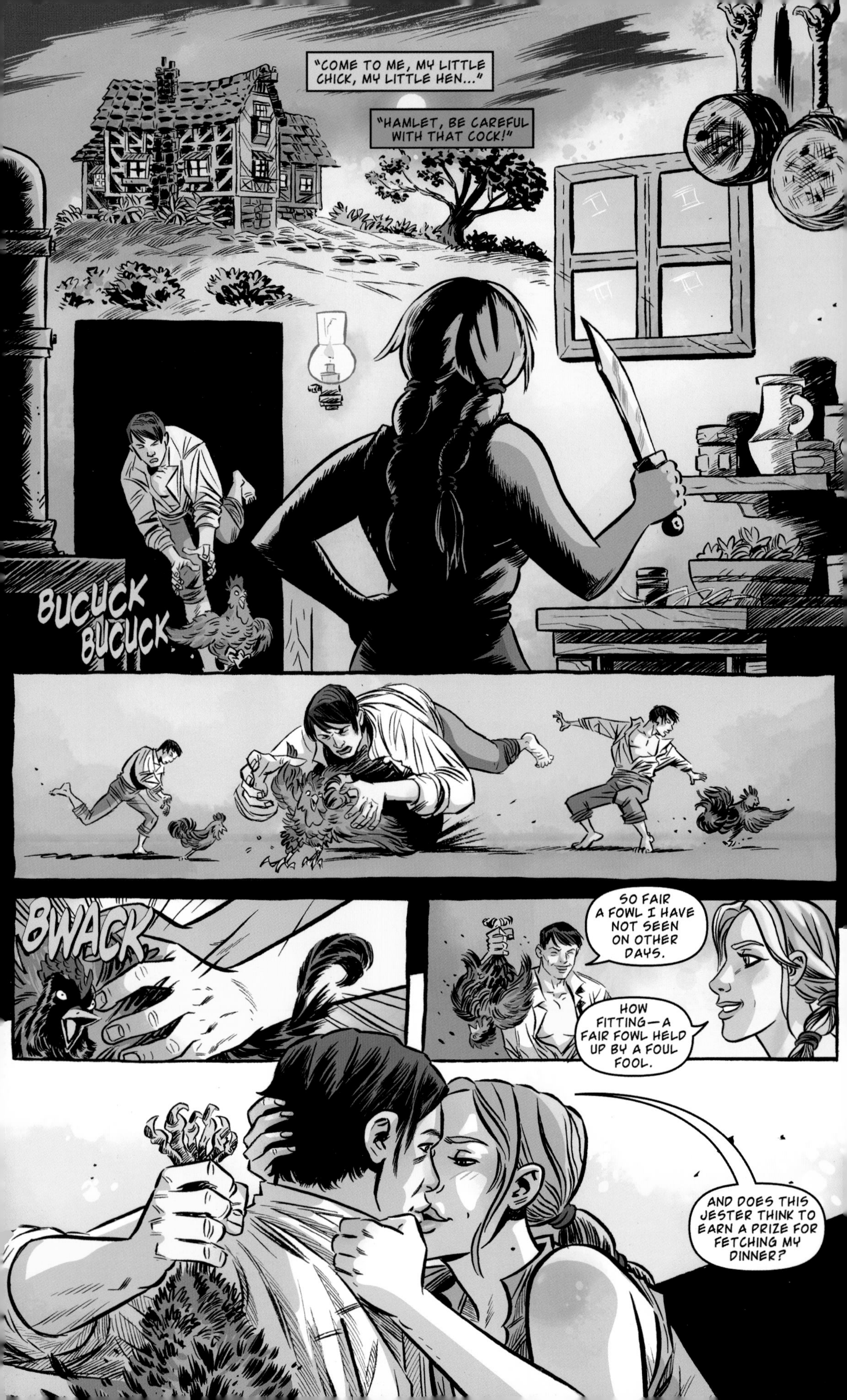

"COME TO ME, MY LITTLE CHICK, MY LITTLE HEN..."
"HAMLET, BE CAREFUL WITH THAT COCK!"
BUCUCK BUCUCK
BWACK
SO FAIR A FOWL I HAVE NOT SEEN ON OTHER DAYS.
HOW FITTING—A FAIR FOWL HELD UP BY A FOUL FOOL.
AND DOES THIS JESTER THINK TO EARN A PRIZE FOR FETCHING MY DINNER?

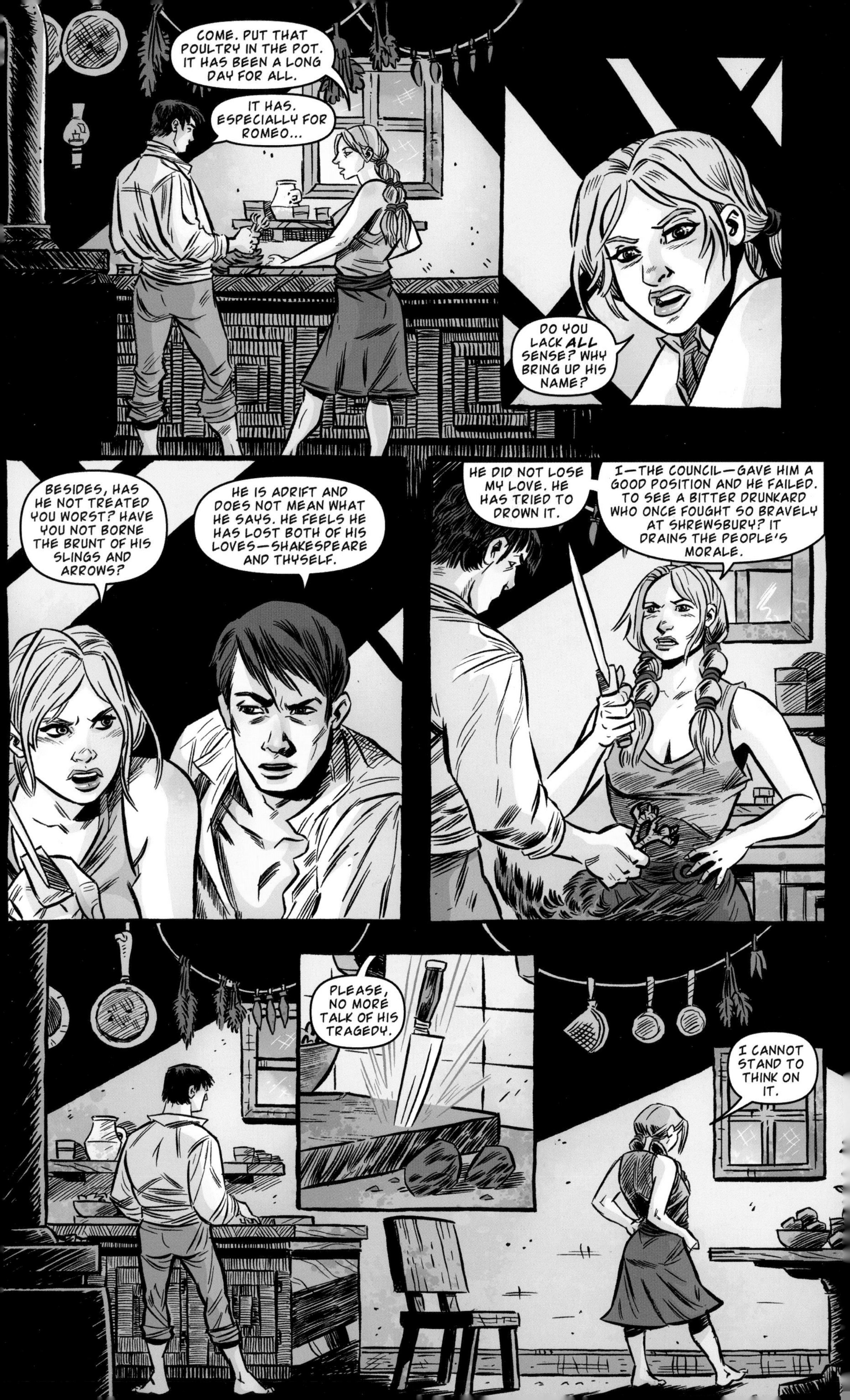
COME. PUT THAT POULTRY IN THE POT. IT HAS BEEN A LONG DAY FOR ALL.
IT HAS. ESPECIALLY FOR ROMEO...
DO YOU LACK ALL SENSE? WHY BRING UP HIS NAME?
BESIDES, HAS HE NOT TREATED YOU WORST? HAVE YOU NOT BORNE THE BRUNT OF HIS SLINGS AND ARROWS?
HE IS ADRIFT AND DOES NOT MEAN WHAT HE SAYS. HE FEELS HE HAS LOST BOTH OF HIS LOVES—SHAKESPEARE AND THYSELF.
HE DID NOT LOSE MY LOVE. HE HAS TRIED TO DROWN IT.
I—THE COUNCIL—GAVE HIM A GOOD POSITION AND HE FAILED. TO SEE A BITTER DRUNKARD WHO ONCE FOUGHT SO BRAVELY AT SHREWSBURY? IT DRAINS THE PEOPLE'S MORALE.
PLEASE, NO MORE TALK OF HIS TRAGEDY.
I CANNOT STAND TO THINK ON IT.

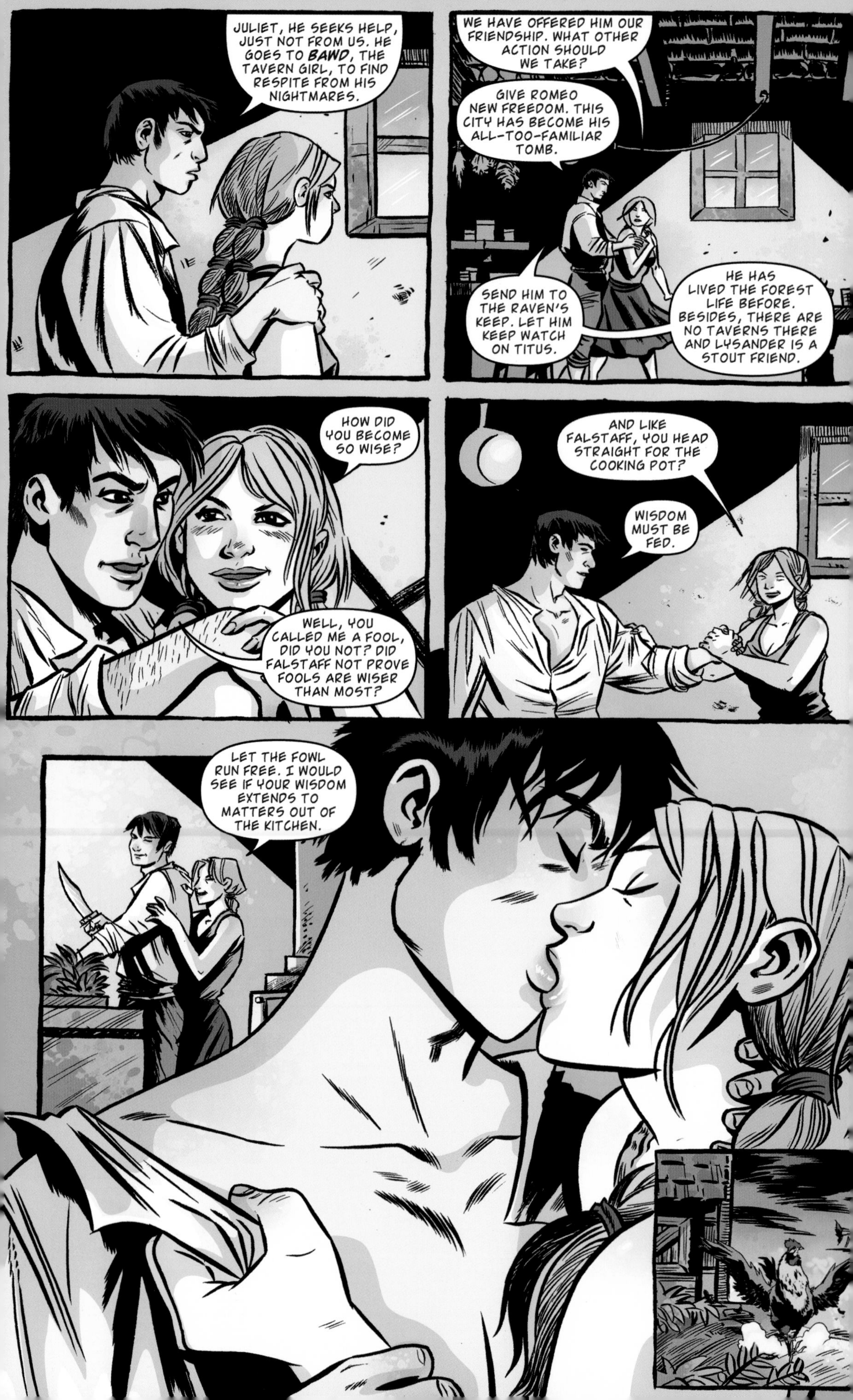
JULIET, HE SEEKS HELP, JUST NOT FROM US. HE GOES TO **BAWD**, THE TAVERN GIRL, TO FIND RESPITE FROM HIS NIGHTMARES.
WE HAVE OFFERED HIM OUR FRIENDSHIP. WHAT OTHER ACTION SHOULD WE TAKE?
GIVE ROMEO NEW FREEDOM. THIS CITY HAS BECOME HIS ALL-TOO-FAMILIAR TOMB.
SEND HIM TO THE RAVEN'S KEEP. LET HIM KEEP WATCH ON TITUS.
HE HAS LIVED THE FOREST LIFE BEFORE. BESIDES, THERE ARE NO TAVERNS THERE AND LYSANDER IS A STOUT FRIEND.
HOW DID YOU BECOME SO WISE?
WELL, YOU CALLED ME A FOOL, DID YOU NOT? DID FALSTAFF NOT PROVE FOOLS ARE WISER THAN MOST?
AND LIKE FALSTAFF, YOU HEAD STRAIGHT FOR THE COOKING POT?
WISDOM MUST BE FED.
LET THE FOWL RUN FREE. I WOULD SEE IF YOUR WISDOM EXTENDS TO MATTERS OUT OF THE KITCHEN.

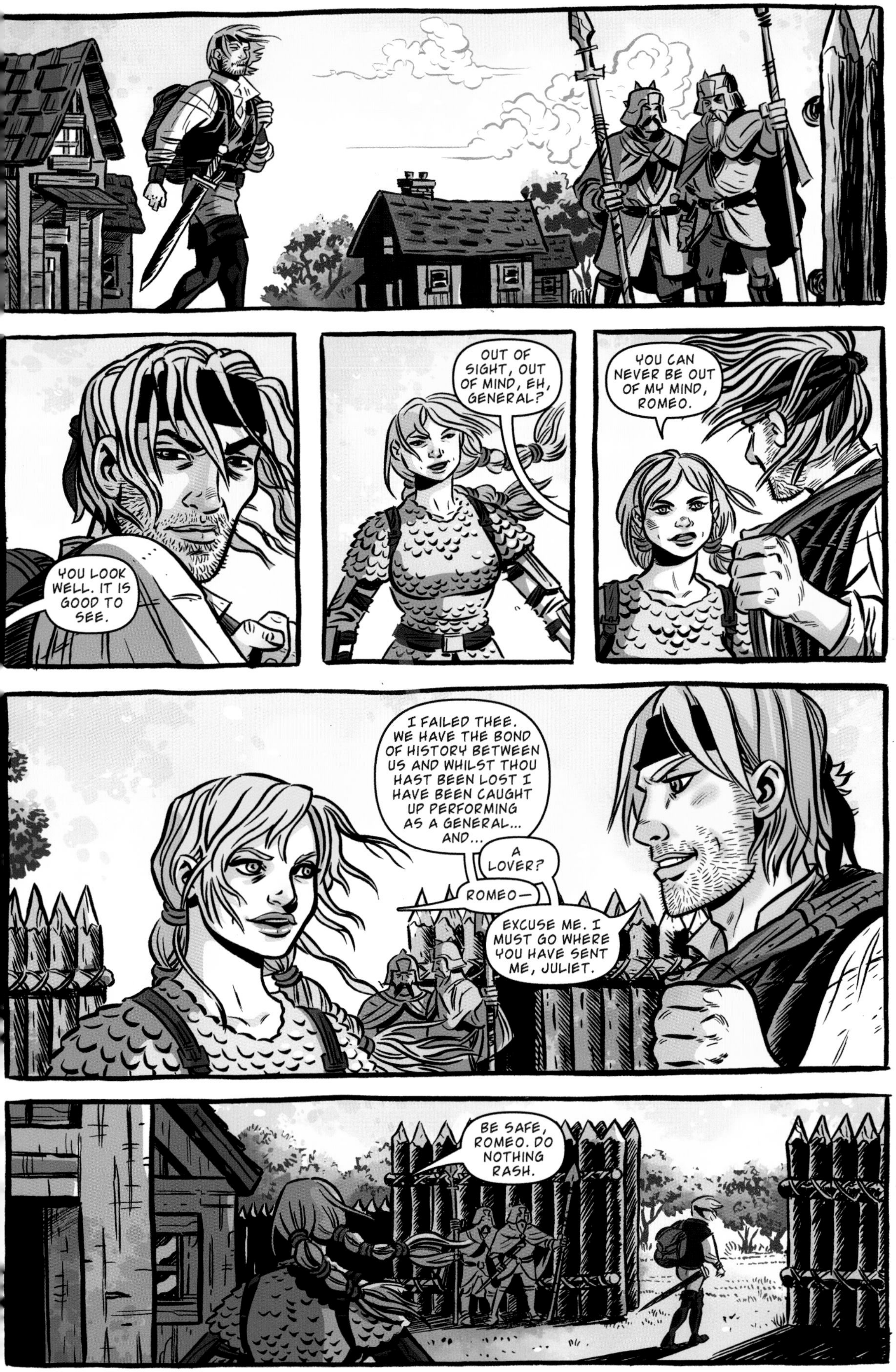
YOU LOOK WELL. IT IS GOOD TO SEE.
OUT OF SIGHT, OUT OF MIND, EH, GENERAL?
YOU CAN NEVER BE OUT OF MY MIND, ROMEO.
I FAILED THEE. WE HAVE THE BOND OF HISTORY BETWEEN US AND WHILST THOU HAST BEEN LOST I HAVE BEEN CAUGHT UP PERFORMING AS A GENERAL... AND...
A LOVER?
ROMEO—
EXCUSE ME. I MUST GO WHERE YOU HAVE SENT ME, JULIET.
BE SAFE, ROMEO. DO NOTHING RASH.

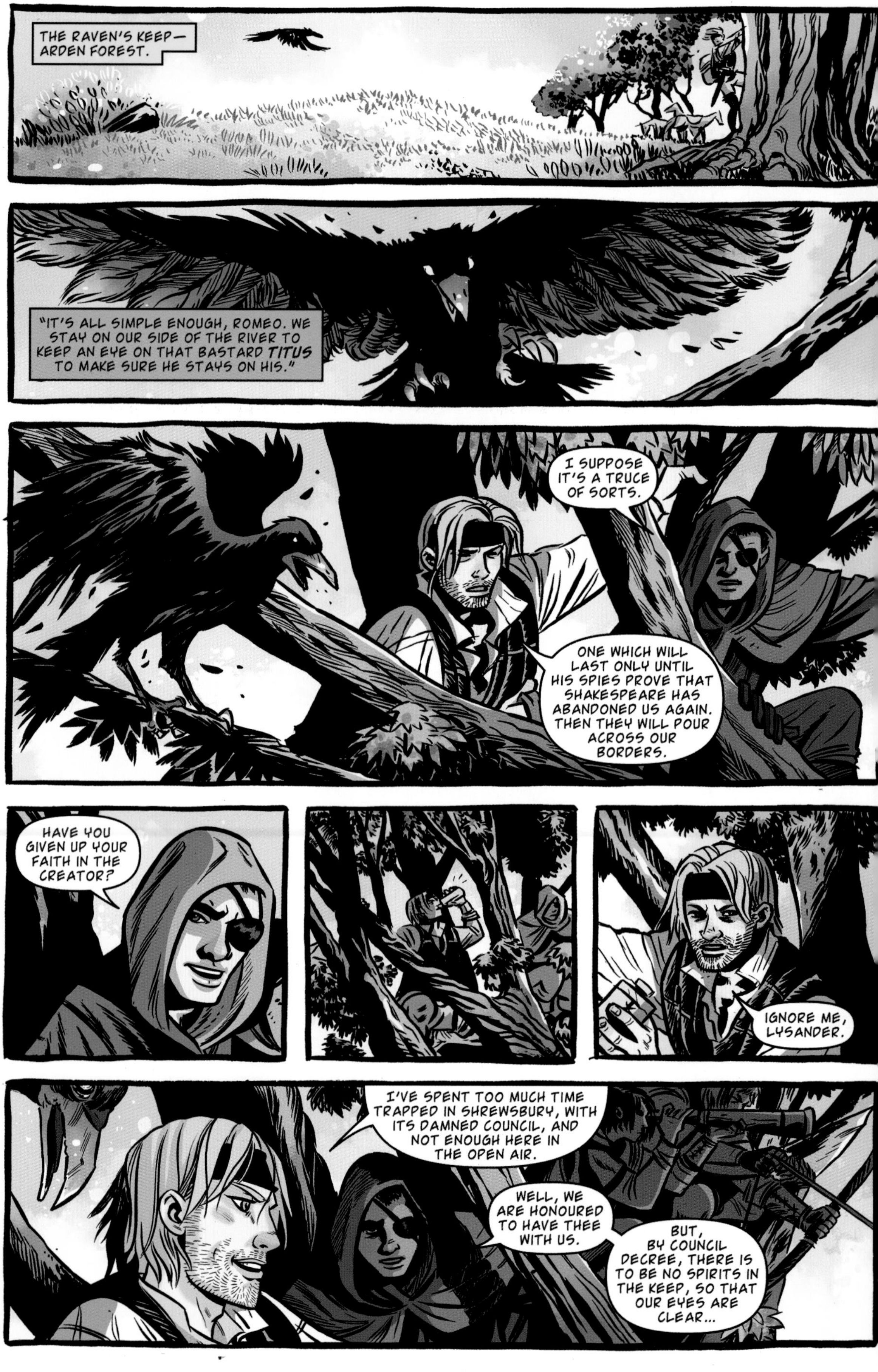
THE RAVEN'S KEEP—ARDEN FOREST.
"IT'S ALL SIMPLE ENOUGH, ROMEO. WE STAY ON OUR SIDE OF THE RIVER TO KEEP AN EYE ON THAT BASTARD *TITUS* TO MAKE SURE HE STAYS ON HIS."
I SUPPOSE IT'S A TRUCE OF SORTS.
ONE WHICH WILL LAST ONLY UNTIL HIS SPIES PROVE THAT SHAKESPEARE HAS ABANDONED US AGAIN. THEN THEY WILL POUR ACROSS OUR BORDERS.
HAVE YOU GIVEN UP YOUR FAITH IN THE CREATOR?
IGNORE ME, LYSANDER.
I'VE SPENT TOO MUCH TIME TRAPPED IN SHREWSBURY, WITH ITS DAMNED COUNCIL, AND NOT ENOUGH HERE IN THE OPEN AIR.
WELL, WE ARE HONOURED TO HAVE THEE WITH US.
BUT, BY COUNCIL DECREE, THERE IS TO BE NO SPIRITS IN THE KEEP, SO THAT OUR EYES ARE CLEAR...

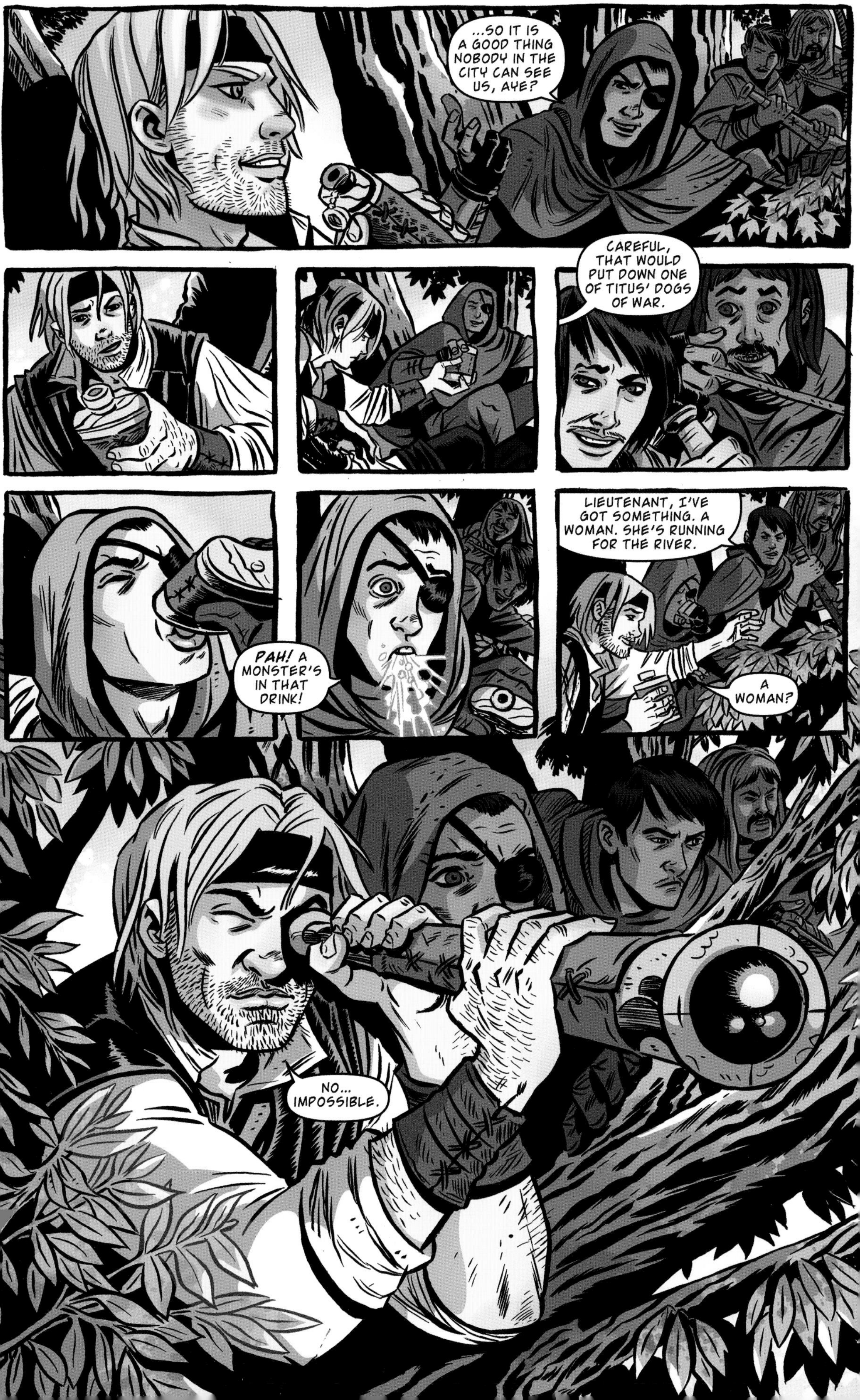
...SO IT IS A GOOD THING NOBODY IN THE CITY CAN SEE US, AYE?
CAREFUL, THAT WOULD PUT DOWN ONE OF TITUS' DOGS OF WAR.
PAH! A MONSTER'S IN THAT DRINK!
LIEUTENANT, I'VE GOT SOMETHING. A WOMAN. SHE'S RUNNING FOR THE RIVER.
A WOMAN?
NO... IMPOSSIBLE.

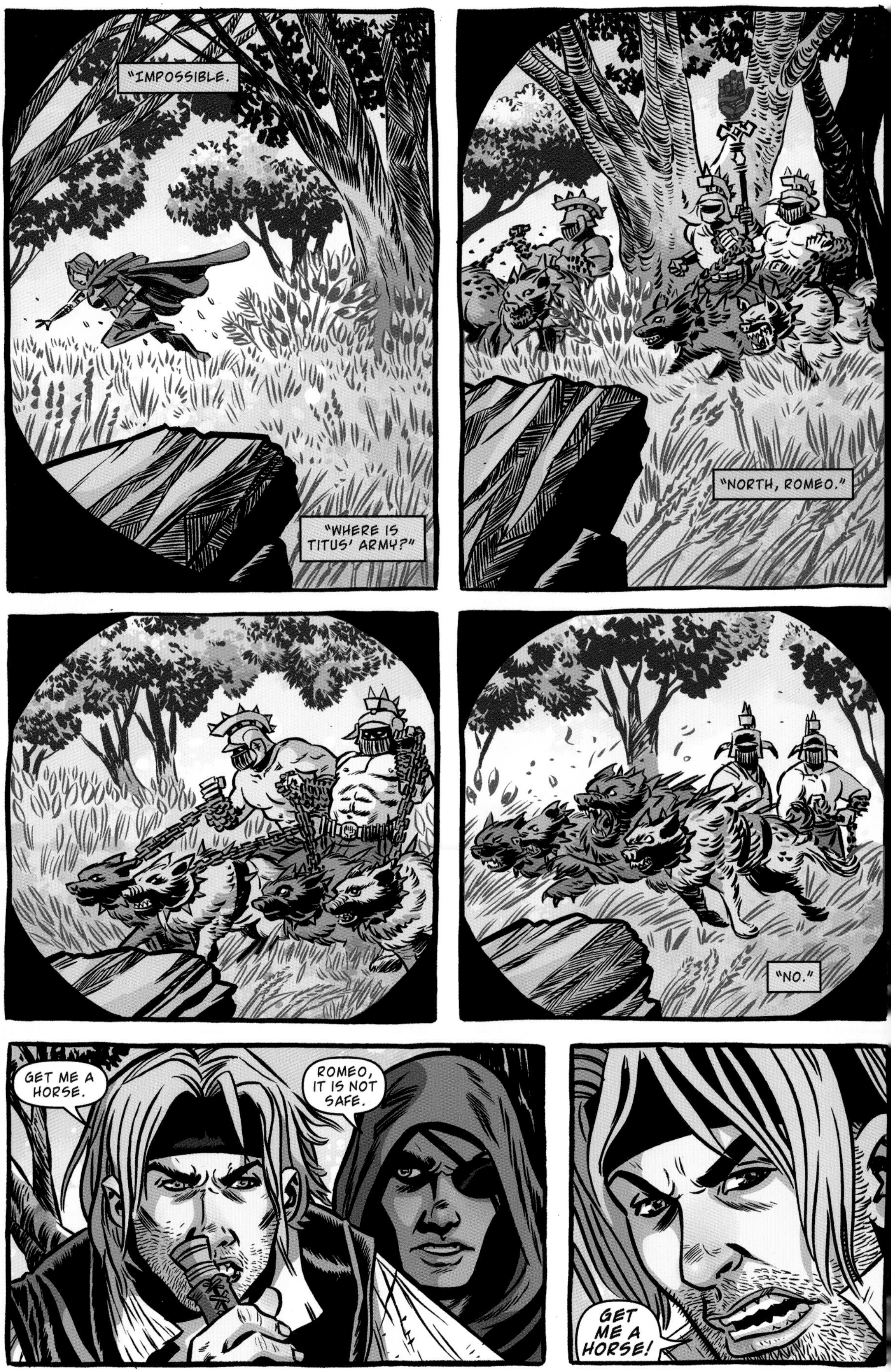
"IMPOSSIBLE.
"WHERE IS TITUS' ARMY?"
"NORTH, ROMEO."
"NO."
GET ME A HORSE.
ROMEO, IT IS NOT SAFE.
GET ME A HORSE!

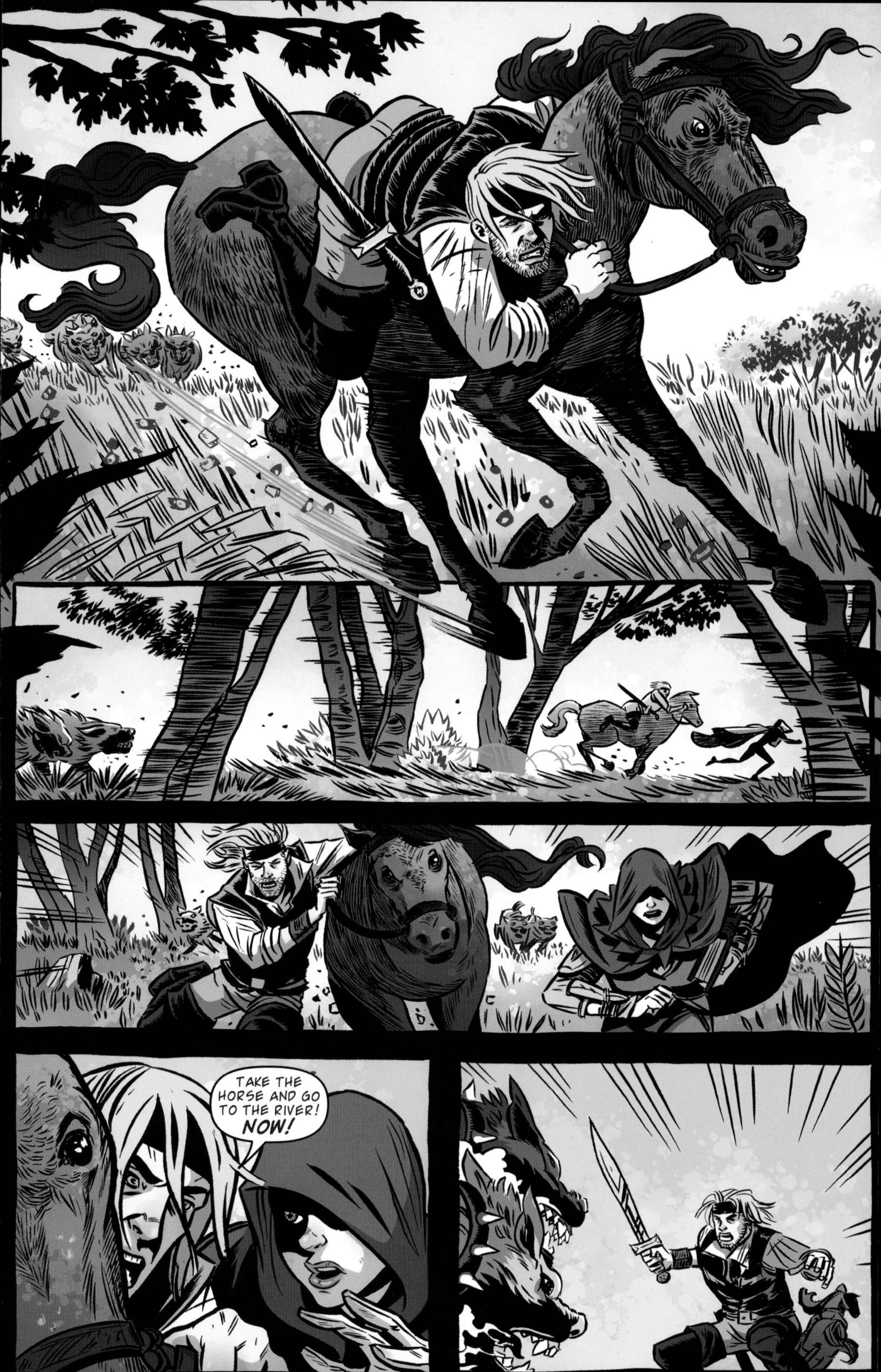
TAKE THE HORSE AND GO TO THE RIVER! NOW!

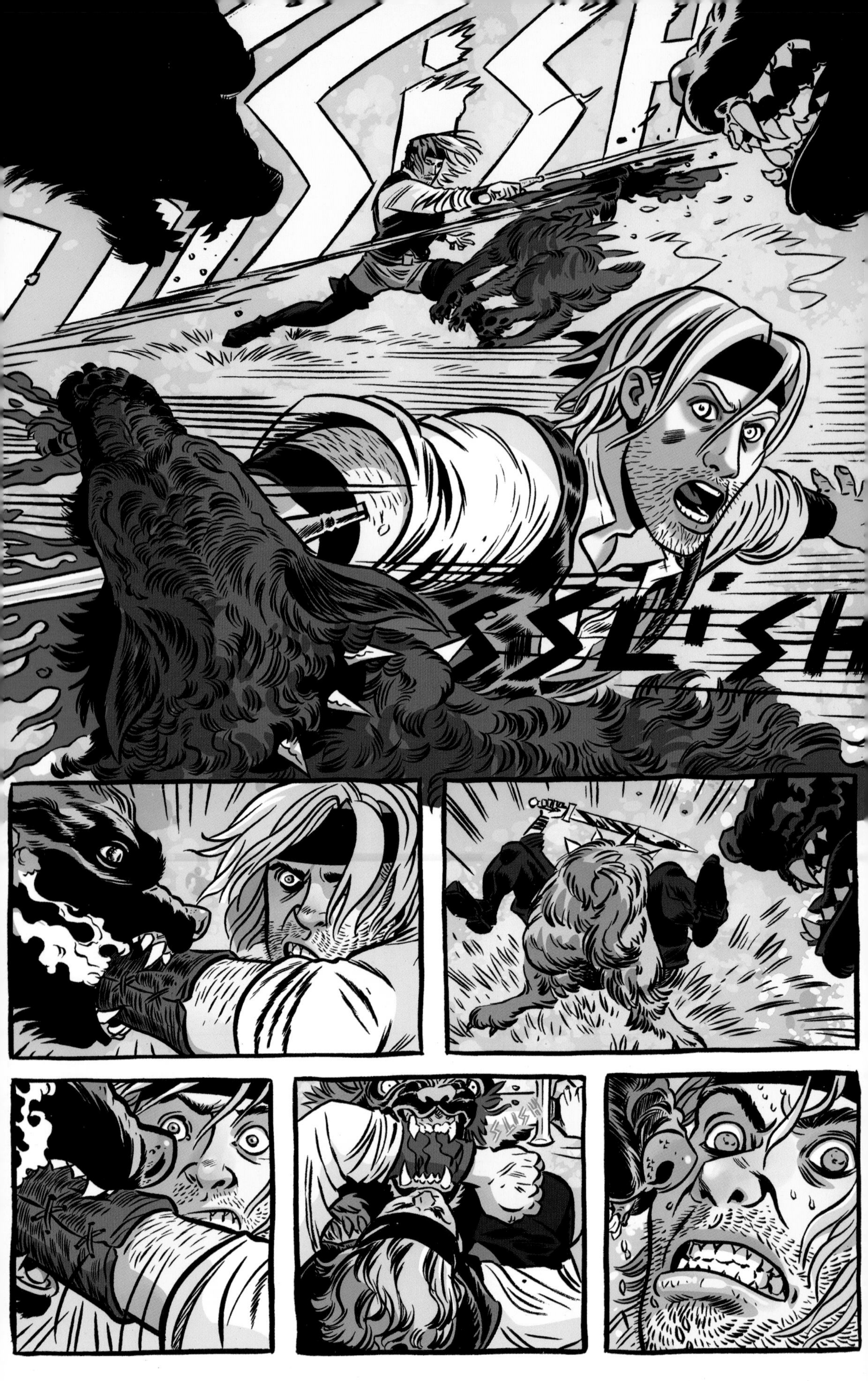
SSLISH
SLISH

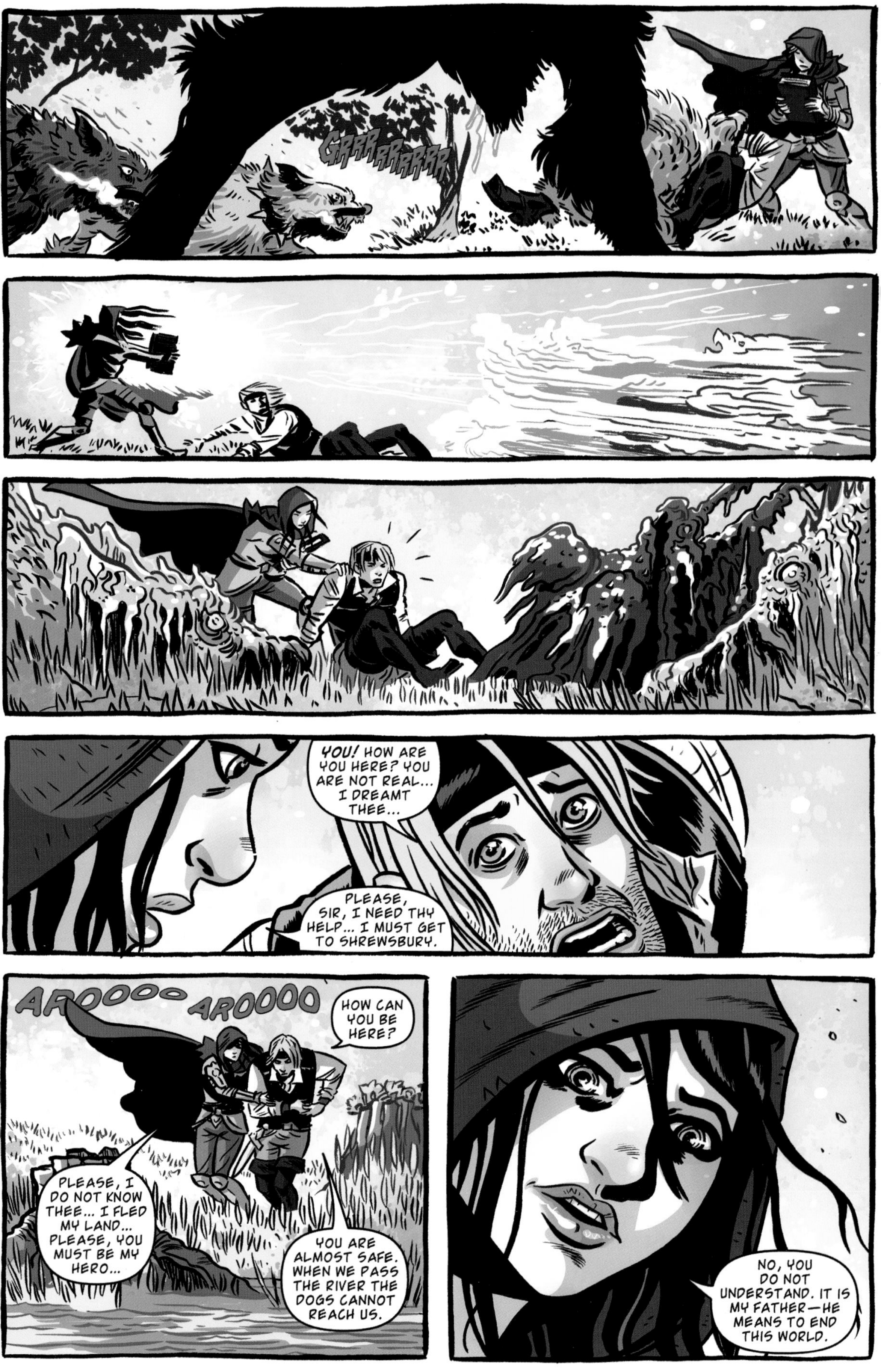
GRRRRRRRRR
YOU! HOW ARE YOU HERE? YOU ARE NOT REAL... I DREAMT THEE...
PLEASE, SIR, I NEED THY HELP... I MUST GET TO SHREWSBURY.
AROOOO AROOOO
HOW CAN YOU BE HERE?
PLEASE, I DO NOT KNOW THEE... I FLED MY LAND... PLEASE, YOU MUST BE MY HERO...
YOU ARE ALMOST SAFE. WHEN WE PASS THE RIVER THE DOGS CANNOT REACH US.
NO, YOU DO NOT UNDERSTAND. IT IS MY FATHER—HE MEANS TO END THIS WORLD.

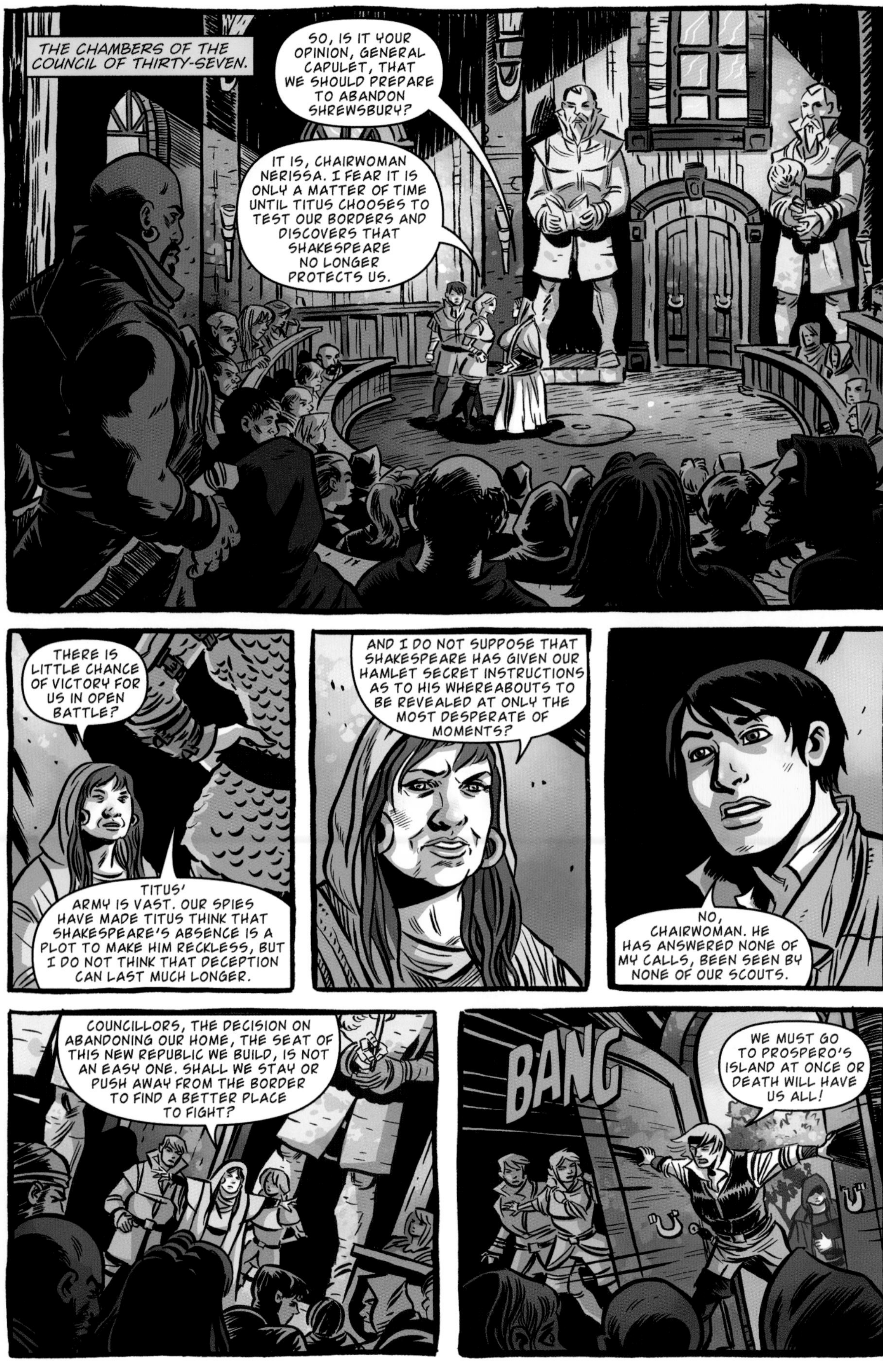
THE CHAMBERS OF THE COUNCIL OF THIRTY-SEVEN.
SO, IS IT YOUR OPINION, GENERAL CAPULET, THAT WE SHOULD PREPARE TO ABANDON SHREWSBURY?
IT IS, CHAIRWOMAN NERISSA. I FEAR IT IS ONLY A MATTER OF TIME UNTIL TITUS CHOOSES TO TEST OUR BORDERS AND DISCOVERS THAT SHAKESPEARE NO LONGER PROTECTS US.
THERE IS LITTLE CHANCE OF VICTORY FOR US IN OPEN BATTLE?
TITUS' ARMY IS VAST. OUR SPIES HAVE MADE TITUS THINK THAT SHAKESPEARE'S ABSENCE IS A PLOT TO MAKE HIM RECKLESS, BUT I DO NOT THINK THAT DECEPTION CAN LAST MUCH LONGER.
AND I DO NOT SUPPOSE THAT SHAKESPEARE HAS GIVEN OUR HAMLET SECRET INSTRUCTIONS AS TO HIS WHEREABOUTS TO BE REVEALED AT ONLY THE MOST DESPERATE OF MOMENTS?
NO, CHAIRWOMAN. HE HAS ANSWERED NONE OF MY CALLS, BEEN SEEN BY NONE OF OUR SCOUTS.
COUNCILLORS, THE DECISION ON ABANDONING OUR HOME, THE SEAT OF THIS NEW REPUBLIC WE BUILD, IS NOT AN EASY ONE. SHALL WE STAY OR PUSH AWAY FROM THE BORDER TO FIND A BETTER PLACE TO FIGHT?
BANG
WE MUST GO TO PROSPERO'S ISLAND AT ONCE OR DEATH WILL HAVE US ALL!

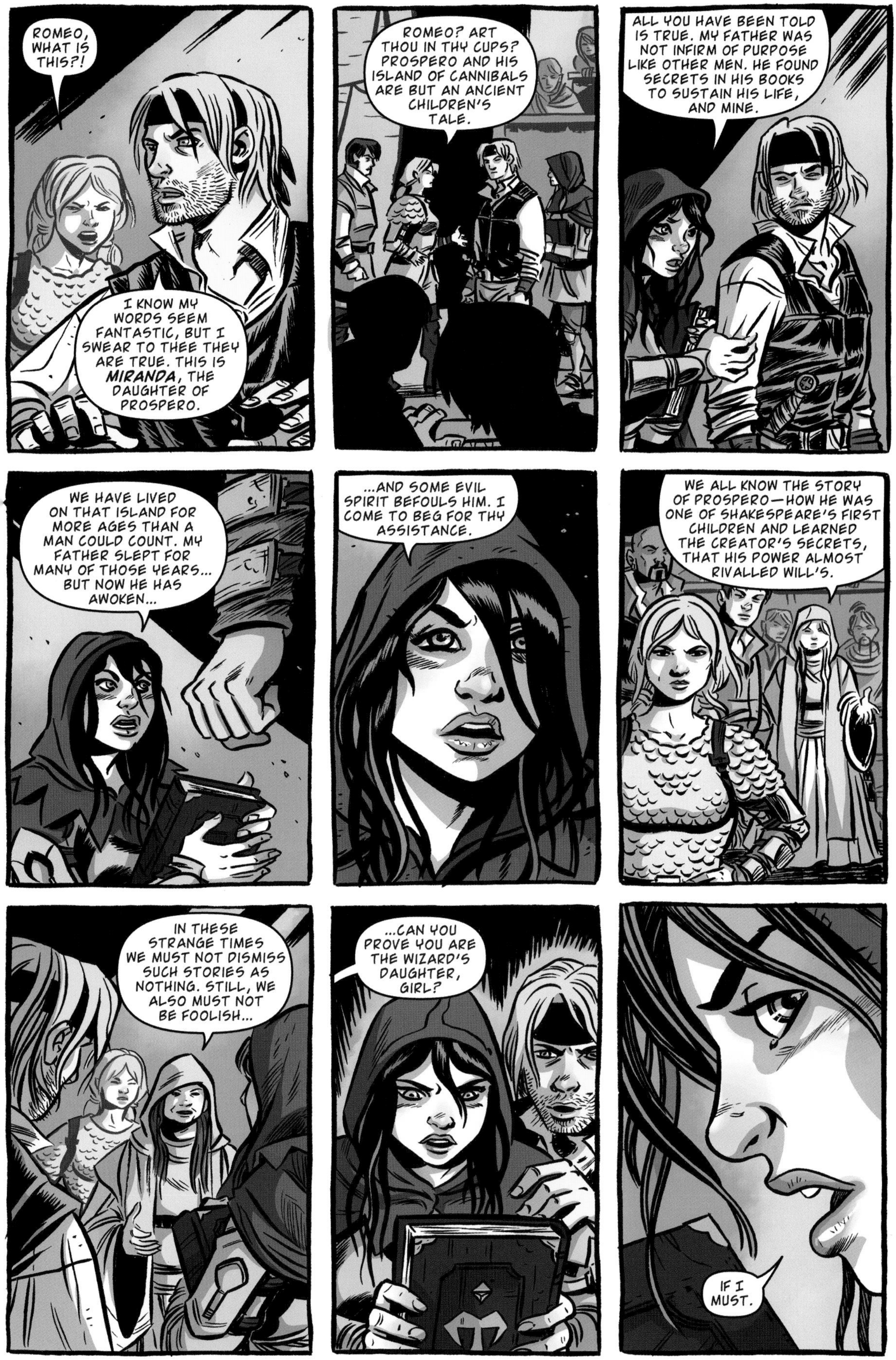
ROMEO, WHAT IS THIS?!
I KNOW MY WORDS SEEM FANTASTIC, BUT I SWEAR TO THEE THEY ARE TRUE. THIS IS MIRANDA, THE DAUGHTER OF PROSPERO.
ROMEO? ART THOU IN THY CUPS? PROSPERO AND HIS ISLAND OF CANNIBALS ARE BUT AN ANCIENT CHILDREN'S TALE.
ALL YOU HAVE BEEN TOLD IS TRUE. MY FATHER WAS NOT INFIRM OF PURPOSE LIKE OTHER MEN. HE FOUND SECRETS IN HIS BOOKS TO SUSTAIN HIS LIFE, AND MINE.
WE HAVE LIVED ON THAT ISLAND FOR MORE AGES THAN A MAN COULD COUNT. MY FATHER SLEPT FOR MANY OF THOSE YEARS... BUT NOW HE HAS AWOKEN...
...AND SOME EVIL SPIRIT BEFOULS HIM. I COME TO BEG FOR THY ASSISTANCE.
WE ALL KNOW THE STORY OF PROSPERO—HOW HE WAS ONE OF SHAKESPEARE'S FIRST CHILDREN AND LEARNED THE CREATOR'S SECRETS, THAT HIS POWER ALMOST RIVALLED WILL'S.
IN THESE STRANGE TIMES WE MUST NOT DISMISS SUCH STORIES AS NOTHING. STILL, WE ALSO MUST NOT BE FOOLISH...
...CAN YOU PROVE YOU ARE THE WIZARD'S DAUGHTER, GIRL?
IF I MUST.

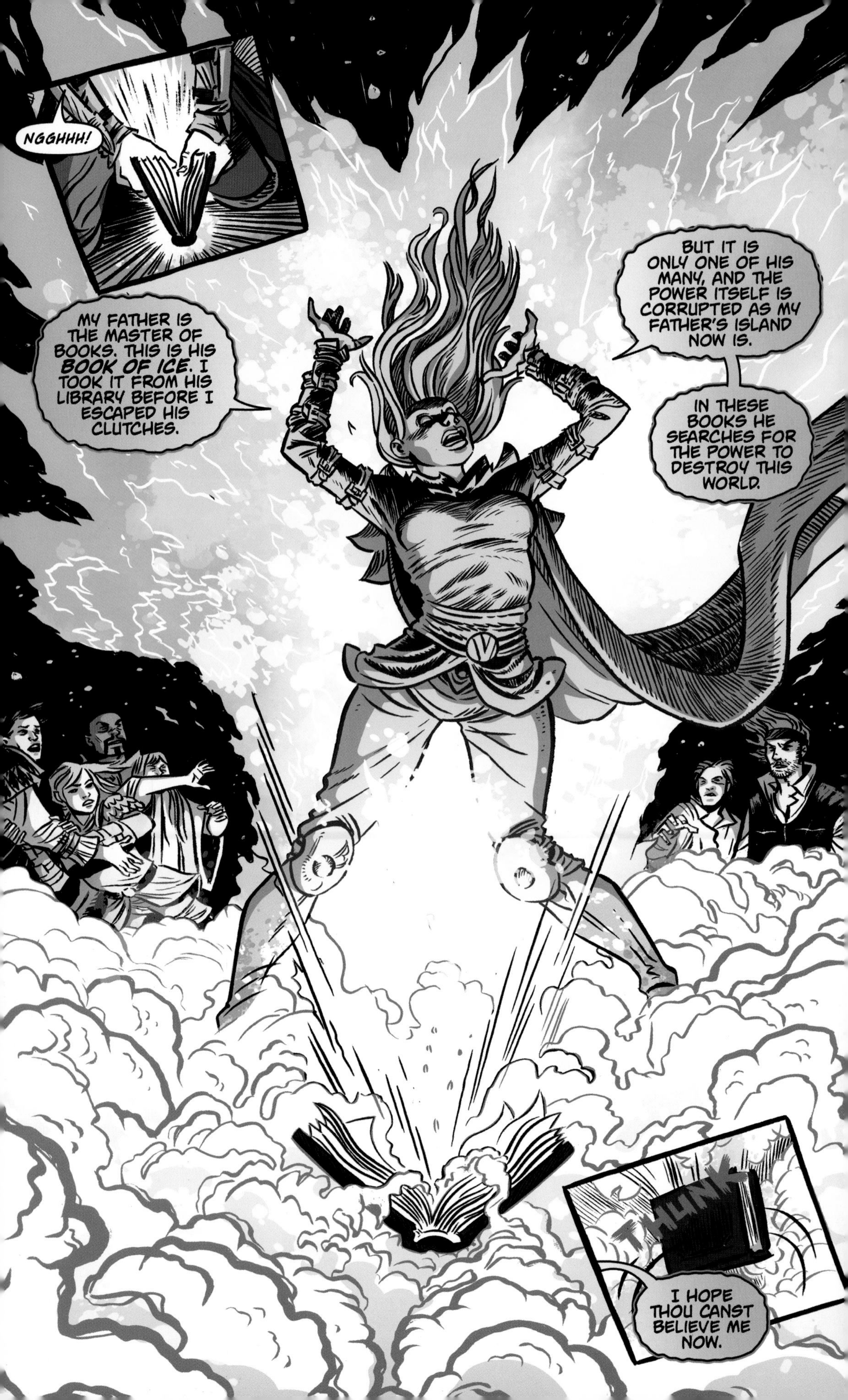
NGGHHH!
MY FATHER IS THE MASTER OF BOOKS. THIS IS HIS BOOK OF ICE. I TOOK IT FROM HIS LIBRARY BEFORE I ESCAPED HIS CLUTCHES.
BUT IT IS ONLY ONE OF HIS MANY, AND THE POWER ITSELF IS CORRUPTED AS MY FATHER'S ISLAND NOW IS.
IN THESE BOOKS HE SEARCHES FOR THE POWER TO DESTROY THIS WORLD.
THUNK
I HOPE THOU CANST BELIEVE ME NOW.

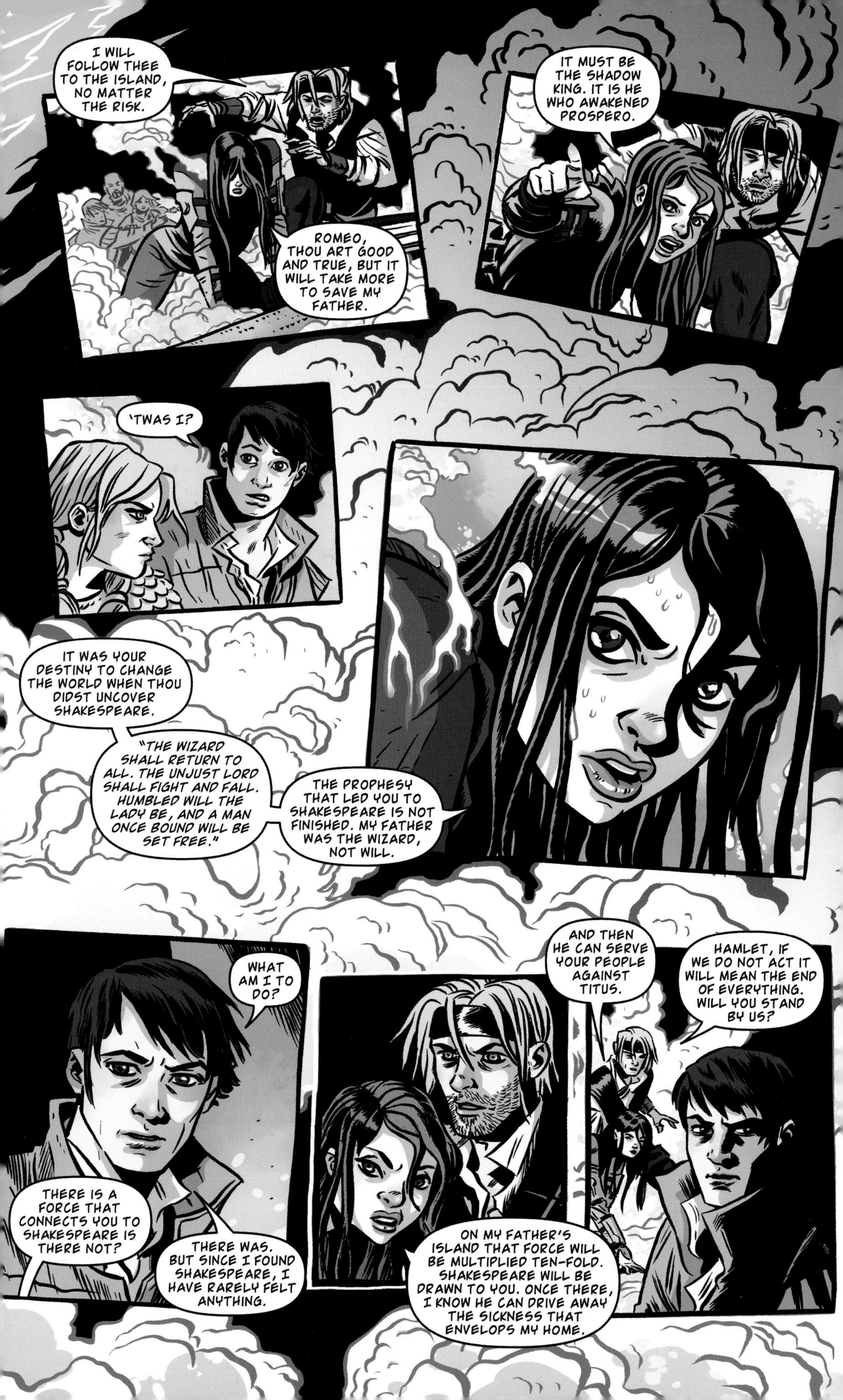
I WILL FOLLOW THEE TO THE ISLAND, NO MATTER THE RISK.
ROMEO, THOU ART GOOD AND TRUE, BUT IT WILL TAKE MORE TO SAVE MY FATHER.
IT MUST BE THE SHADOW KING. IT IS HE WHO AWAKENED PROSPERO.
'TWAS I?
IT WAS YOUR DESTINY TO CHANGE THE WORLD WHEN THOU DIDST UNCOVER SHAKESPEARE.
"THE WIZARD SHALL RETURN TO ALL. THE UNJUST LORD SHALL FIGHT AND FALL. HUMBLED WILL THE LADY BE, AND A MAN ONCE BOUND WILL BE SET FREE."
THE PROPHESY THAT LED YOU TO SHAKESPEARE IS NOT FINISHED. MY FATHER WAS THE WIZARD, NOT WILL.
WHAT AM I TO DO?
THERE IS A FORCE THAT CONNECTS YOU TO SHAKESPEARE IS THERE NOT?
THERE WAS. BUT SINCE I FOUND SHAKESPEARE, I HAVE RARELY FELT ANYTHING.
ON MY FATHER'S ISLAND THAT FORCE WILL BE MULTIPLIED TEN-FOLD. SHAKESPEARE WILL BE DRAWN TO YOU. ONCE THERE, I KNOW HE CAN DRIVE AWAY THE SICKNESS THAT ENVELOPS MY HOME.
AND THEN HE CAN SERVE YOUR PEOPLE AGAINST TITUS.
HAMLET, IF WE DO NOT ACT IT WILL MEAN THE END OF EVERYTHING. WILL YOU STAND BY US?

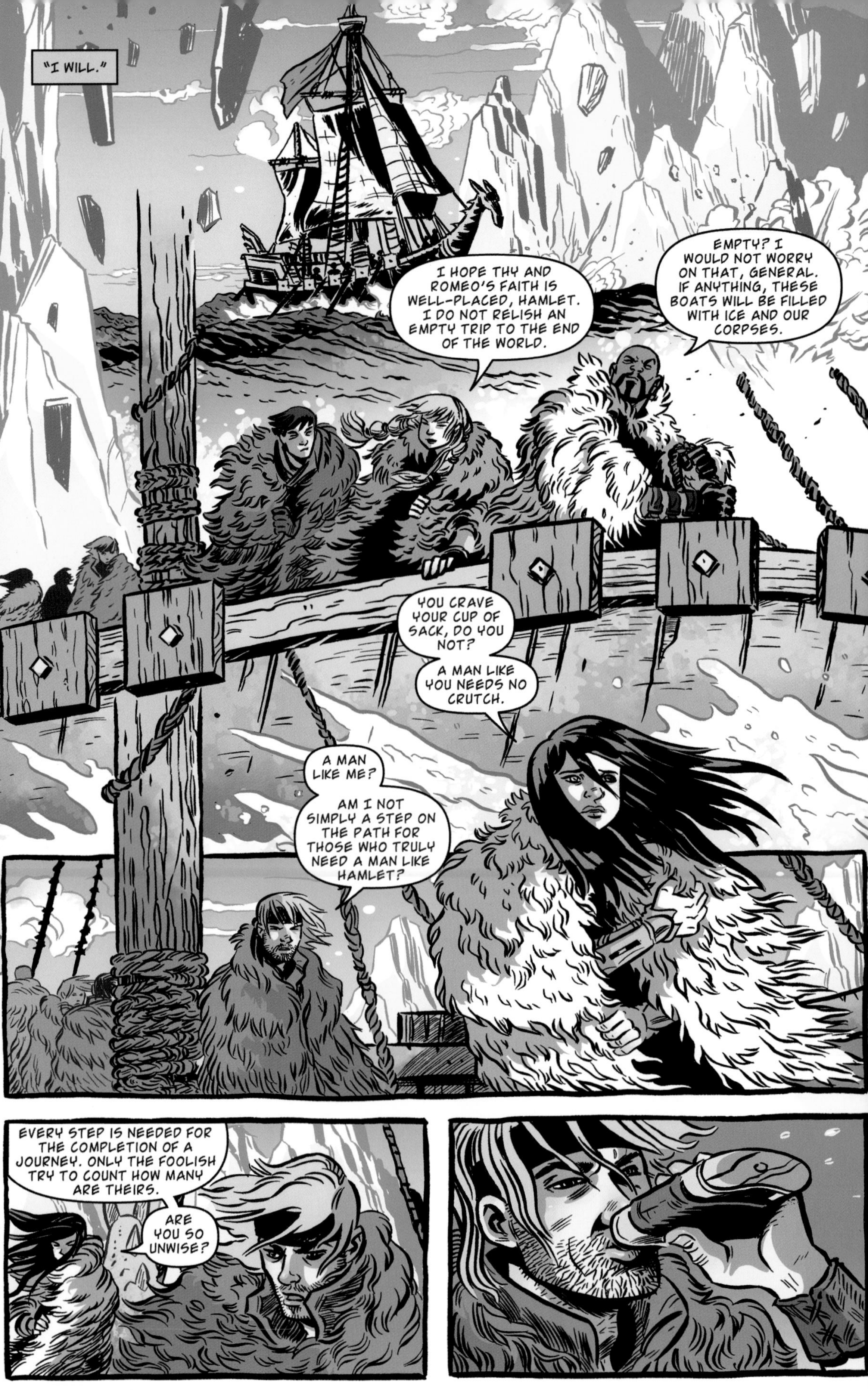
"I WILL."
I HOPE THY AND ROMEO'S FAITH IS WELL-PLACED, HAMLET. I DO NOT RELISH AN EMPTY TRIP TO THE END OF THE WORLD.
EMPTY? I WOULD NOT WORRY ON THAT, GENERAL. IF ANYTHING, THESE BOATS WILL BE FILLED WITH ICE AND OUR CORPSES.
YOU CRAVE YOUR CUP OF SACK, DO YOU NOT?
A MAN LIKE YOU NEEDS NO CRUTCH.
A MAN LIKE ME?
AM I NOT SIMPLY A STEP ON THE PATH FOR THOSE WHO TRULY NEED A MAN LIKE HAMLET?
EVERY STEP IS NEEDED FOR THE COMPLETION OF A JOURNEY. ONLY THE FOOLISH TRY TO COUNT HOW MANY ARE THEIRS.
ARE YOU SO UNWISE?

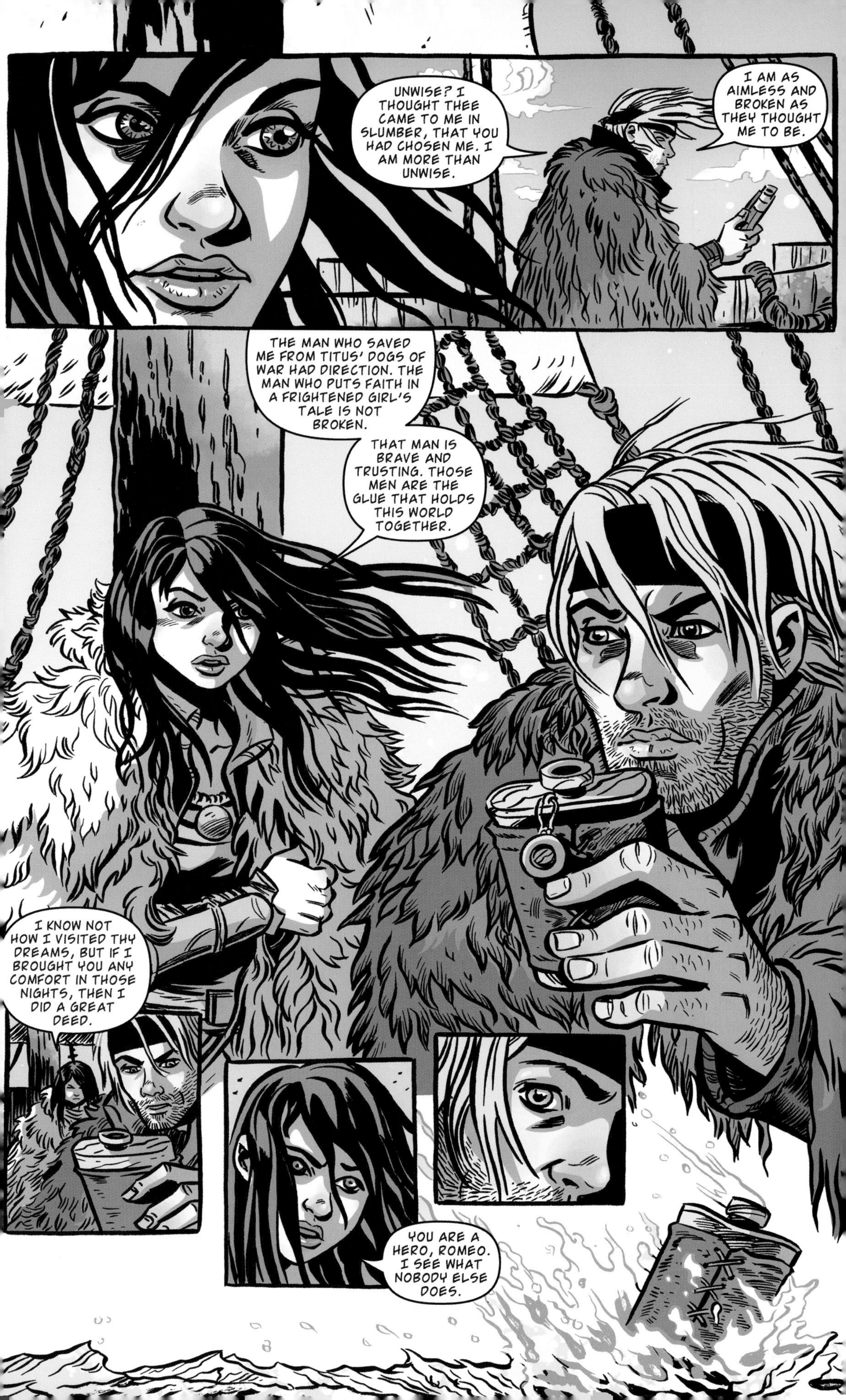
UNWISE? I THOUGHT THEE CAME TO ME IN SLUMBER, THAT YOU HAD CHOSEN ME. I AM MORE THAN UNWISE.
I AM AS AIMLESS AND BROKEN AS THEY THOUGHT ME TO BE.
THE MAN WHO SAVED ME FROM TITUS' DOGS OF WAR HAD DIRECTION. THE MAN WHO PUTS FAITH IN A FRIGHTENED GIRL'S TALE IS NOT BROKEN.
THAT MAN IS BRAVE AND TRUSTING. THOSE MEN ARE THE GLUE THAT HOLDS THIS WORLD TOGETHER.
I KNOW NOT HOW I VISITED THY DREAMS, BUT IF I BROUGHT YOU ANY COMFORT IN THOSE NIGHTS, THEN I DID A GREAT DEED.
YOU ARE A HERO, ROMEO. I SEE WHAT NOBODY ELSE DOES.

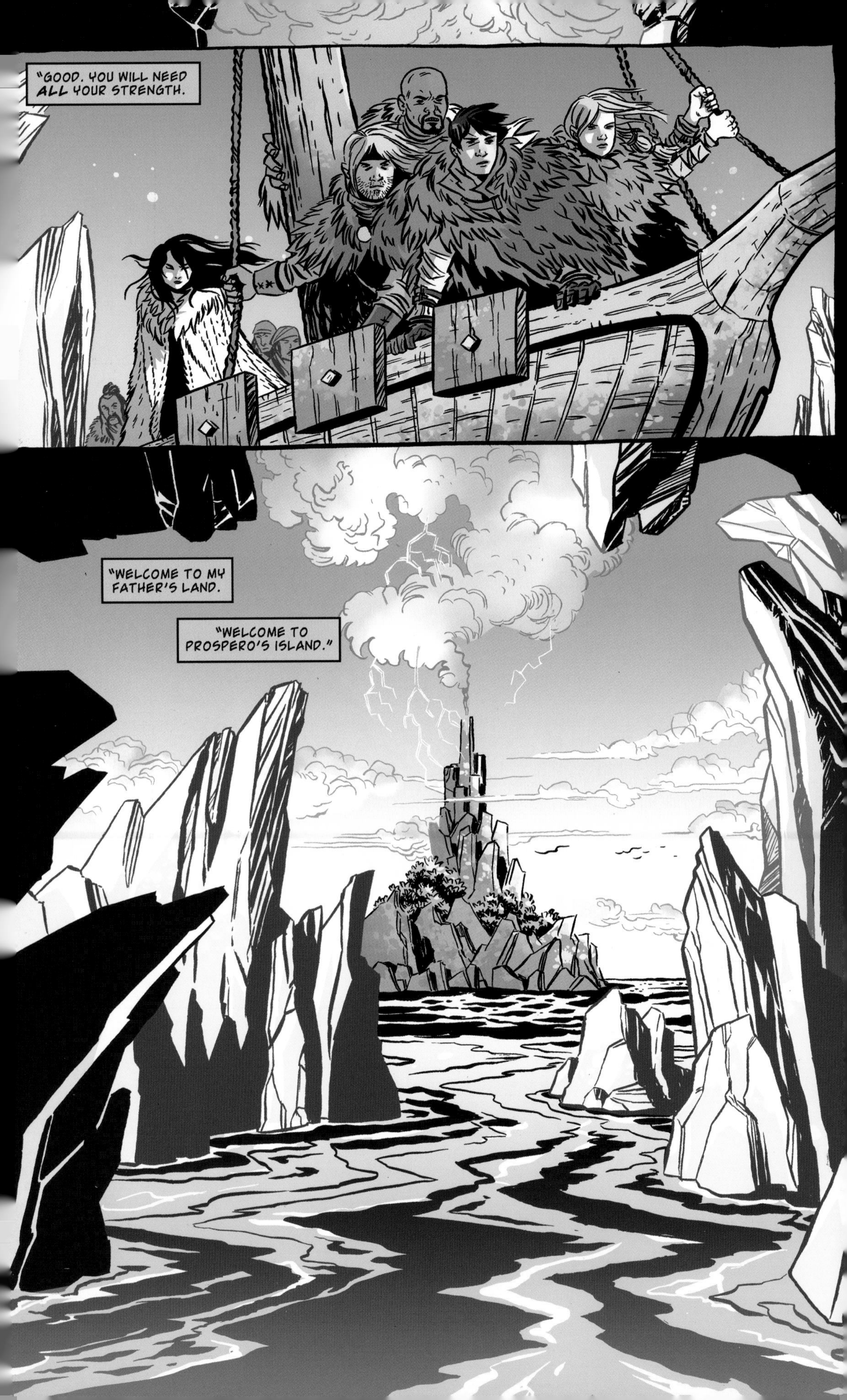
"GOOD. YOU WILL NEED ALL YOUR STRENGTH.
"WELCOME TO MY FATHER'S LAND.
"WELCOME TO PROSPERO'S ISLAND."

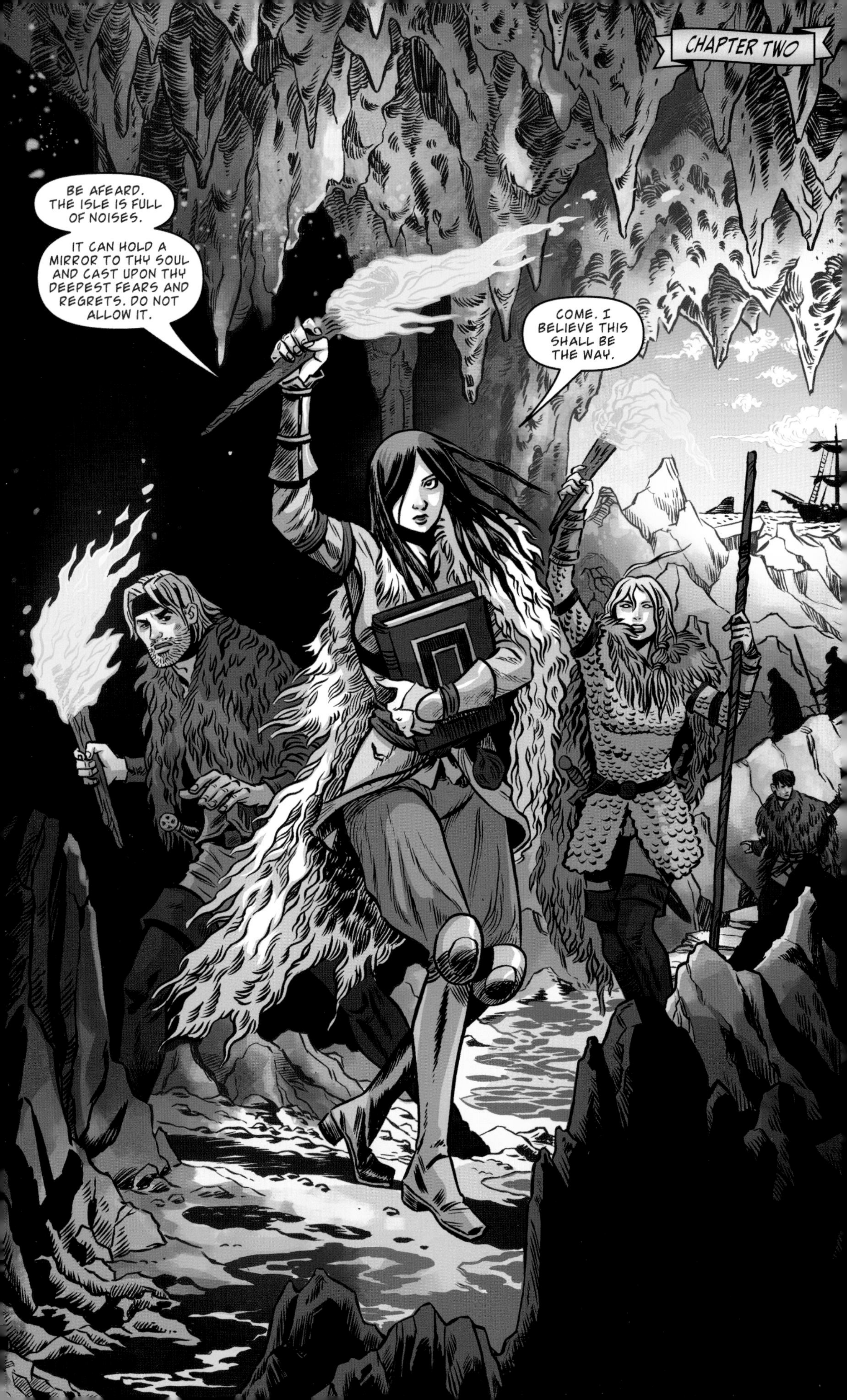
CHAPTER TWO
BE AFEARD. THE ISLE IS FULL OF NOISES.
IT CAN HOLD A MIRROR TO THY SOUL AND CAST UPON THY DEEPEST FEARS AND REGRETS. DO NOT ALLOW IT.
COME. I BELIEVE THIS SHALL BE THE WAY.

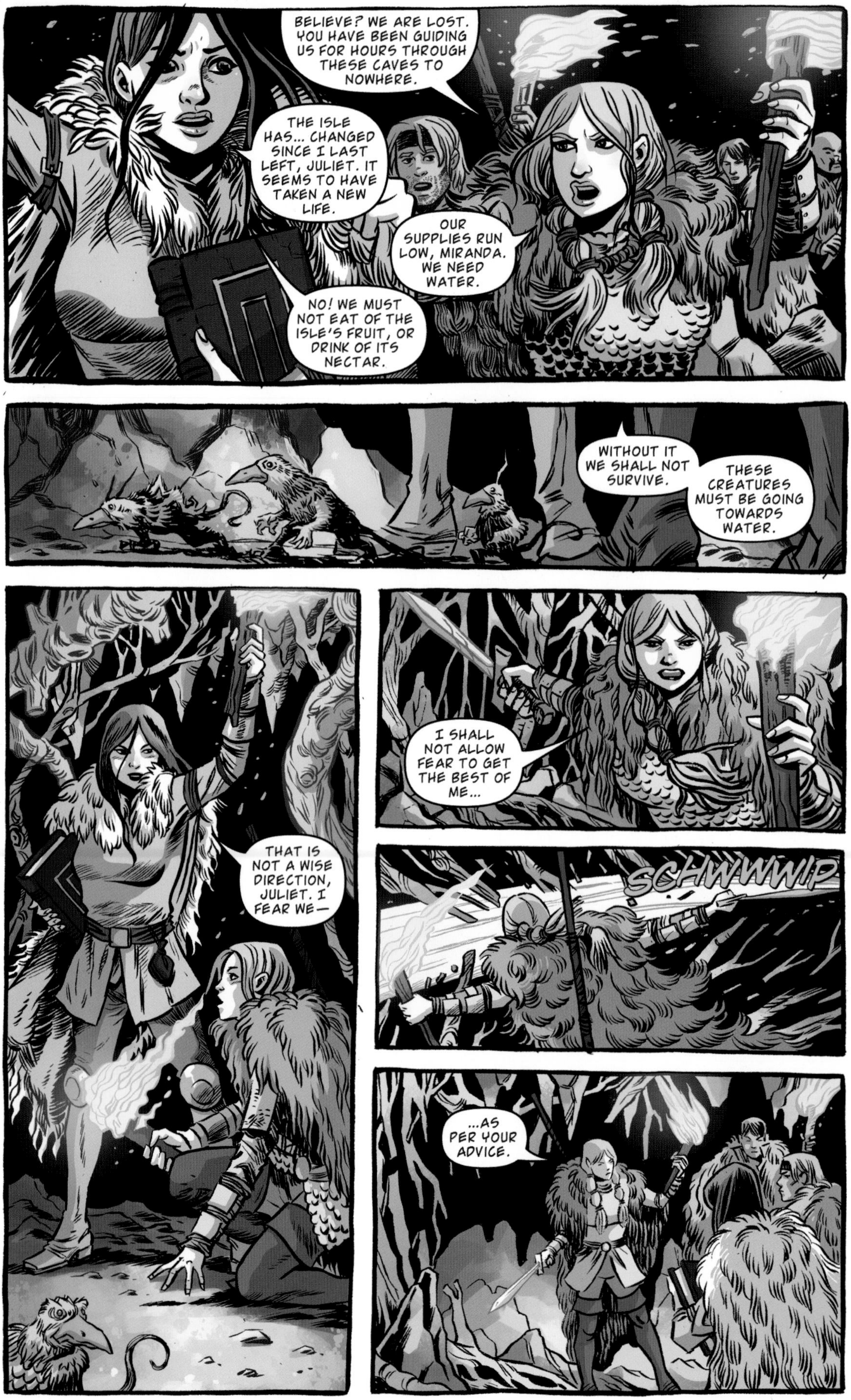
BELIEVE? WE ARE LOST. YOU HAVE BEEN GUIDING US FOR HOURS THROUGH THESE CAVES TO NOWHERE.
THE ISLE HAS... CHANGED SINCE I LAST LEFT, JULIET. IT SEEMS TO HAVE TAKEN A NEW LIFE.
OUR SUPPLIES RUN LOW, MIRANDA. WE NEED WATER.
NO! WE MUST NOT EAT OF THE ISLE'S FRUIT, OR DRINK OF ITS NECTAR.
WITHOUT IT WE SHALL NOT SURVIVE.
THESE CREATURES MUST BE GOING TOWARDS WATER.
THAT IS NOT A WISE DIRECTION, JULIET. I FEAR WE—
I SHALL NOT ALLOW FEAR TO GET THE BEST OF ME...
SCHWWWIP
...AS PER YOUR ADVICE.

DRINK. FILL UP THY SKINS. THE JOURNEY STILL LOOKS TO BE LONG.

WE SHOULD SET UP CAMP HERE. I LOSE FAITH IN MIRANDA.

DOES YOUR SENSE OF SHAKESPEARE GROW, HAMLET?

WHY PRESS ON BLINDLY THEN? IF THAT STIRRING DOES NOT STRENGTHEN THEN HER TALE WAS A LIE AND WE LEAVE THIS LAND.

CAMP? HERE?

I FEEL... SOMETHING.

WE MADE A PROMISE, JULIET.

I SWORE TO MIRANDA TO FREE HER FATHER OF THIS ISLAND'S CURSE.

I APPLAUD THY DESIRE TO HELP HER BUT WE ARE LOST. MIRANDA KNOWS NOT THE WAY. HER BOOK DOES NOT GUIDE HER AS I BELIEVED IT WOULD.

I FEAR THAT WITHOUT SHAKESPEARE WE MAY NOT BE ABLE TO ESCAPE THIS ISLAND AS IT IS—

WE... WE CANNOT WAIT FOR SHAKESPEARE TO COME AND PROVIDE SALVATION. WE MUST FREE PROSPERO OURSELVES.

HAMLET

DO YOU HEAR THAT?

WHY THOU THOU HAST HAST THOU HAST THOU HAST

DO YOU—?

FORGOTTEN ME

HAMLET?

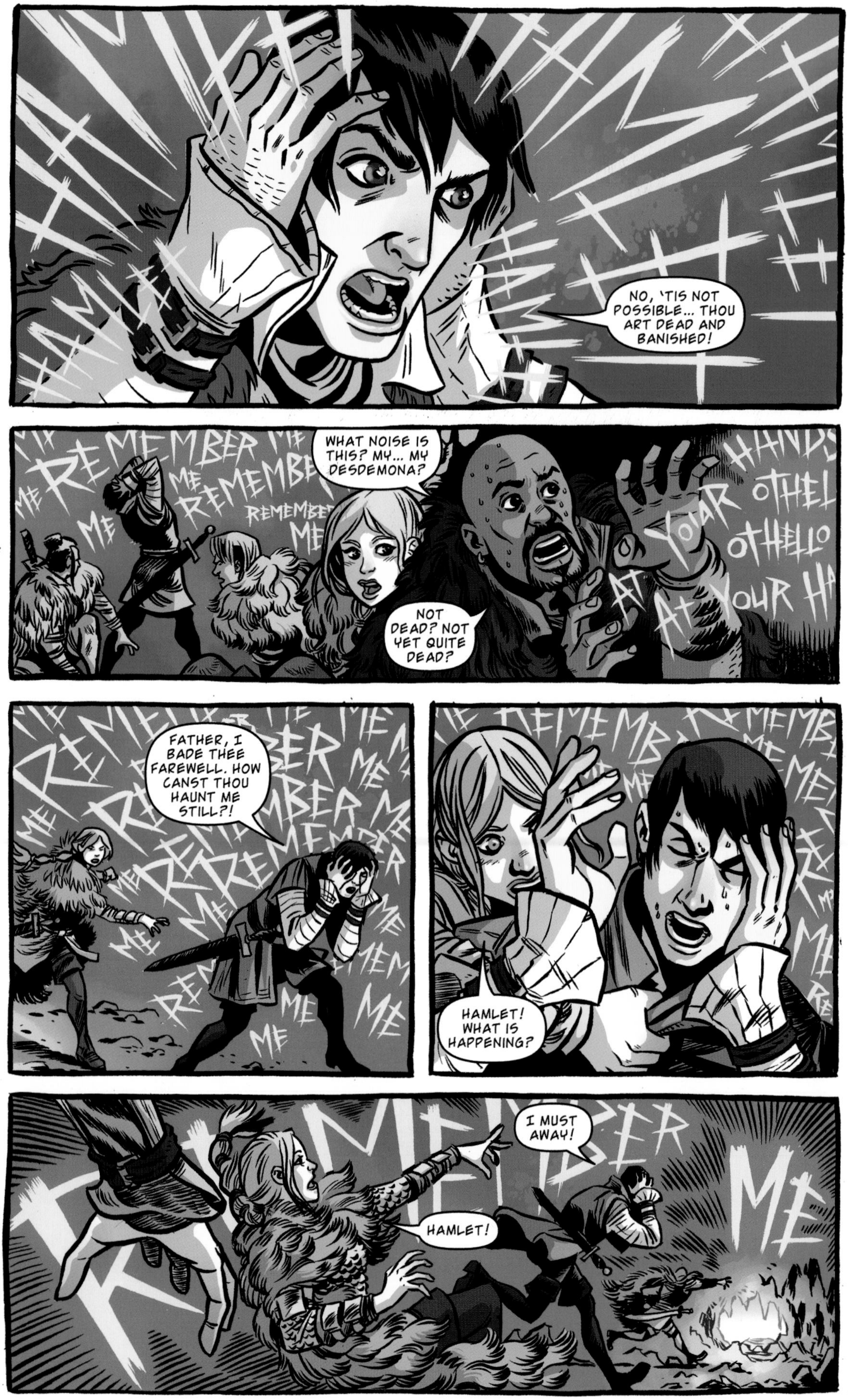
NO, 'TIS NOT POSSIBLE... THOU ART DEAD AND BANISHED!
REMEMBER ME
WHAT NOISE IS THIS? MY... MY DESDEMONA?
NOT DEAD? NOT YET QUITE DEAD?
FATHER, I BADE THEE FAREWELL. HOW CANST THOU HAUNT ME STILL?!
HAMLET! WHAT IS HAPPENING?
I MUST AWAY!
HAMLET!

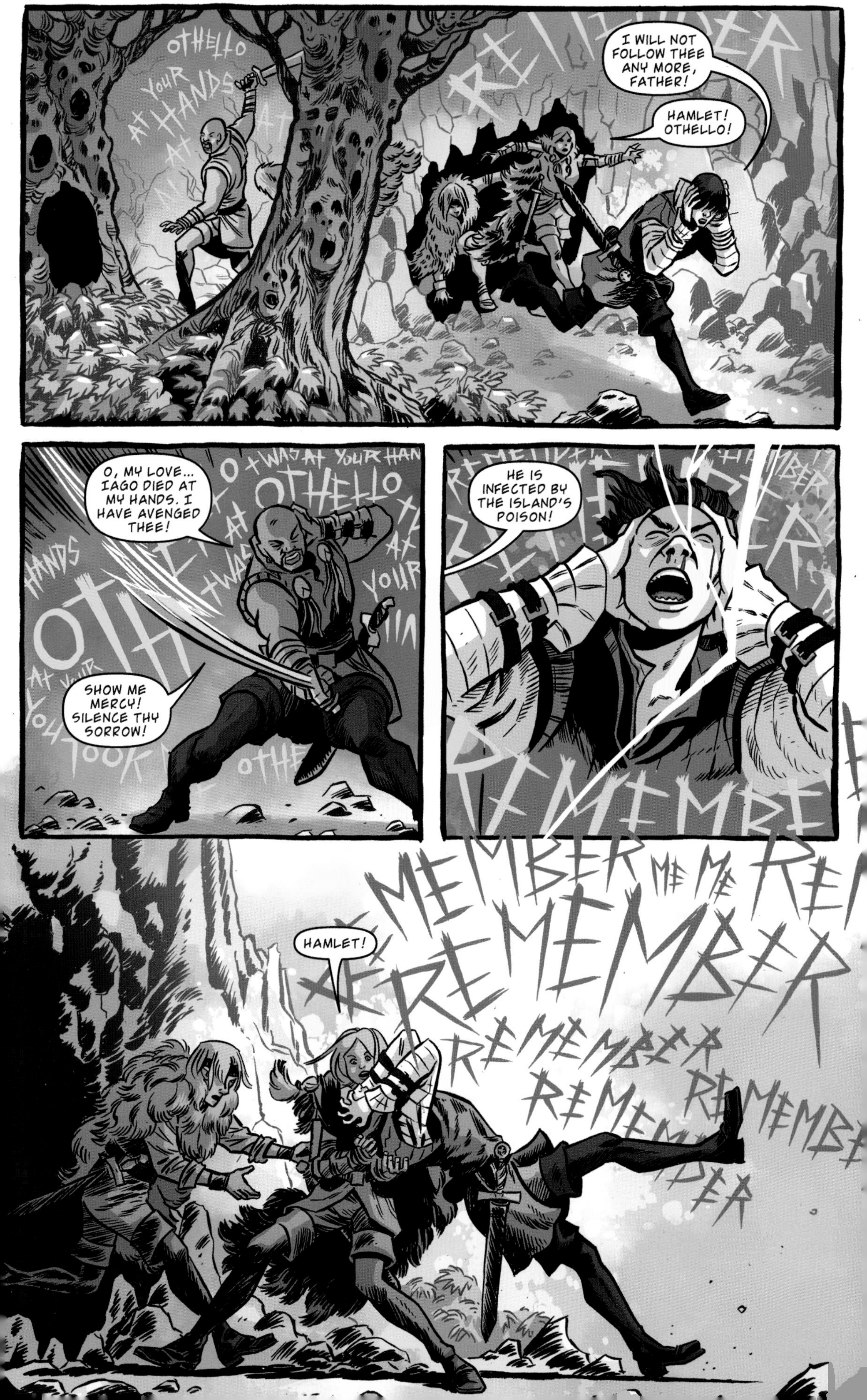
I WILL NOT FOLLOW THEE ANY MORE, FATHER!
HAMLET! OTHELLO!
O, MY LOVE... IAGO DIED AT MY HANDS. I HAVE AVENGED THEE!
SHOW ME MERCY! SILENCE THY SORROW!
HE IS INFECTED BY THE ISLAND'S POISON!
HAMLET!
REMEMBER
REMEMBER
REMEMBER
REMEMBER

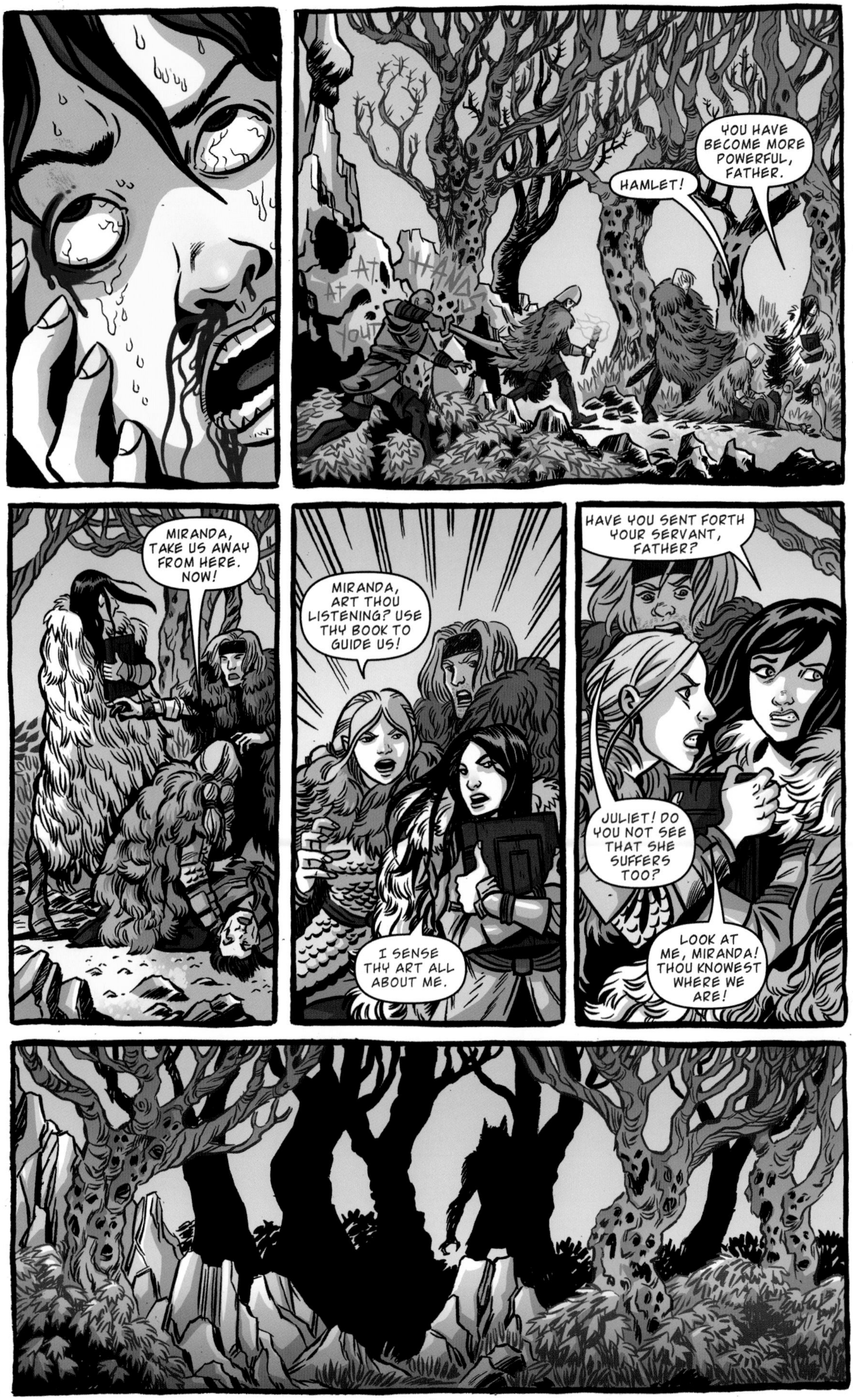
HAMLET!
YOU HAVE BECOME MORE POWERFUL, FATHER.
MIRANDA, TAKE US AWAY FROM HERE. NOW!
MIRANDA, ART THOU LISTENING? USE THY BOOK TO GUIDE US!
I SENSE THY ART ALL ABOUT ME.
HAVE YOU SENT FORTH YOUR SERVANT, FATHER?
JULIET! DO YOU NOT SEE THAT SHE SUFFERS TOO?
LOOK AT ME, MIRANDA! THOU KNOWEST WHERE WE ARE!

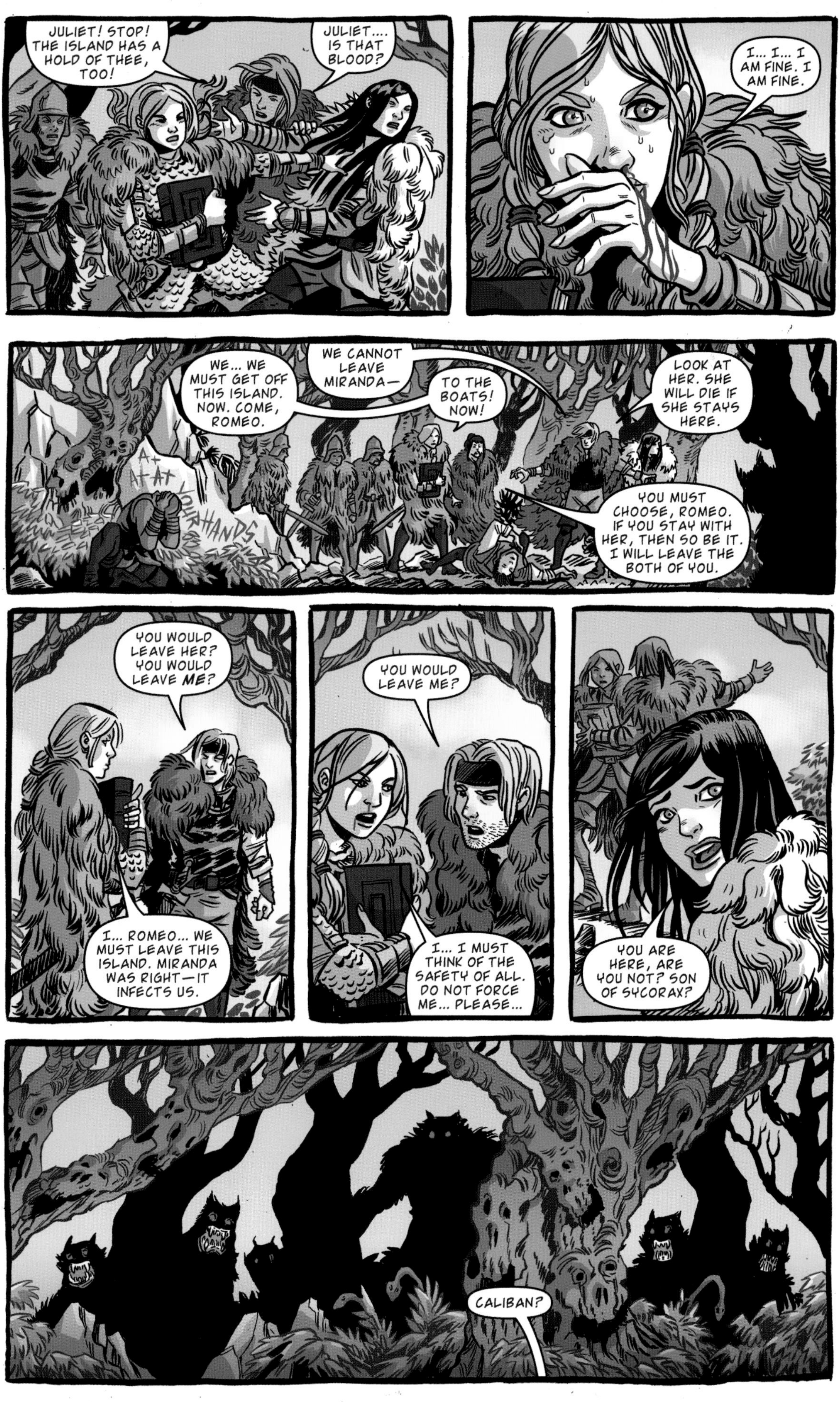
JULIET! STOP! THE ISLAND HAS A HOLD OF THEE, TOO!
JULIET.... IS THAT BLOOD?
I... I... I AM FINE. I AM FINE.
WE... WE MUST GET OFF THIS ISLAND. NOW. COME, ROMEO.
WE CANNOT LEAVE MIRANDA—
TO THE BOATS! NOW!
LOOK AT HER. SHE WILL DIE IF SHE STAYS HERE.
YOU MUST CHOOSE, ROMEO. IF YOU STAY WITH HER, THEN SO BE IT. I WILL LEAVE THE BOTH OF YOU.
YOU WOULD LEAVE HER? YOU WOULD LEAVE *ME*?
I... ROMEO... WE MUST LEAVE THIS ISLAND. MIRANDA WAS RIGHT—IT INFECTS US.
YOU WOULD LEAVE ME?
I... I MUST THINK OF THE SAFETY OF ALL. DO NOT FORCE ME... PLEASE...
YOU ARE HERE, ARE YOU NOT? SON OF SYCORAX?
CALIBAN?

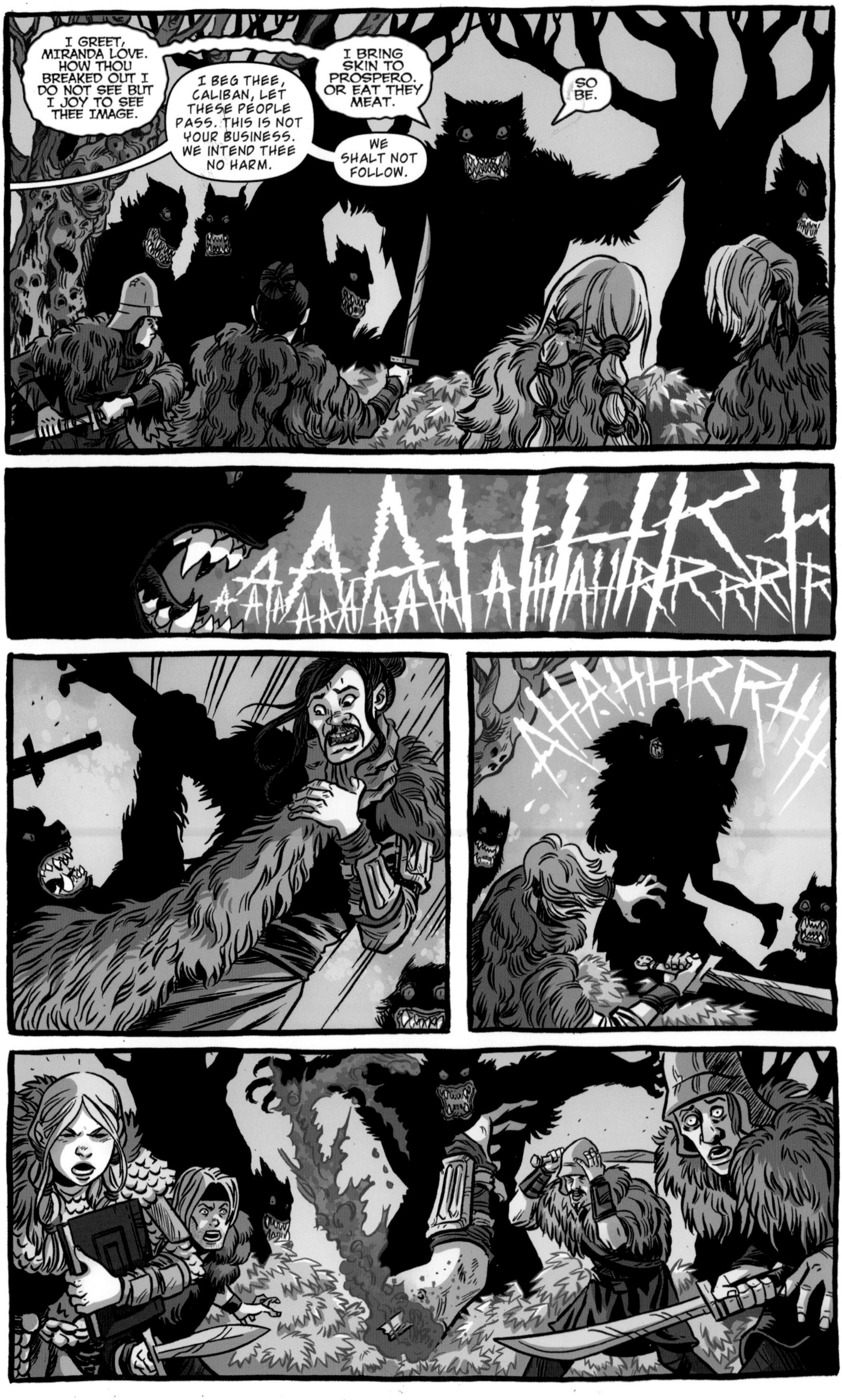
I GREET, MIRANDA LOVE. HOW THOU BREAKED OUT I DO NOT SEE BUT I JOY TO SEE THEE IMAGE.
I BEG THEE, CALIBAN, LET THESE PEOPLE PASS. THIS IS NOT YOUR BUSINESS. WE INTEND THEE NO HARM.
I BRING SKIN TO PROSPERO. OR EAT THEY MEAT.
WE SHALT NOT FOLLOW.
SO BE.

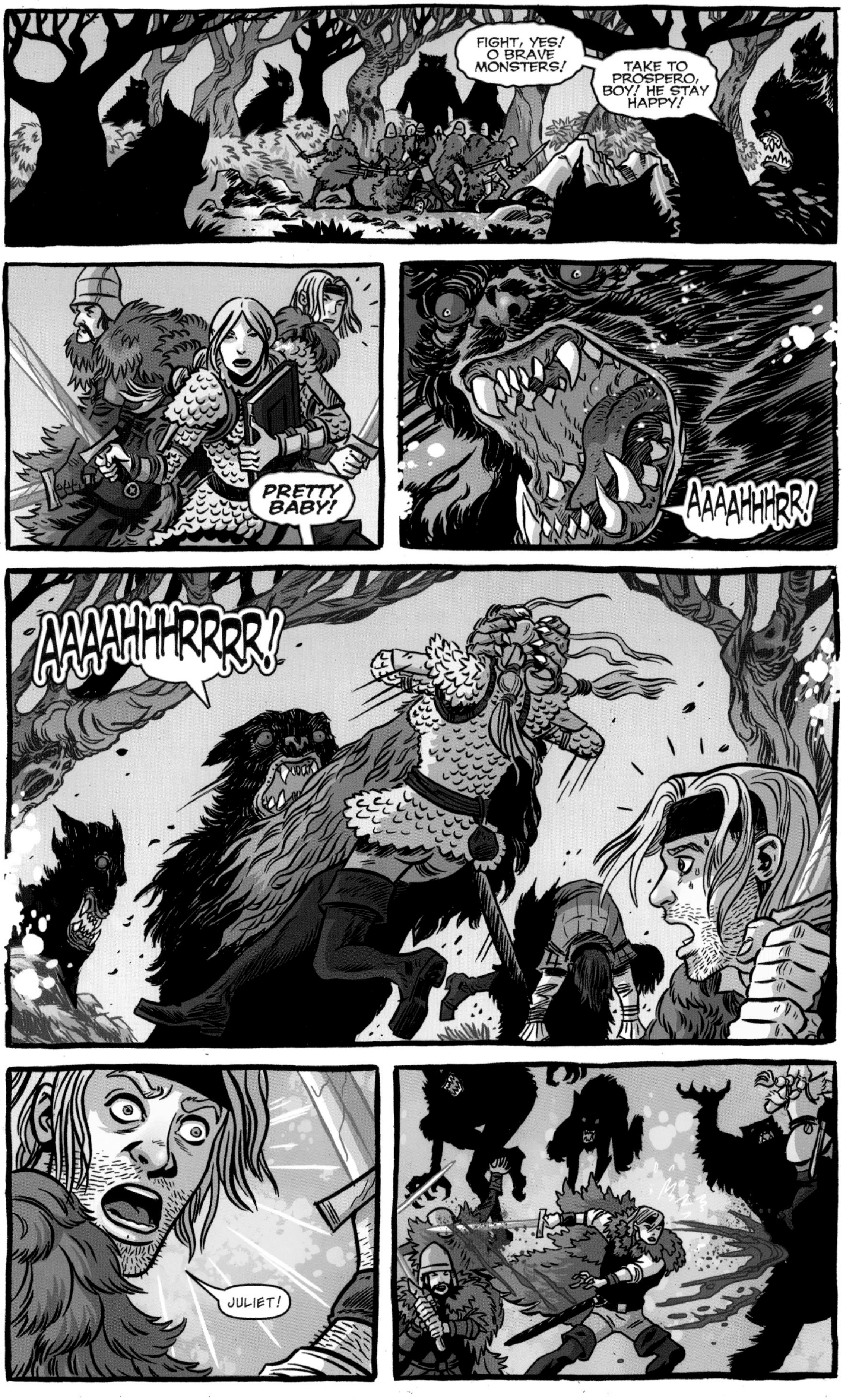
FIGHT, YES! O BRAVE MONSTERS!
TAKE TO PROSPERO, BOY! HE STAY HAPPY!
PRETTY BABY!
AAAAHHHRR!
AAAAHHHRRRR!
JULIET!

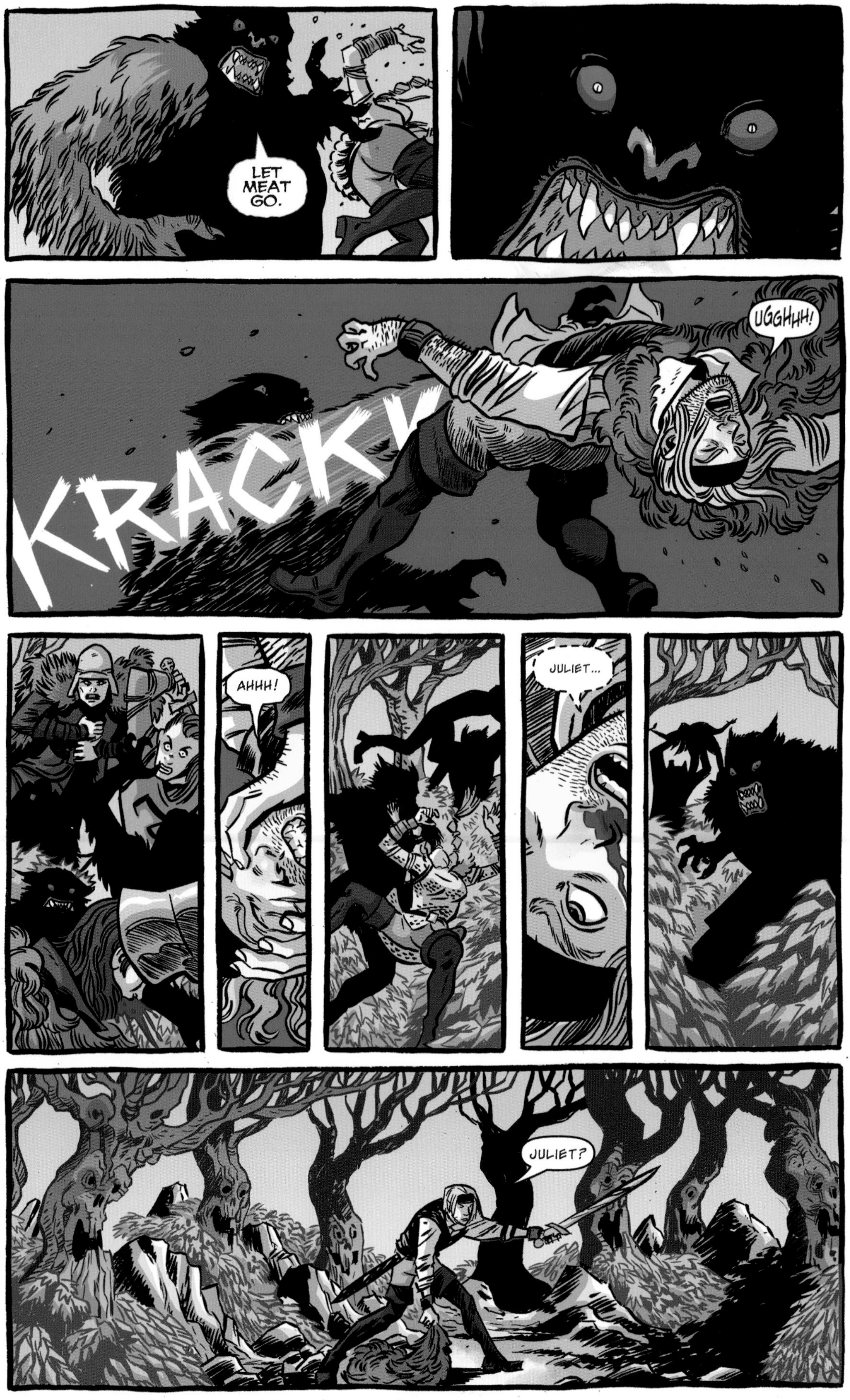
LET MEAT GO.
UGGHHH!
KRACK
AHHH!
JULIET...
JULIET?

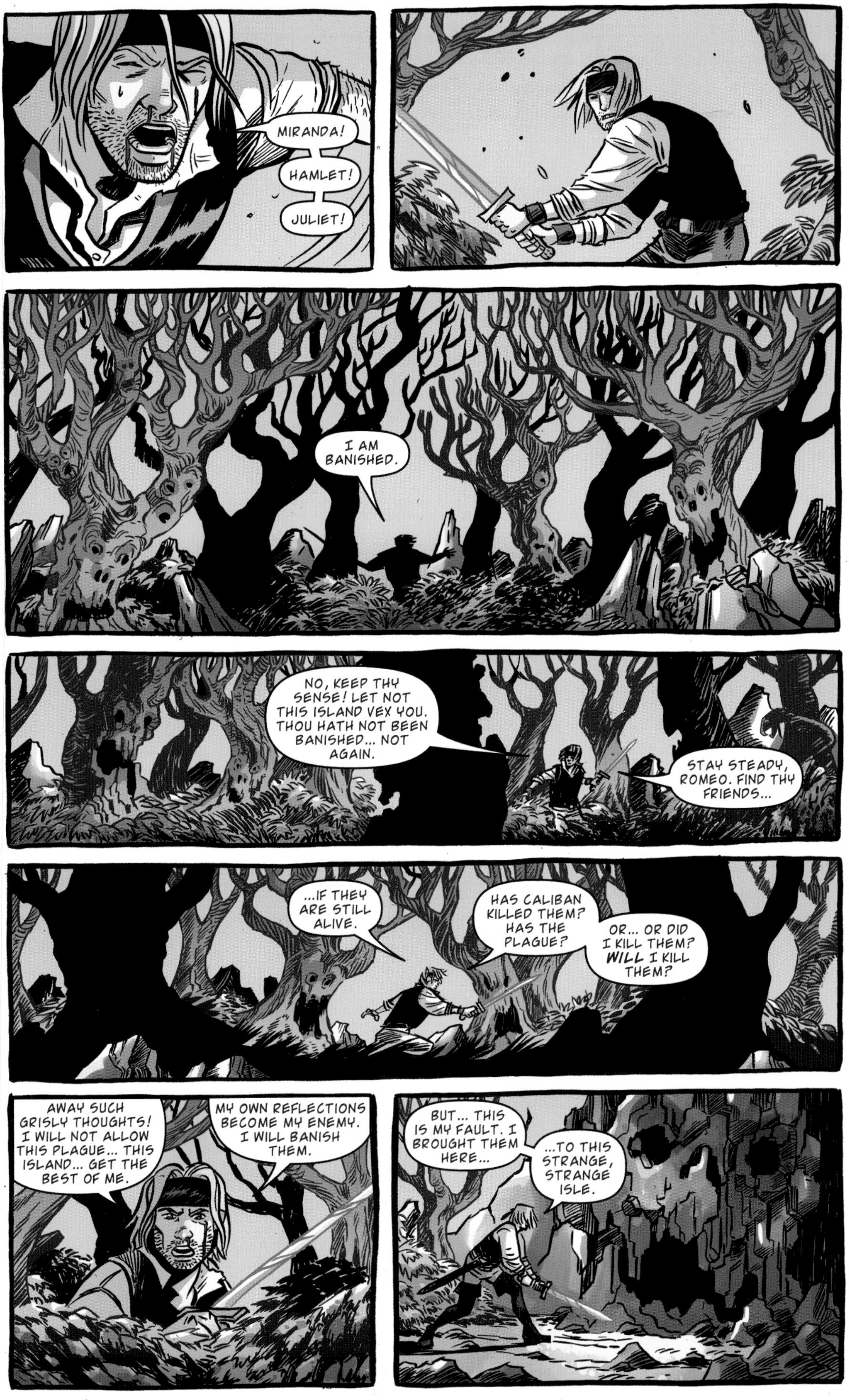
MIRANDA!
HAMLET!
JULIET!
I AM BANISHED.
NO, KEEP THY SENSE! LET NOT THIS ISLAND VEX YOU. THOU HATH NOT BEEN BANISHED... NOT AGAIN.
STAY STEADY, ROMEO. FIND THY FRIENDS...
...IF THEY ARE STILL ALIVE.
HAS CALIBAN KILLED THEM? HAS THE PLAGUE?
OR... OR DID I KILL THEM? WILL I KILL THEM?
AWAY SUCH GRISLY THOUGHTS! I WILL NOT ALLOW THIS PLAGUE... THIS ISLAND... GET THE BEST OF ME.
MY OWN REFLECTIONS BECOME MY ENEMY. I WILL BANISH THEM.
BUT... THIS IS MY FAULT. I BROUGHT THEM HERE...
...TO THIS STRANGE, STRANGE ISLE.

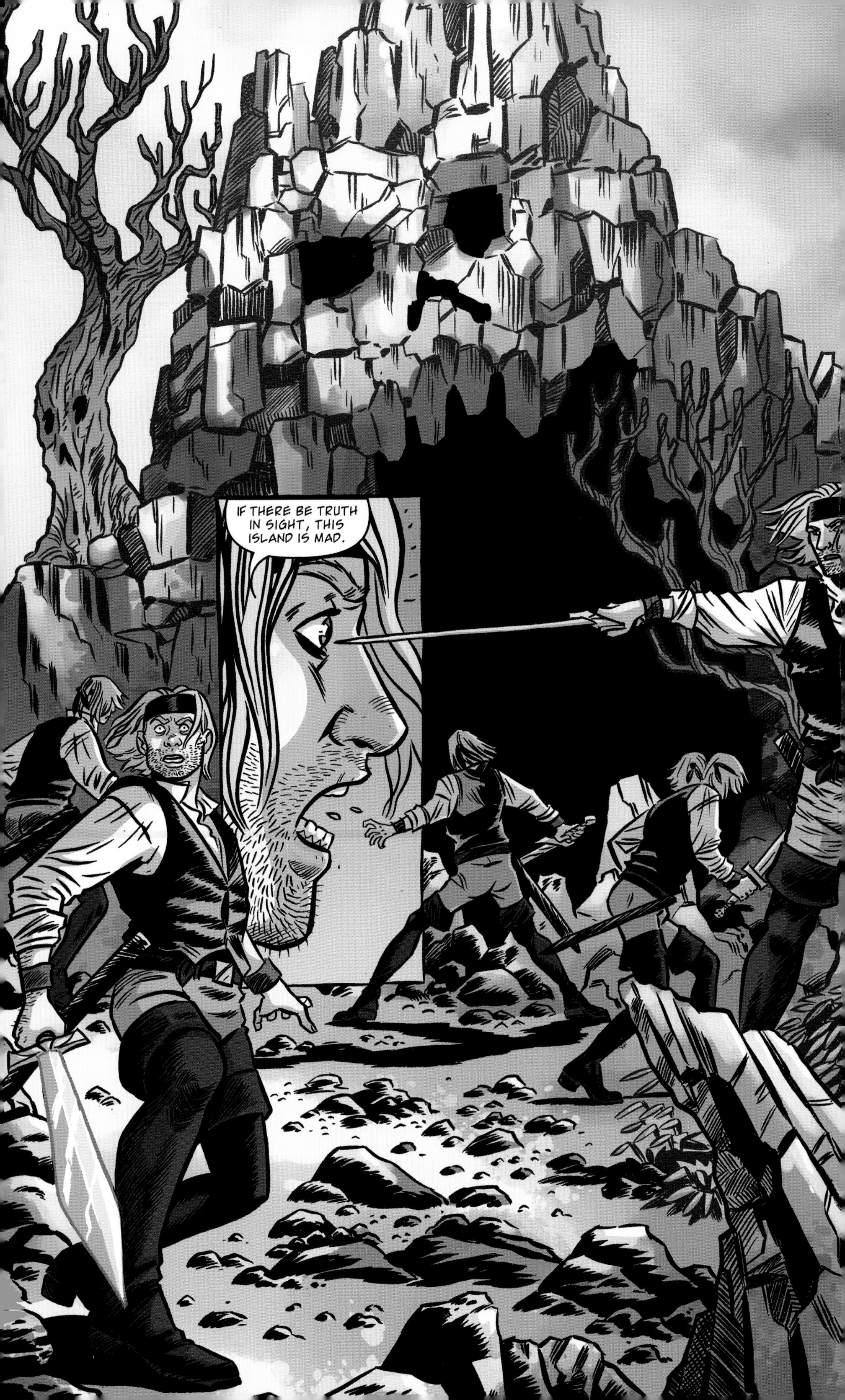
IF THERE BE TRUTH IN SIGHT, THIS ISLAND IS MAD.

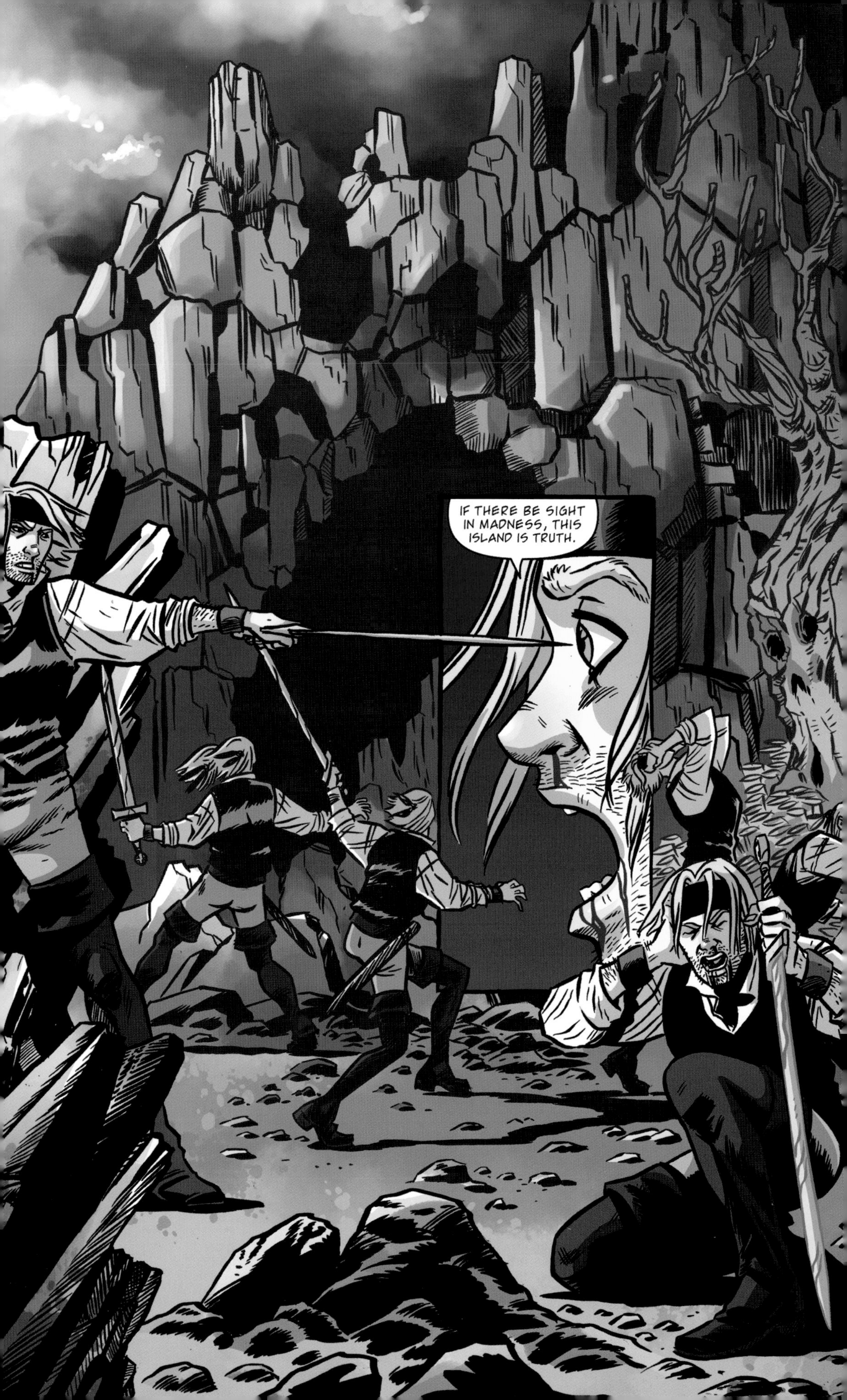
IF THERE BE SIGHT IN MADNESS, THIS ISLAND IS TRUTH.

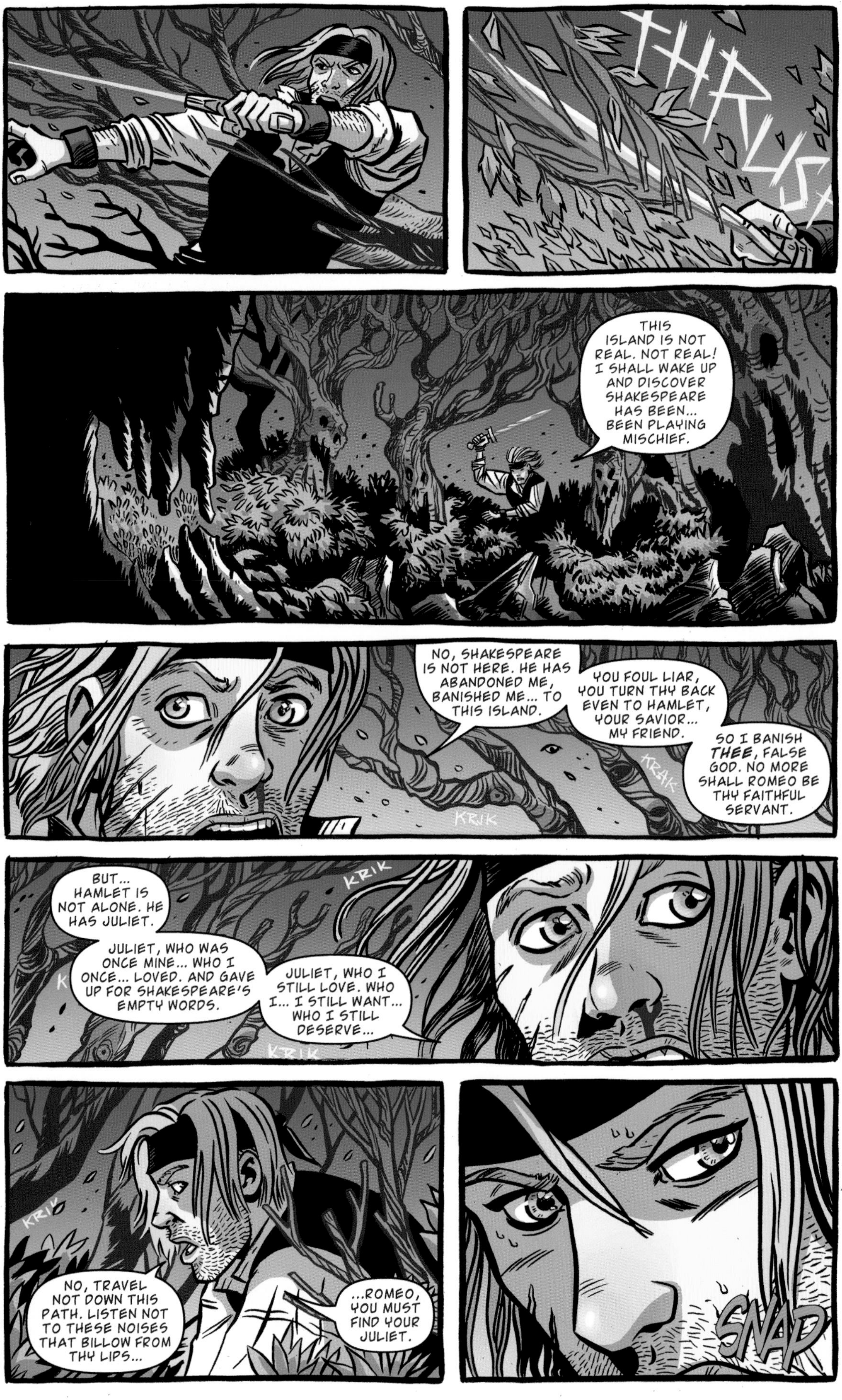
THRUST
THIS ISLAND IS NOT REAL. NOT REAL! I SHALL WAKE UP AND DISCOVER SHAKESPEARE HAS BEEN... BEEN PLAYING MISCHIEF.
NO, SHAKESPEARE IS NOT HERE. HE HAS ABANDONED ME, BANISHED ME... TO THIS ISLAND.
YOU FOUL LIAR, YOU TURN THY BACK EVEN TO HAMLET, YOUR SAVIOR... MY FRIEND.
SO I BANISH THEE, FALSE GOD. NO MORE SHALL ROMEO BE THY FAITHFUL SERVANT.
KRAK
KRIK
BUT... HAMLET IS NOT ALONE. HE HAS JULIET.
KRIK
JULIET, WHO WAS ONCE MINE... WHO I ONCE... LOVED. AND GAVE UP FOR SHAKESPEARE'S EMPTY WORDS.
JULIET, WHO I STILL LOVE. WHO I... I STILL WANT... WHO I STILL DESERVE...
KRIK
KRIK
NO, TRAVEL NOT DOWN THIS PATH. LISTEN NOT TO THESE NOISES THAT BILLOW FROM THY LIPS...
...ROMEO, YOU MUST FIND YOUR JULIET.
SNAP

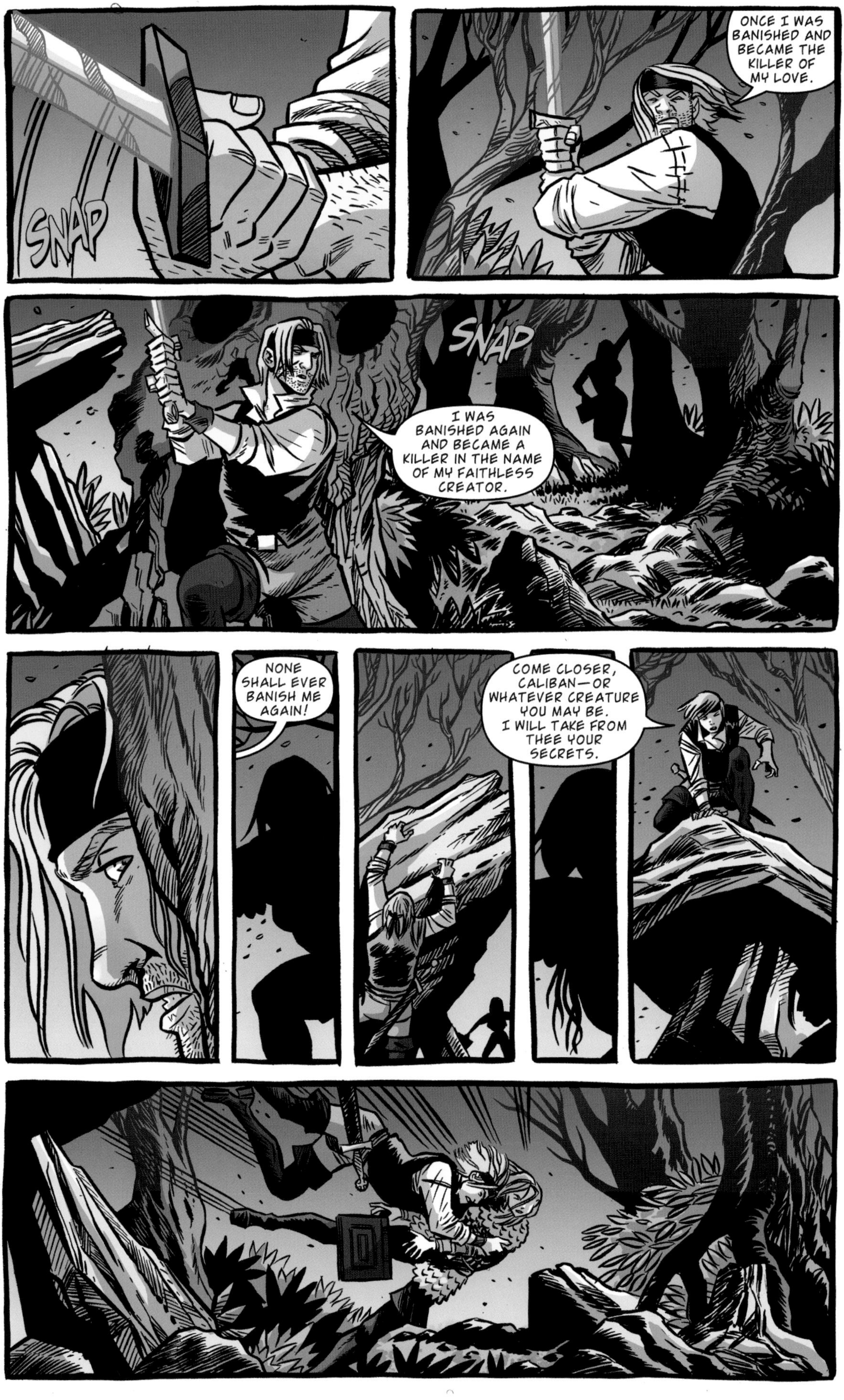
SNAP
ONCE I WAS BANISHED AND BECAME THE KILLER OF MY LOVE.
SNAP
I WAS BANISHED AGAIN AND BECAME A KILLER IN THE NAME OF MY FAITHLESS CREATOR.
NONE SHALL EVER BANISH ME AGAIN!
COME CLOSER, CALIBAN—OR WHATEVER CREATURE YOU MAY BE. I WILL TAKE FROM THEE YOUR SECRETS.

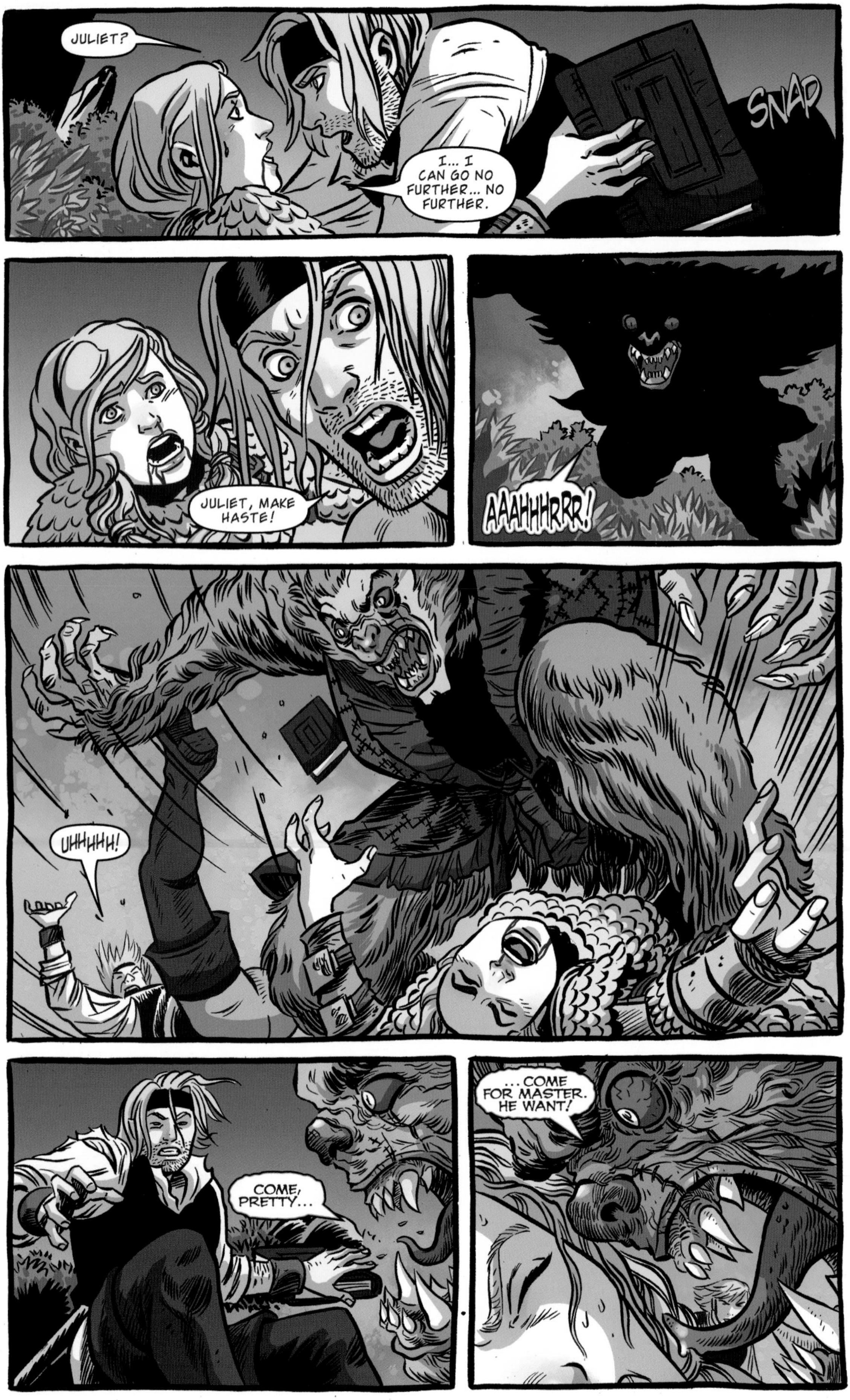
JULIET?
SNAP
I... I CAN GO NO FURTHER... NO FURTHER.
JULIET, MAKE HASTE!
AAAHHHRRR!
UHHHHH!
COME, PRETTY...
...COME FOR MASTER. HE WANT!

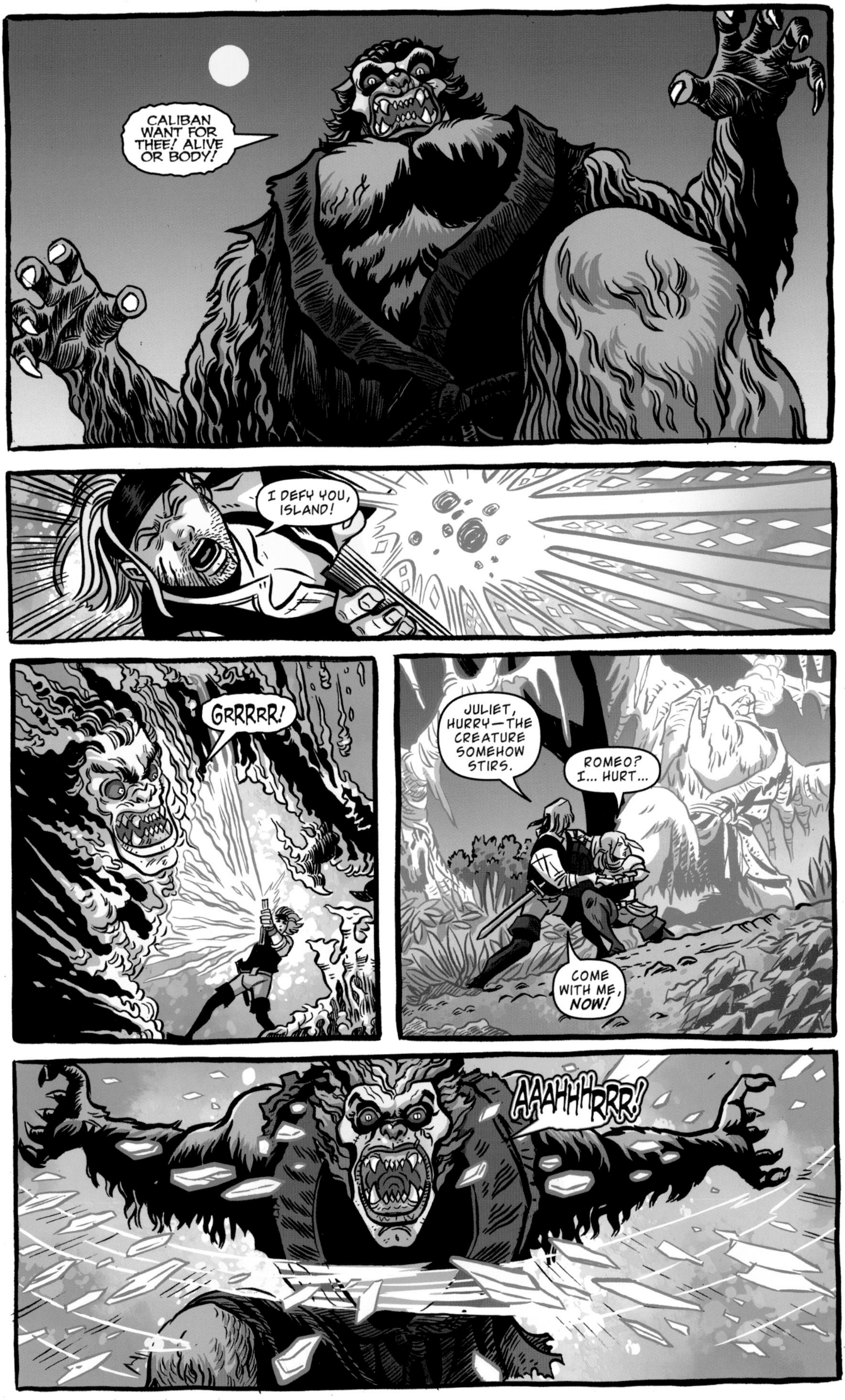
CALIBAN WANT FOR THEE! ALIVE OR BODY!
I DEFY YOU, ISLAND!
GRRRRR!
JULIET, HURRY—THE CREATURE SOMEHOW STIRS.
ROMEO? I... HURT...
COME WITH ME, NOW!
AAAHHHRRR!

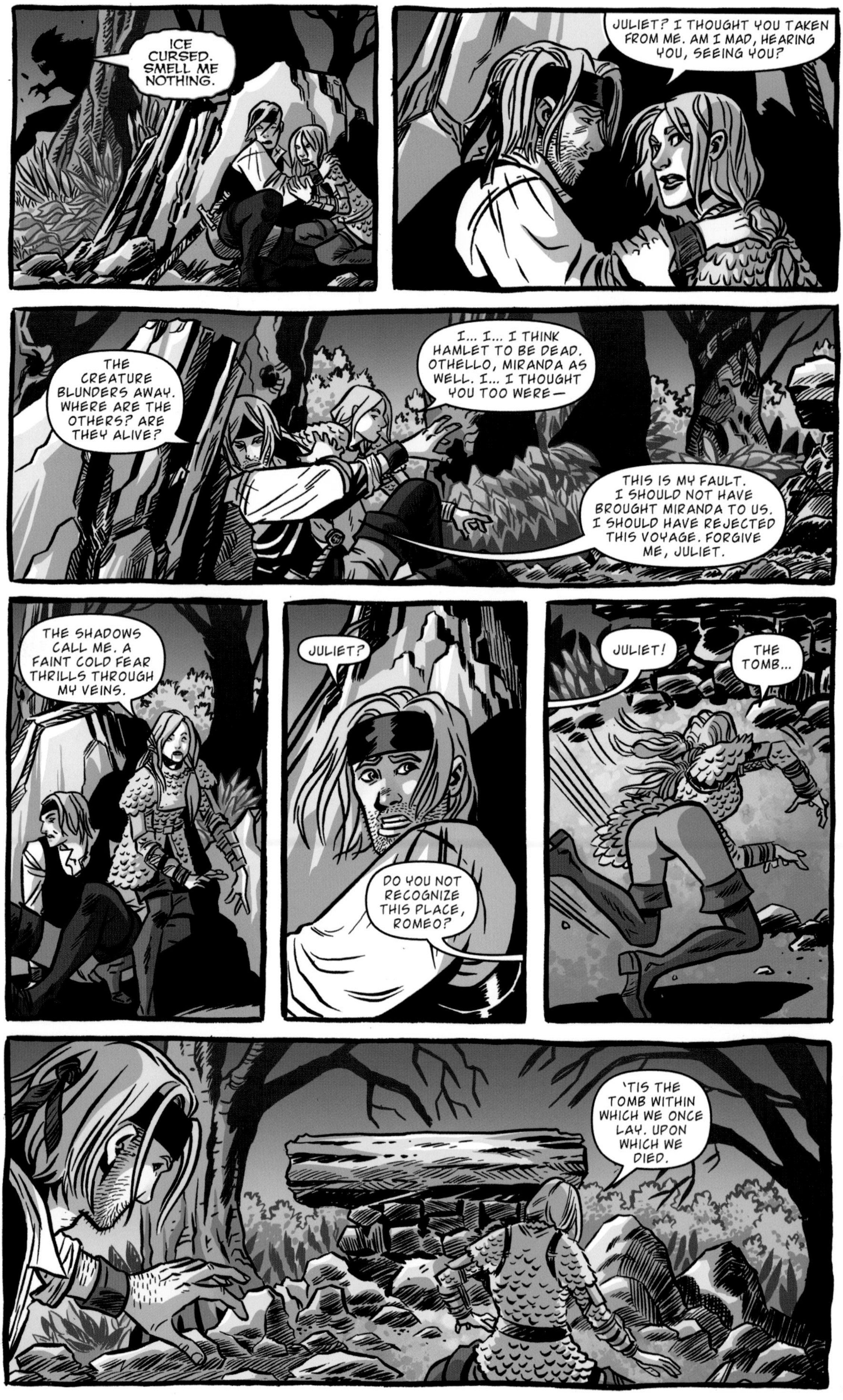
ICE CURSED. SMELL ME NOTHING.
JULIET? I THOUGHT YOU TAKEN FROM ME. AM I MAD, HEARING YOU, SEEING YOU?
THE CREATURE BLUNDERS AWAY. WHERE ARE THE OTHERS? ARE THEY ALIVE?
I... I... I THINK HAMLET TO BE DEAD. OTHELLO, MIRANDA AS WELL. I... I THOUGHT YOU TOO WERE—
THIS IS MY FAULT. I SHOULD NOT HAVE BROUGHT MIRANDA TO US. I SHOULD HAVE REJECTED THIS VOYAGE. FORGIVE ME, JULIET.
THE SHADOWS CALL ME. A FAINT COLD FEAR THRILLS THROUGH MY VEINS.
JULIET?
DO YOU NOT RECOGNIZE THIS PLACE, ROMEO?
JULIET!
THE TOMB...
'TIS THE TOMB WITHIN WHICH WE ONCE LAY. UPON WHICH WE DIED.

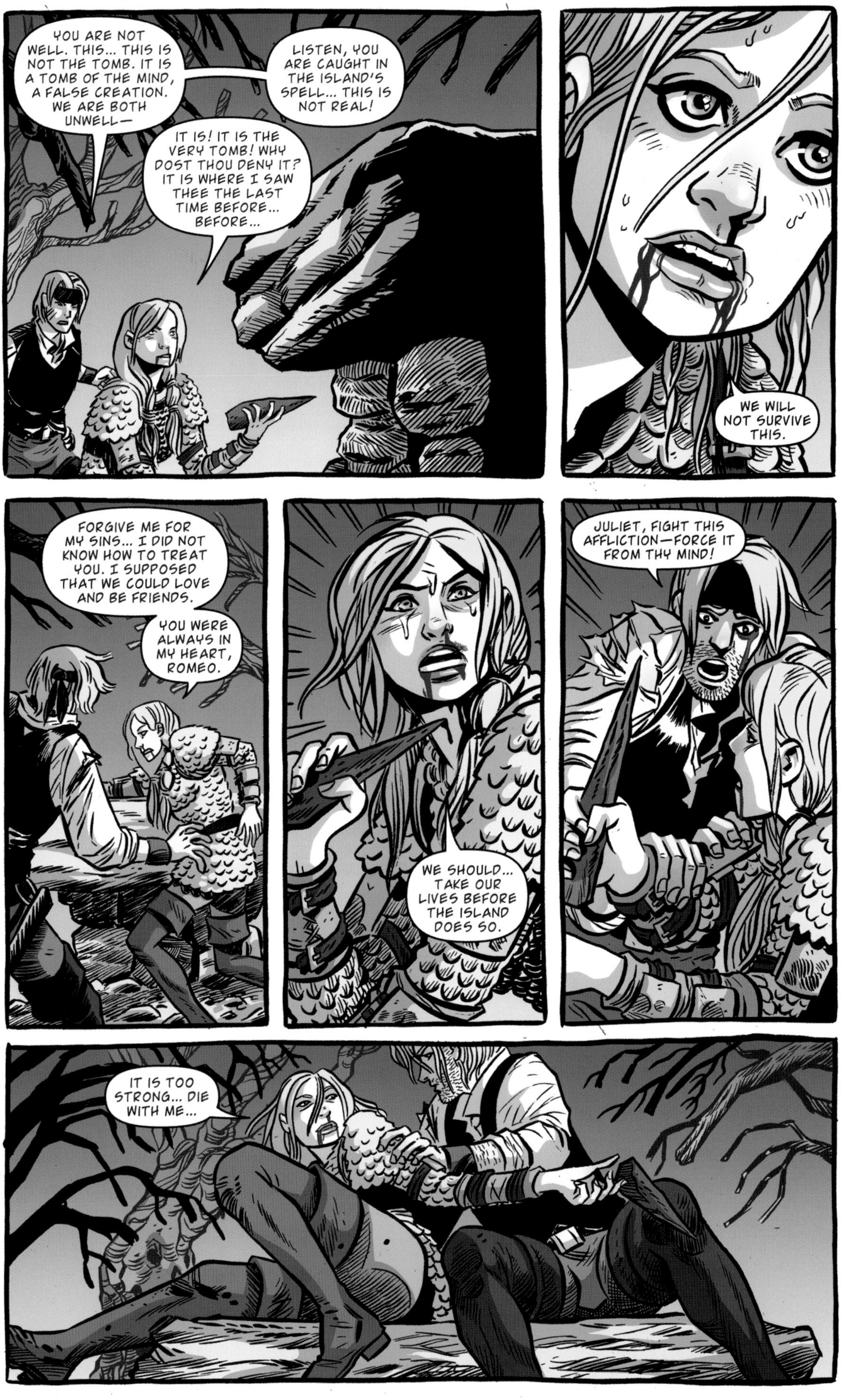
YOU ARE NOT WELL. THIS... THIS IS NOT THE TOMB. IT IS A TOMB OF THE MIND, A FALSE CREATION. WE ARE BOTH UNWELL—
LISTEN, YOU ARE CAUGHT IN THE ISLAND'S SPELL... THIS IS NOT REAL!
IT IS! IT IS THE VERY TOMB! WHY DOST THOU DENY IT? IT IS WHERE I SAW THEE THE LAST TIME BEFORE... BEFORE...
WE WILL NOT SURVIVE THIS.
FORGIVE ME FOR MY SINS... I DID NOT KNOW HOW TO TREAT YOU. I SUPPOSED THAT WE COULD LOVE AND BE FRIENDS.
YOU WERE ALWAYS IN MY HEART, ROMEO.
WE SHOULD... TAKE OUR LIVES BEFORE THE ISLAND DOES SO.
JULIET, FIGHT THIS AFFLICTION—FORCE IT FROM THY MIND!
IT IS TOO STRONG... DIE WITH ME...

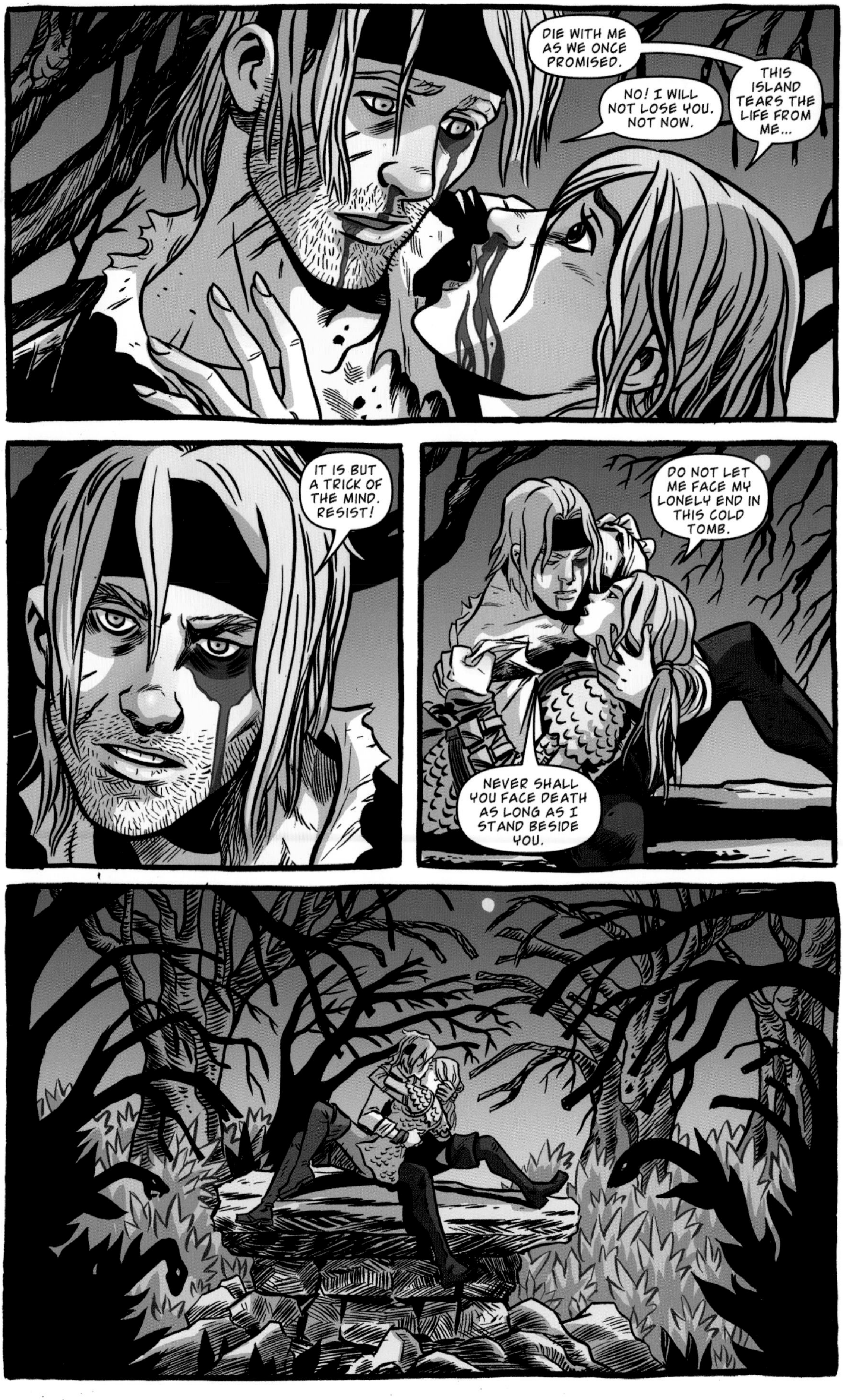
DIE WITH ME AS WE ONCE PROMISED.
THIS ISLAND TEARS THE LIFE FROM ME...
NO! I WILL NOT LOSE YOU. NOT NOW.
IT IS BUT A TRICK OF THE MIND. RESIST!
DO NOT LET ME FACE MY LONELY END IN THIS COLD TOMB.
NEVER SHALL YOU FACE DEATH AS LONG AS I STAND BESIDE YOU.

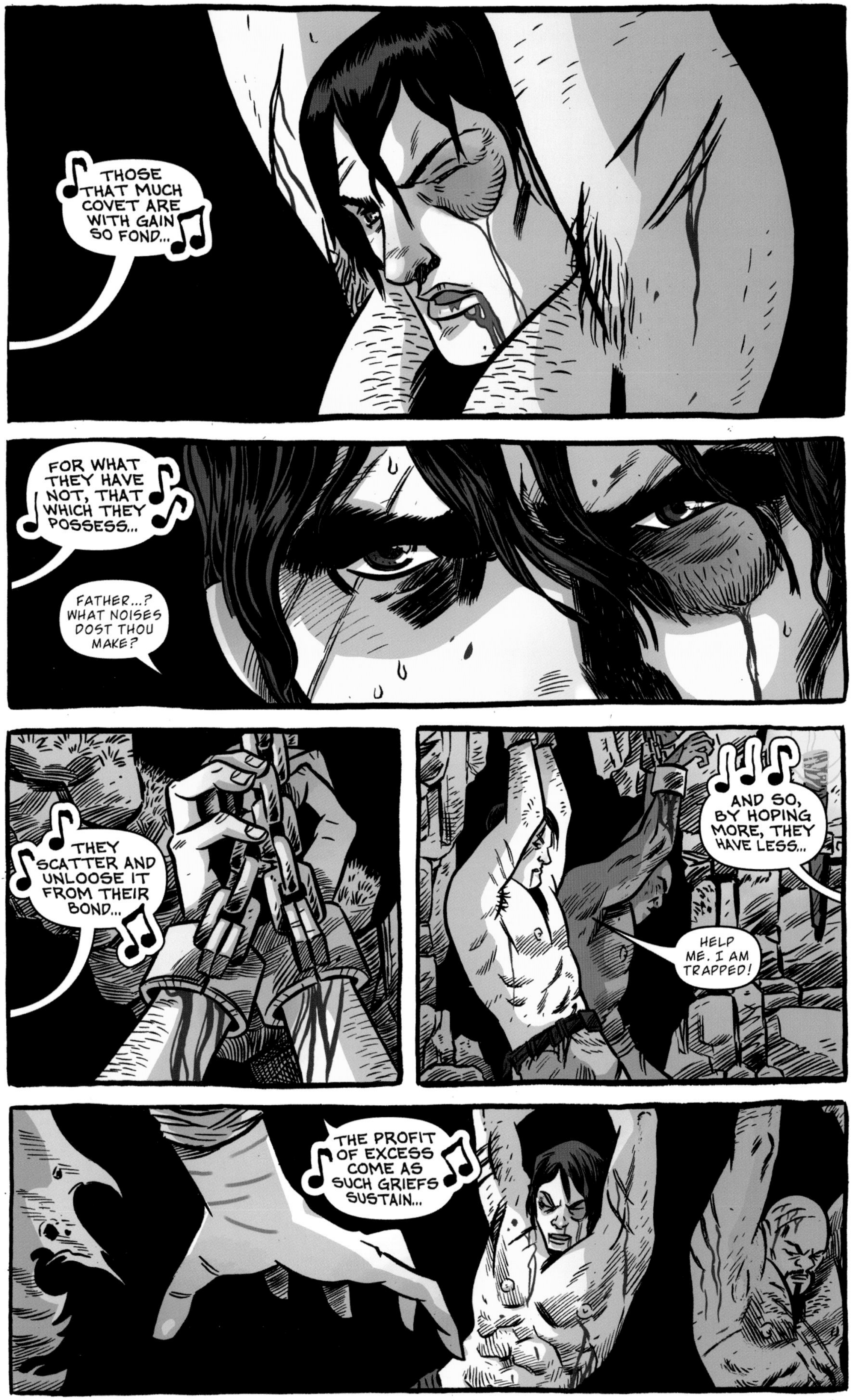
THOSE THAT MUCH COVET ARE WITH GAIN SO FOND...
FOR WHAT THEY HAVE NOT, THAT WHICH THEY POSSESS...
FATHER...? WHAT NOISES DOST THOU MAKE?
THEY SCATTER AND UNLOOSE IT FROM THEIR BOND...
AND SO, BY HOPING MORE, THEY HAVE LESS...
HELP ME. I AM TRAPPED!
THE PROFIT OF EXCESS COME AS SUCH GRIEFS SUSTAIN...

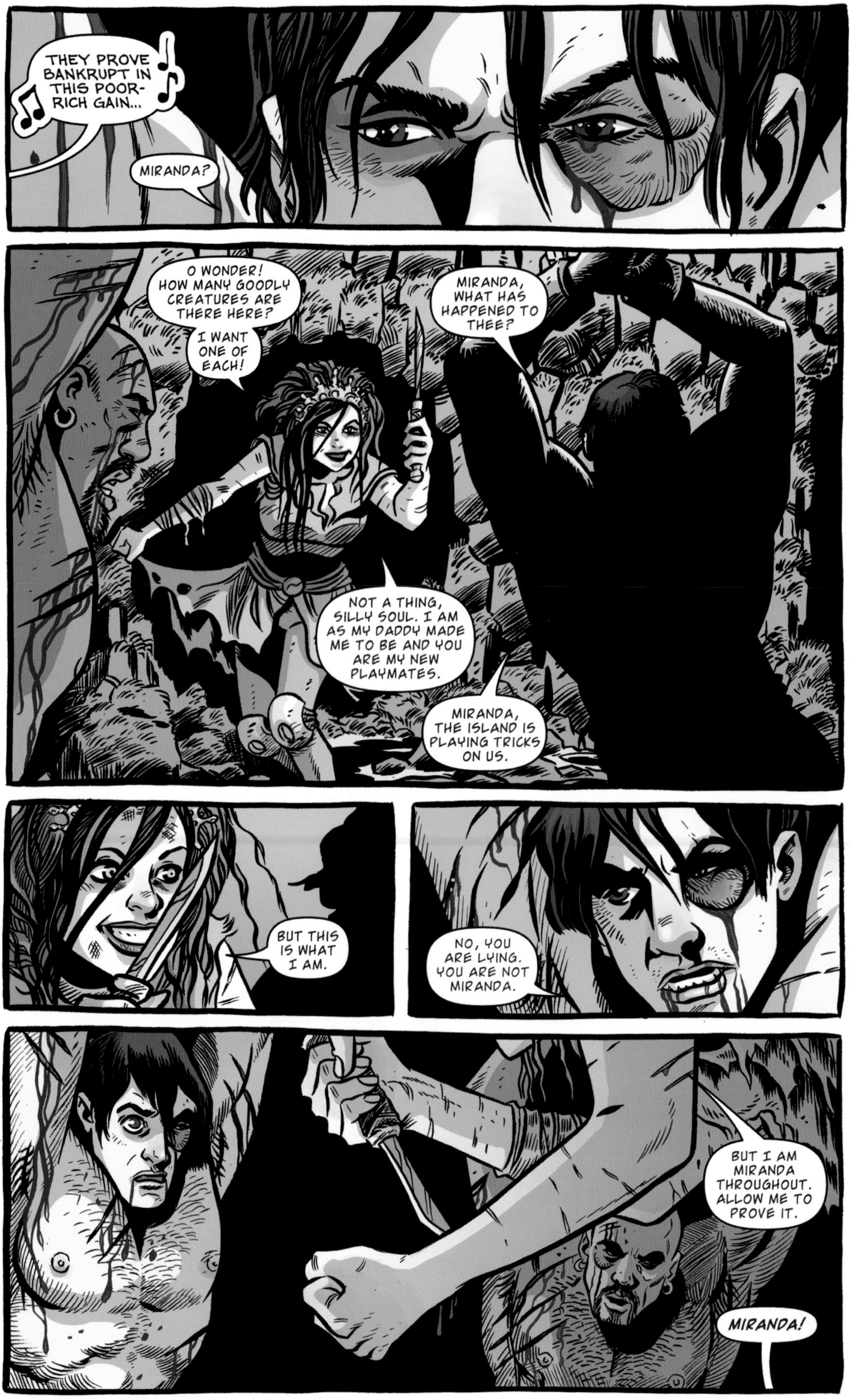
THEY PROVE BANKRUPT IN THIS POOR-RICH GAIN...
MIRANDA?
O WONDER! HOW MANY GOODLY CREATURES ARE THERE HERE?
I WANT ONE OF EACH!
MIRANDA, WHAT HAS HAPPENED TO THEE?
NOT A THING, SILLY SOUL. I AM AS MY DADDY MADE ME TO BE AND YOU ARE MY NEW PLAYMATES.
MIRANDA, THE ISLAND IS PLAYING TRICKS ON US.
BUT THIS IS WHAT I AM.
NO, YOU ARE LYING. YOU ARE NOT MIRANDA.
BUT I AM MIRANDA THROUGHOUT. ALLOW ME TO PROVE IT.
MIRANDA!

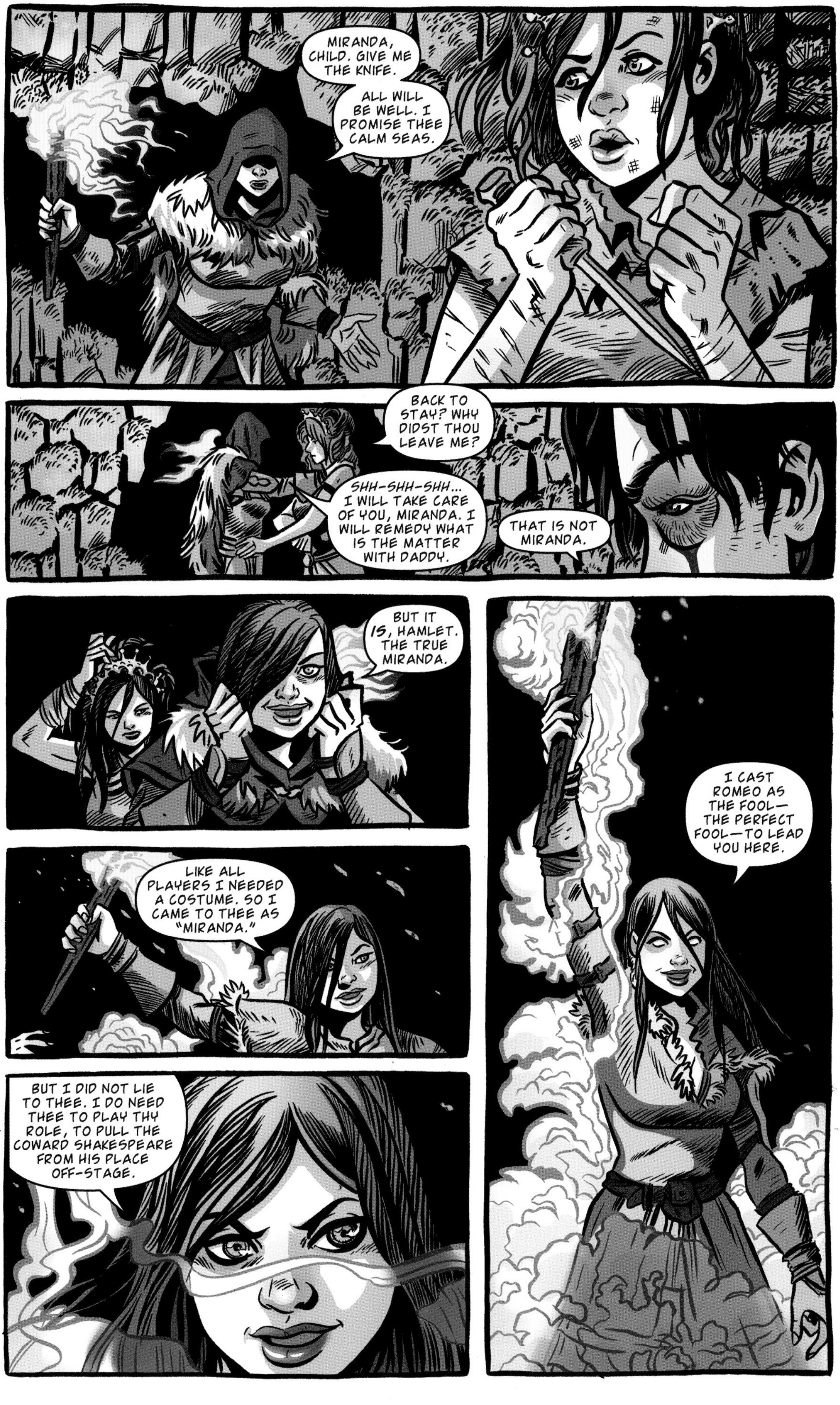
MIRANDA, CHILD. GIVE ME THE KNIFE.
ALL WILL BE WELL. I PROMISE THEE CALM SEAS.
BACK TO STAY? WHY DIDST THOU LEAVE ME?
SHH-SHH-SHH... I WILL TAKE CARE OF YOU, MIRANDA. I WILL REMEDY WHAT IS THE MATTER WITH DADDY.
THAT IS NOT MIRANDA.
BUT IT IS, HAMLET. THE TRUE MIRANDA.
LIKE ALL PLAYERS I NEEDED A COSTUME. SO I CAME TO THEE AS "MIRANDA."
BUT I DID NOT LIE TO THEE. I DO NEED THEE TO PLAY THY ROLE, TO PULL THE COWARD SHAKESPEARE FROM HIS PLACE OFF-STAGE.
I CAST ROMEO AS THE FOOL—THE PERFECT FOOL—TO LEAD YOU HERE.

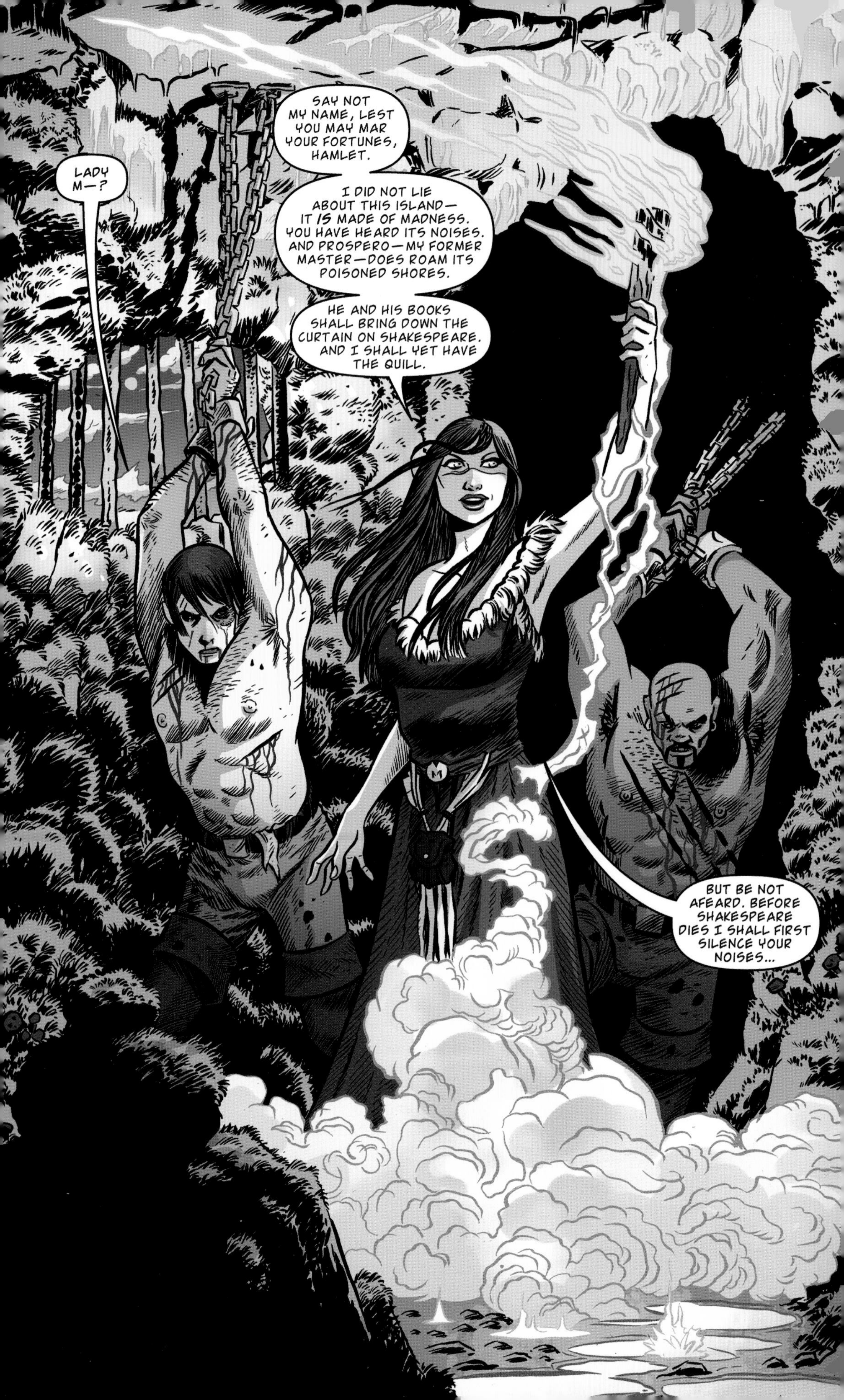
LADY M—?
SAY NOT MY NAME, LEST YOU MAY MAR YOUR FORTUNES, HAMLET.
I DID NOT LIE ABOUT THIS ISLAND— IT IS MADE OF MADNESS. YOU HAVE HEARD ITS NOISES. AND PROSPERO—MY FORMER MASTER—DOES ROAM ITS POISONED SHORES.
HE AND HIS BOOKS SHALL BRING DOWN THE CURTAIN ON SHAKESPEARE. AND I SHALL YET HAVE THE QUILL.
BUT BE NOT AFEARD. BEFORE SHAKESPEARE DIES I SHALL FIRST SILENCE YOUR NOISES...

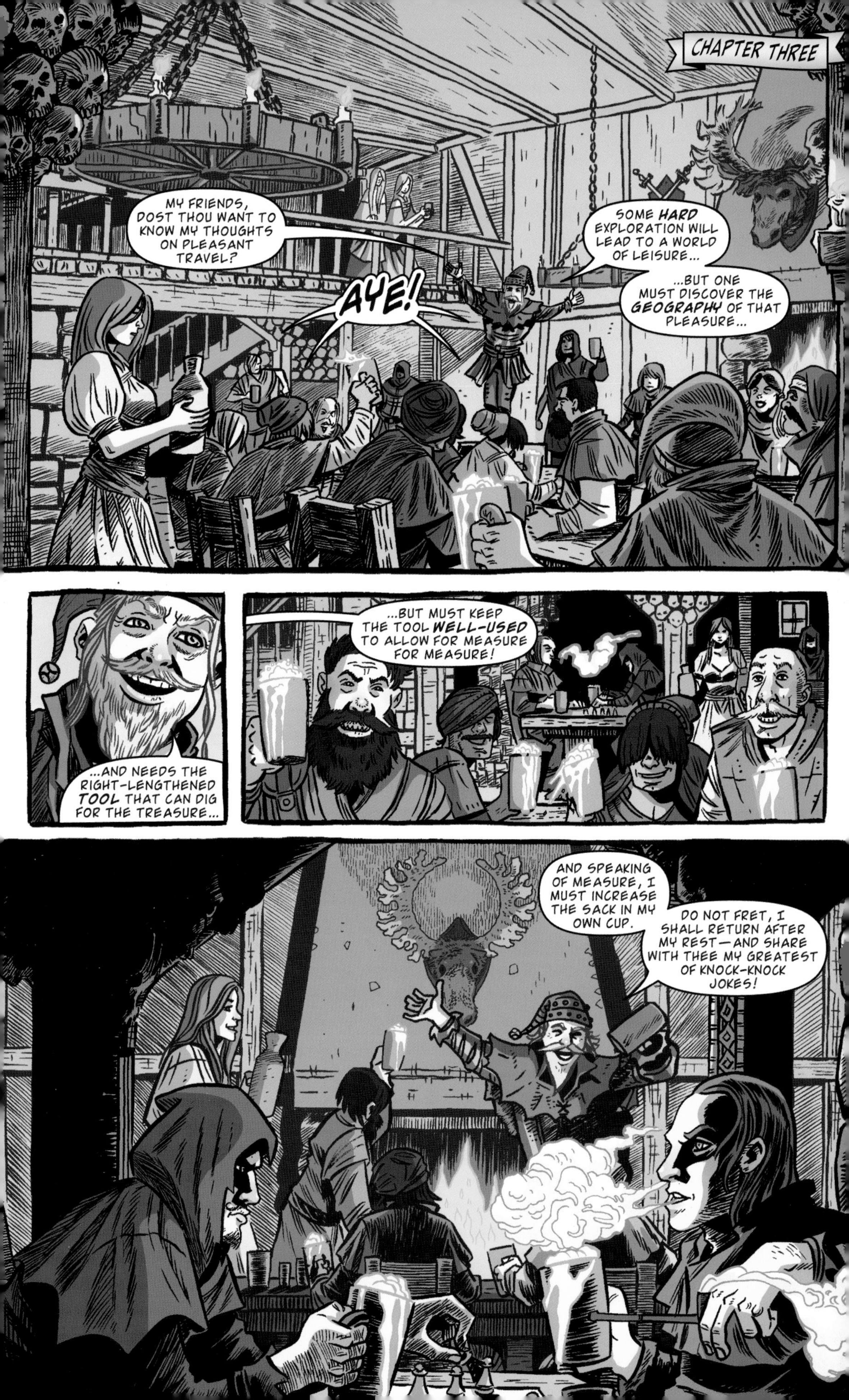
CHAPTER THREE
MY FRIENDS, DOST THOU WANT TO KNOW MY THOUGHTS ON PLEASANT TRAVEL?
AYE!
SOME HARD EXPLORATION WILL LEAD TO A WORLD OF LEISURE...
...BUT ONE MUST DISCOVER THE GEOGRAPHY OF THAT PLEASURE...
...AND NEEDS THE RIGHT-LENGTHENED TOOL THAT CAN DIG FOR THE TREASURE...
...BUT MUST KEEP THE TOOL WELL-USED TO ALLOW FOR MEASURE FOR MEASURE!
AND SPEAKING OF MEASURE, I MUST INCREASE THE SACK IN MY OWN CUP.
DO NOT FRET, I SHALL RETURN AFTER MY REST—AND SHARE WITH THEE MY GREATEST OF KNOCK-KNOCK JOKES!

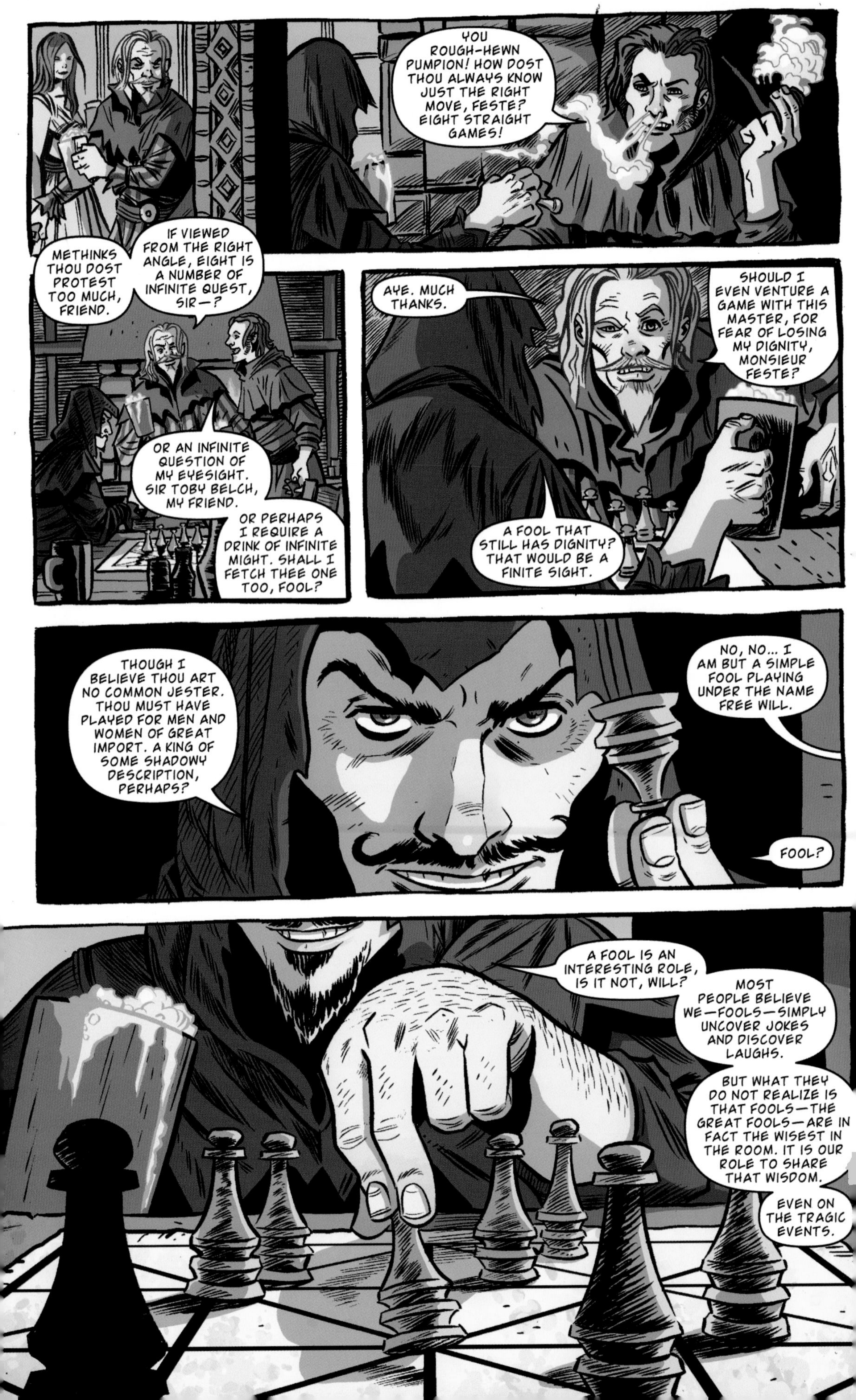
YOU ROUGH-HEWN PUMPION! HOW DOST THOU ALWAYS KNOW JUST THE RIGHT MOVE, FESTE? EIGHT STRAIGHT GAMES!
METHINKS THOU DOST PROTEST TOO MUCH, FRIEND.
IF VIEWED FROM THE RIGHT ANGLE, EIGHT IS A NUMBER OF INFINITE QUEST, SIR—?
OR AN INFINITE QUESTION OF MY EYESIGHT. SIR TOBY BELCH, MY FRIEND.
OR PERHAPS I REQUIRE A DRINK OF INFINITE MIGHT. SHALL I FETCH THEE ONE TOO, FOOL?
AYE. MUCH THANKS.
SHOULD I EVEN VENTURE A GAME WITH THIS MASTER, FOR FEAR OF LOSING MY DIGNITY, MONSIEUR FESTE?
A FOOL THAT STILL HAS DIGNITY? THAT WOULD BE A FINITE SIGHT.
THOUGH I BELIEVE THOU ART NO COMMON JESTER. THOU MUST HAVE PLAYED FOR MEN AND WOMEN OF GREAT IMPORT. A KING OF SOME SHADOWY DESCRIPTION, PERHAPS?
NO, NO... I AM BUT A SIMPLE FOOL PLAYING UNDER THE NAME FREE WILL.
FOOL?
A FOOL IS AN INTERESTING ROLE, IS IT NOT, WILL?
MOST PEOPLE BELIEVE WE—FOOLS—SIMPLY UNCOVER JOKES AND DISCOVER LAUGHS.
BUT WHAT THEY DO NOT REALIZE IS THAT FOOLS—THE GREAT FOOLS—ARE IN FACT THE WISEST IN THE ROOM. IT IS OUR ROLE TO SHARE THAT WISDOM.
EVEN ON THE TRAGIC EVENTS.

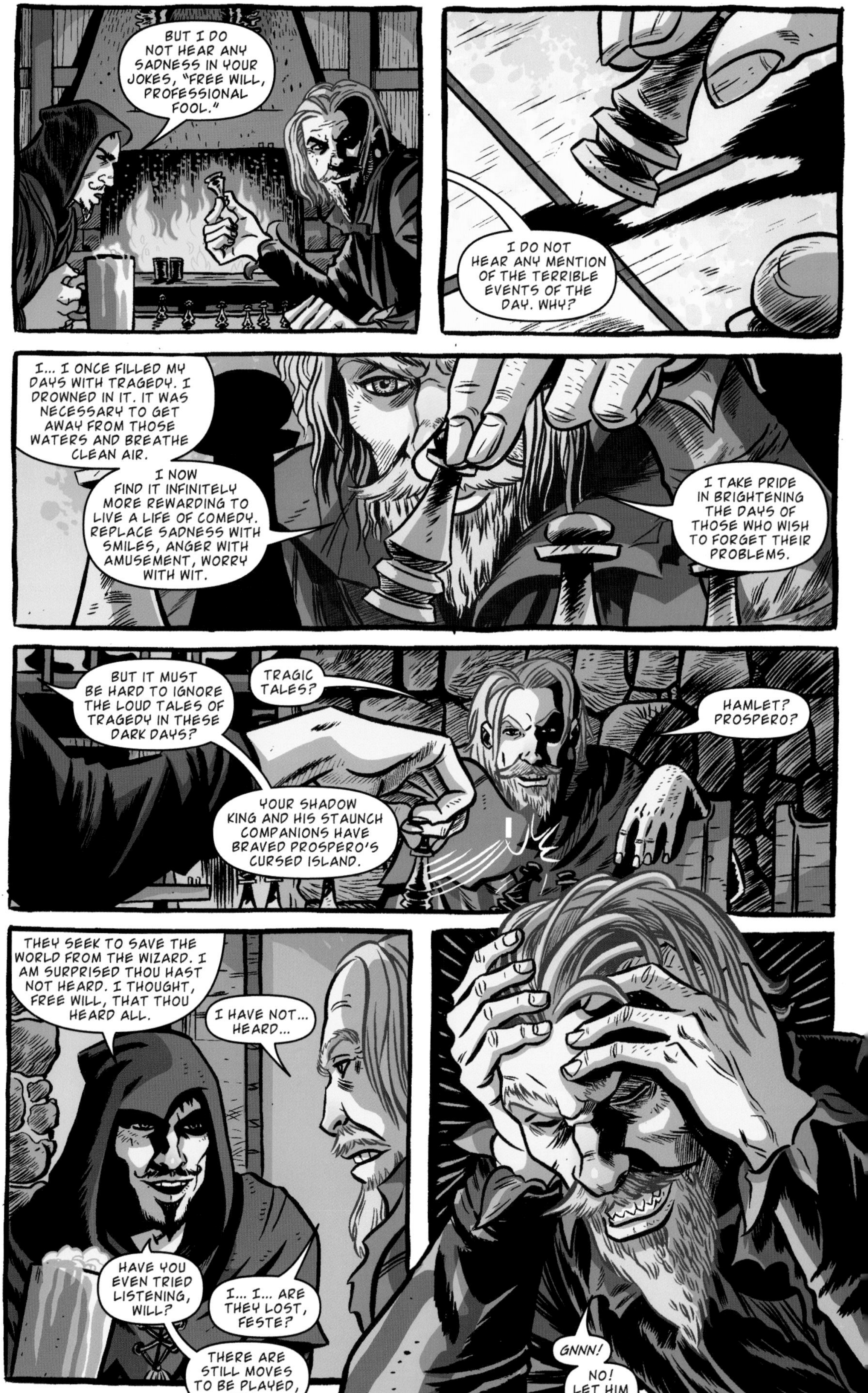

BUT I DO NOT HEAR ANY SADNESS IN YOUR JOKES, "FREE WILL, PROFESSIONAL FOOL."
I DO NOT HEAR ANY MENTION OF THE TERRIBLE EVENTS OF THE DAY. WHY?
I... I ONCE FILLED MY DAYS WITH TRAGEDY. I DROWNED IN IT. IT WAS NECESSARY TO GET AWAY FROM THOSE WATERS AND BREATHE CLEAN AIR.
I NOW FIND IT INFINITELY MORE REWARDING TO LIVE A LIFE OF COMEDY. REPLACE SADNESS WITH SMILES, ANGER WITH AMUSEMENT, WORRY WITH WIT.
I TAKE PRIDE IN BRIGHTENING THE DAYS OF THOSE WHO WISH TO FORGET THEIR PROBLEMS.
BUT IT MUST BE HARD TO IGNORE THE LOUD TALES OF TRAGEDY IN THESE DARK DAYS?
TRAGIC TALES?
HAMLET? PROSPERO?
YOUR SHADOW KING AND HIS STAUNCH COMPANIONS HAVE BRAVED PROSPERO'S CURSED ISLAND.
THEY SEEK TO SAVE THE WORLD FROM THE WIZARD. I AM SURPRISED THOU HAST NOT HEARD. I THOUGHT, FREE WILL, THAT THOU HEARD ALL.
I HAVE NOT... HEARD...
HAVE YOU EVEN TRIED LISTENING, WILL?
I... I... ARE THEY LOST, FESTE?
THERE ARE STILL MOVES TO BE PLAYED, WILL.
GNNN!
NO! LET HIM FREE!

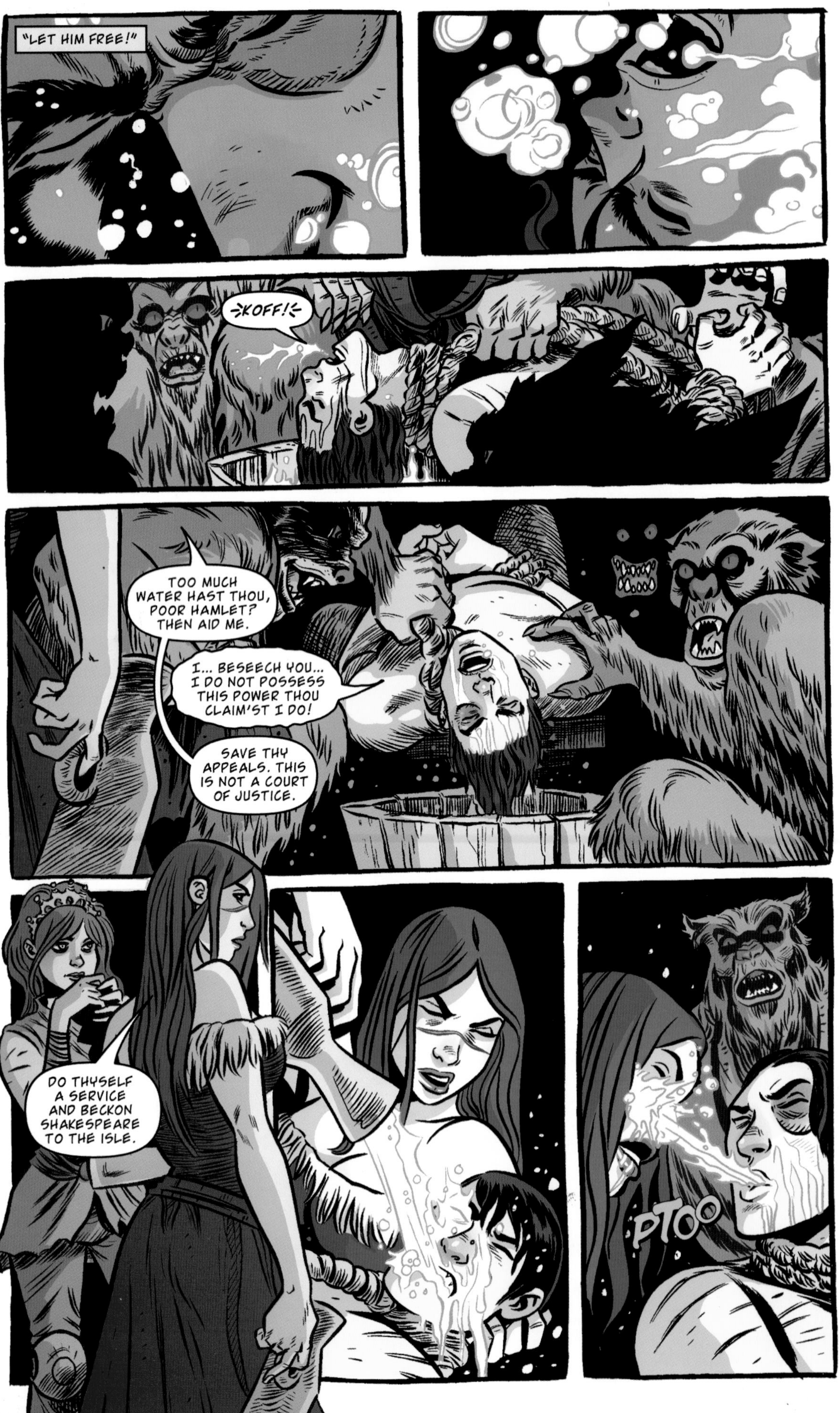

"LET HIM FREE!"
KOFF!
TOO MUCH WATER HAST THOU, POOR HAMLET? THEN AID ME.
I... BESEECH YOU... I DO NOT POSSESS THIS POWER THOU CLAIM'ST I DO!
SAVE THY APPEALS. THIS IS NOT A COURT OF JUSTICE.
DO THYSELF A SERVICE AND BECKON SHAKESPEARE TO THE ISLE.
PTOO

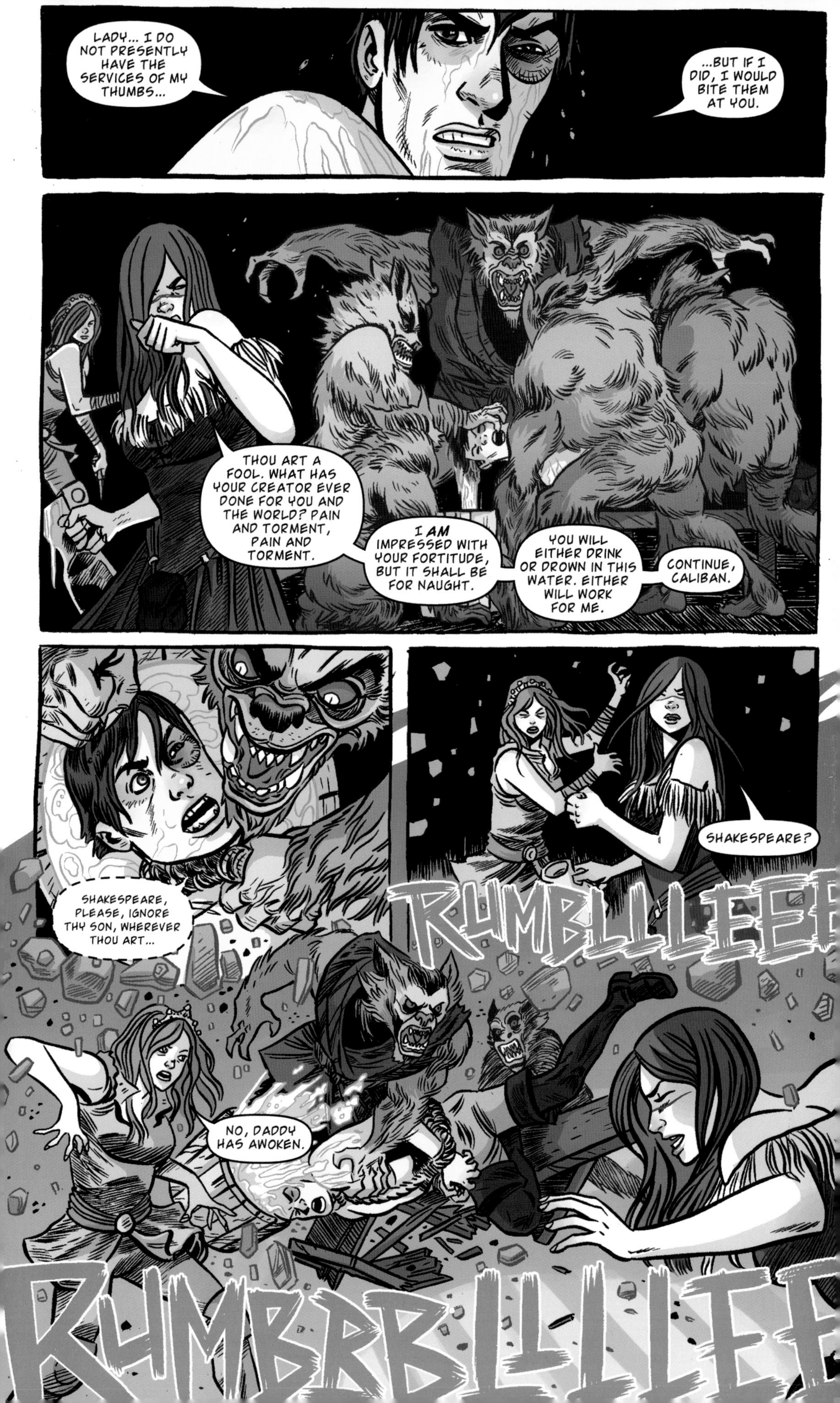

LADY... I DO NOT PRESENTLY HAVE THE SERVICES OF MY THUMBS...
...BUT IF I DID, I WOULD BITE THEM AT YOU.
THOU ART A FOOL. WHAT HAS YOUR CREATOR EVER DONE FOR YOU AND THE WORLD? PAIN AND TORMENT, PAIN AND TORMENT.
I AM IMPRESSED WITH YOUR FORTITUDE, BUT IT SHALL BE FOR NAUGHT.
YOU WILL EITHER DRINK OR DROWN IN THIS WATER. EITHER WILL WORK FOR ME.
CONTINUE, CALIBAN.
SHAKESPEARE, PLEASE, IGNORE THY SON, WHEREVER THOU ART...
SHAKESPEARE?
RUMBLLLEE
NO, DADDY HAS AWOKEN.
RUMBRBLLLEE

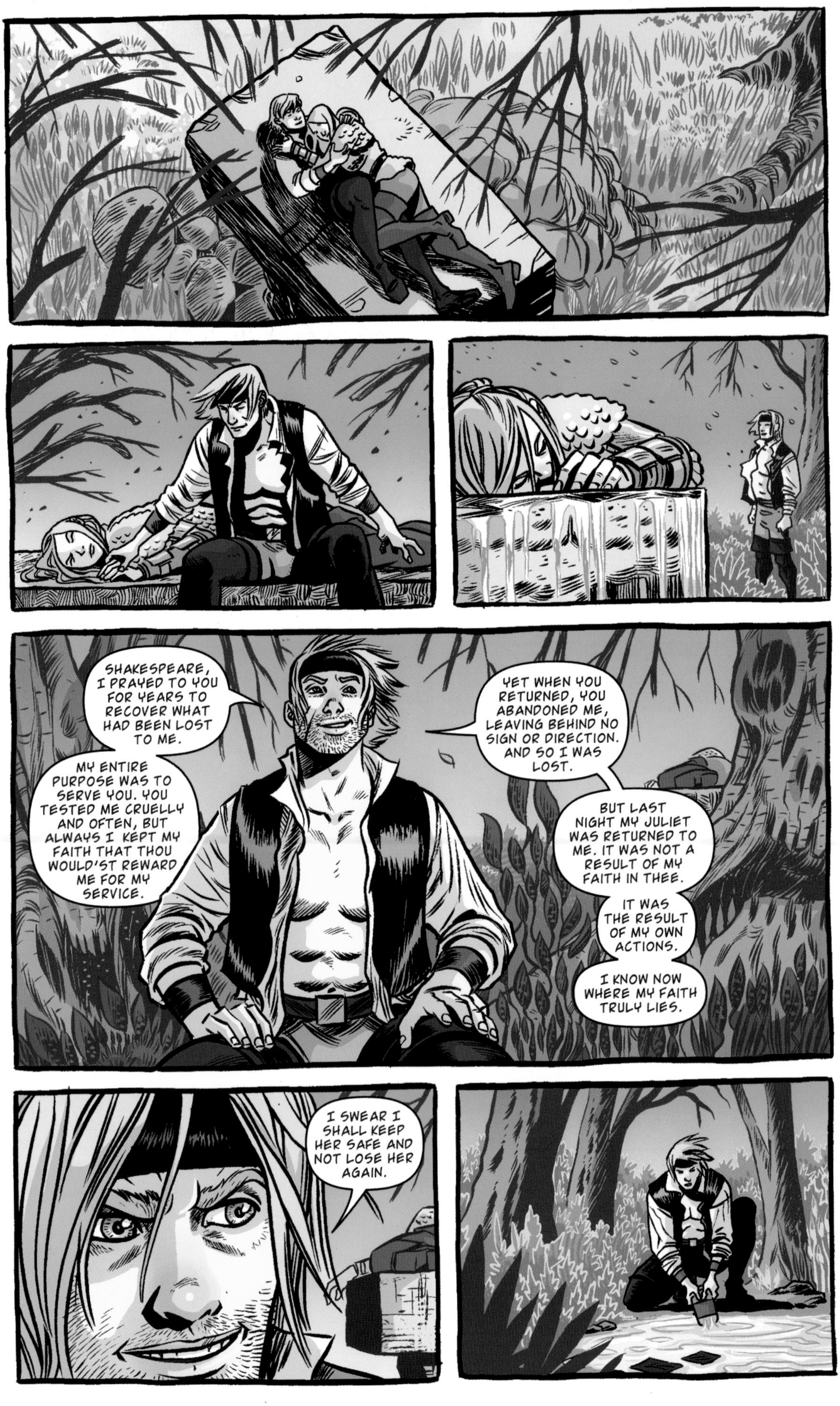
SHAKESPEARE, I PRAYED TO YOU FOR YEARS TO RECOVER WHAT HAD BEEN LOST TO ME.
MY ENTIRE PURPOSE WAS TO SERVE YOU. YOU TESTED ME CRUELLY AND OFTEN, BUT ALWAYS I KEPT MY FAITH THAT THOU WOULD'ST REWARD ME FOR MY SERVICE.
YET WHEN YOU RETURNED, YOU ABANDONED ME, LEAVING BEHIND NO SIGN OR DIRECTION. AND SO I WAS LOST.
BUT LAST NIGHT MY JULIET WAS RETURNED TO ME. IT WAS NOT A RESULT OF MY FAITH IN THEE.
IT WAS THE RESULT OF MY OWN ACTIONS.
I KNOW NOW WHERE MY FAITH TRULY LIES.
I SWEAR I SHALL KEEP HER SAFE AND NOT LOSE HER AGAIN.

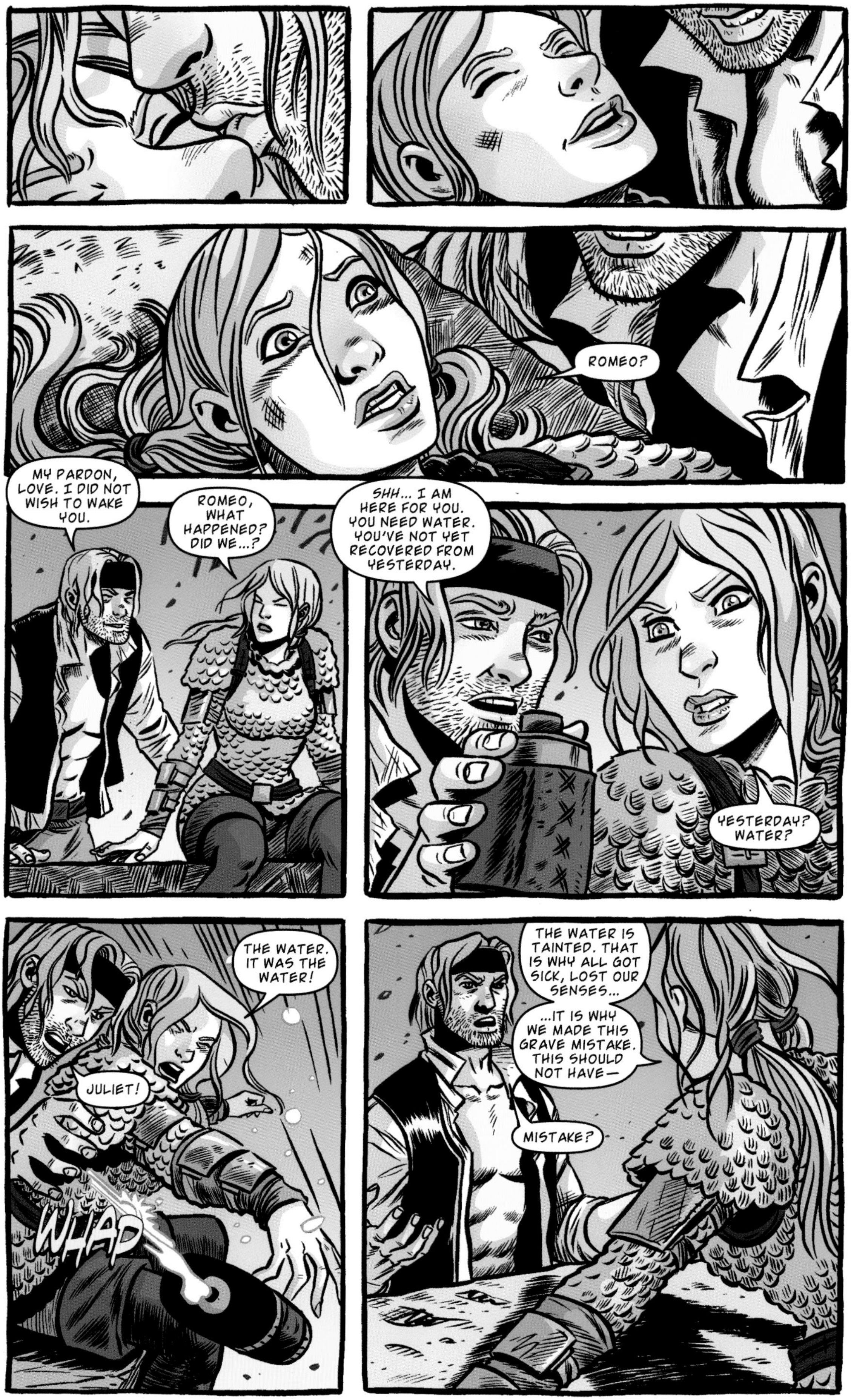
ROMEO?
MY PARDON, LOVE. I DID NOT WISH TO WAKE YOU.
ROMEO, WHAT HAPPENED? DID WE...?
SHH... I AM HERE FOR YOU. YOU NEED WATER. YOU'VE NOT YET RECOVERED FROM YESTERDAY.
YESTERDAY? WATER?
THE WATER. IT WAS THE WATER!
JULIET!
WHAP
THE WATER IS TAINTED. THAT IS WHY ALL GOT SICK, LOST OUR SENSES...
...IT IS WHY WE MADE THIS GRAVE MISTAKE. THIS SHOULD NOT HAVE—
MISTAKE?

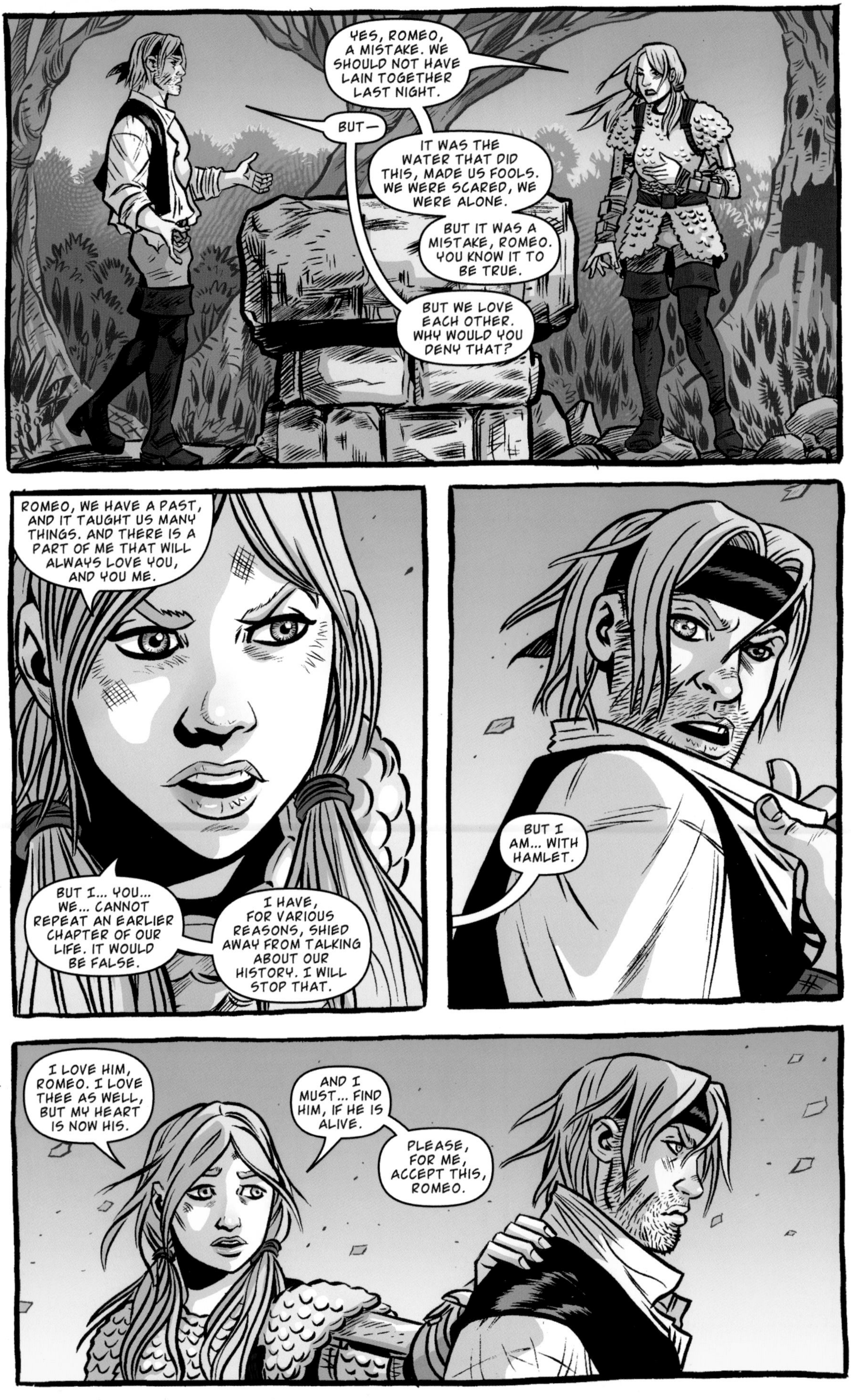
YES, ROMEO, A MISTAKE. WE SHOULD NOT HAVE LAIN TOGETHER LAST NIGHT.
BUT—
IT WAS THE WATER THAT DID THIS, MADE US FOOLS. WE WERE SCARED, WE WERE ALONE.
BUT IT WAS A MISTAKE, ROMEO. YOU KNOW IT TO BE TRUE.
BUT WE LOVE EACH OTHER. WHY WOULD YOU DENY THAT?
ROMEO, WE HAVE A PAST, AND IT TAUGHT US MANY THINGS. AND THERE IS A PART OF ME THAT WILL ALWAYS LOVE YOU, AND YOU ME.
BUT I... YOU... WE... CANNOT REPEAT AN EARLIER CHAPTER OF OUR LIFE. IT WOULD BE FALSE.
I HAVE, FOR VARIOUS REASONS, SHIED AWAY FROM TALKING ABOUT OUR HISTORY. I WILL STOP THAT.
BUT I AM... WITH HAMLET.
I LOVE HIM, ROMEO. I LOVE THEE AS WELL, BUT MY HEART IS NOW HIS.
AND I MUST... FIND HIM, IF HE IS ALIVE.
PLEASE, FOR ME, ACCEPT THIS, ROMEO.

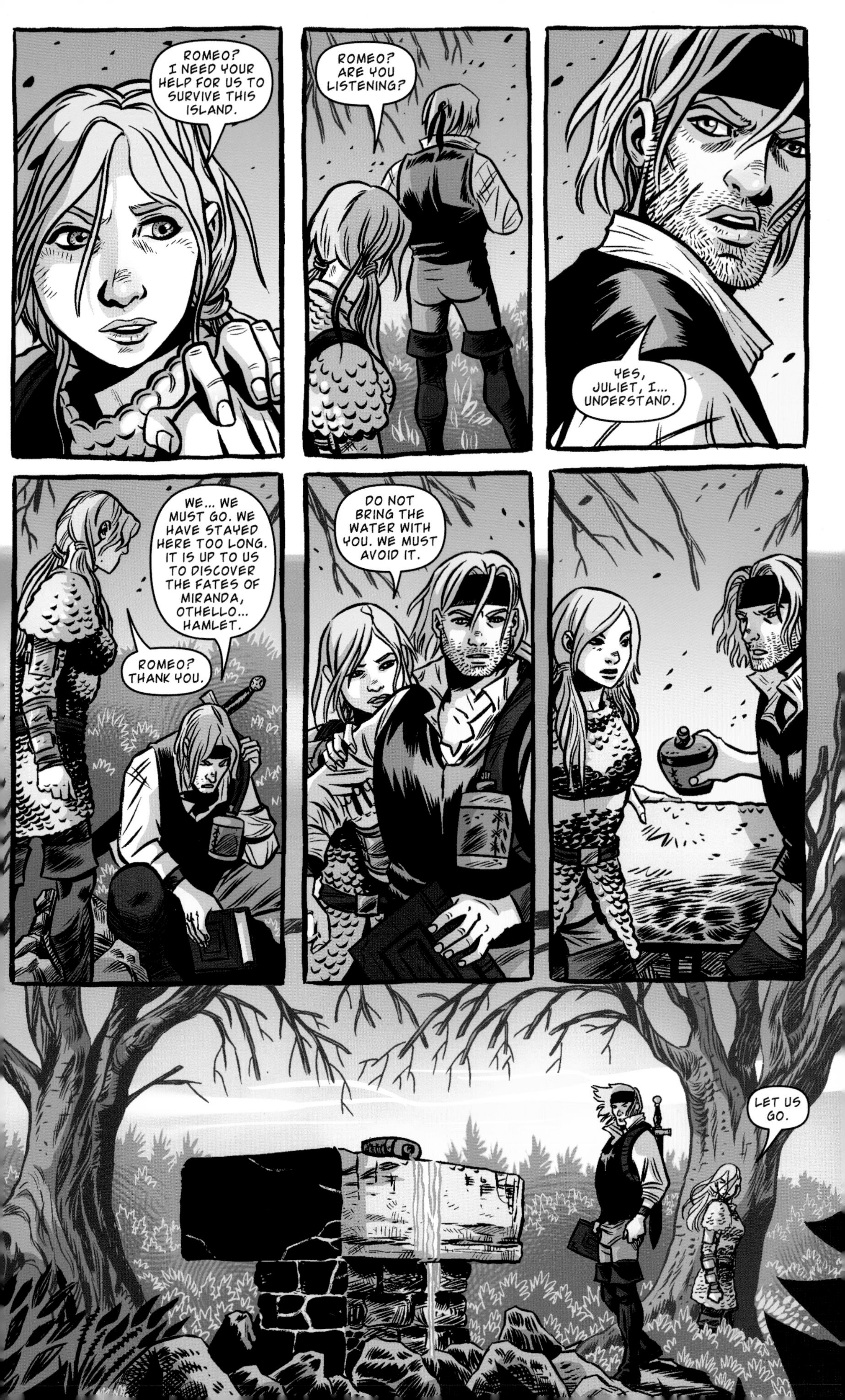
ROMEO? I NEED YOUR HELP FOR US TO SURVIVE THIS ISLAND.
ROMEO? ARE YOU LISTENING?
YES, JULIET, I... UNDERSTAND.
WE... WE MUST GO. WE HAVE STAYED HERE TOO LONG. IT IS UP TO US TO DISCOVER THE FATES OF MIRANDA, OTHELLO... HAMLET.
ROMEO? THANK YOU.
DO NOT BRING THE WATER WITH YOU. WE MUST AVOID IT.
LET US GO.

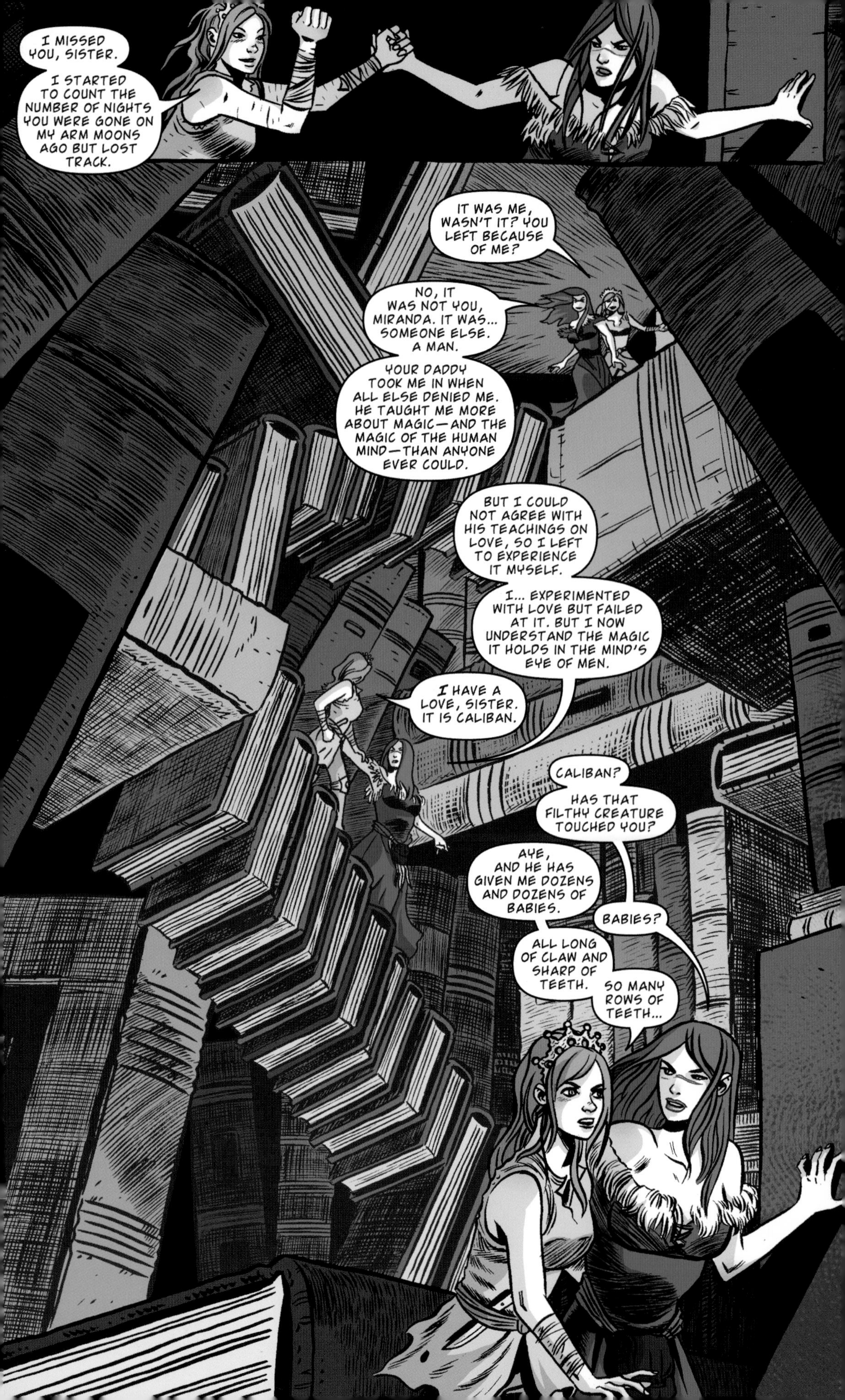

I MISSED YOU, SISTER.
I STARTED TO COUNT THE NUMBER OF NIGHTS YOU WERE GONE ON MY ARM MOONS AGO BUT LOST TRACK.
IT WAS ME, WASN'T IT? YOU LEFT BECAUSE OF ME?
NO, IT WAS NOT YOU, MIRANDA. IT WAS... SOMEONE ELSE. A MAN.
YOUR DADDY TOOK ME IN WHEN ALL ELSE DENIED ME. HE TAUGHT ME MORE ABOUT MAGIC—AND THE MAGIC OF THE HUMAN MIND—THAN ANYONE EVER COULD.
BUT I COULD NOT AGREE WITH HIS TEACHINGS ON LOVE, SO I LEFT TO EXPERIENCE IT MYSELF.
I... EXPERIMENTED WITH LOVE BUT FAILED AT IT. BUT I NOW UNDERSTAND THE MAGIC IT HOLDS IN THE MIND'S EYE OF MEN.
I HAVE A LOVE, SISTER. IT IS CALIBAN.
CALIBAN?
HAS THAT FILTHY CREATURE TOUCHED YOU?
AYE, AND HE HAS GIVEN ME DOZENS AND DOZENS OF BABIES.
BABIES?
ALL LONG OF CLAW AND SHARP OF TEETH.
SO MANY ROWS OF TEETH...

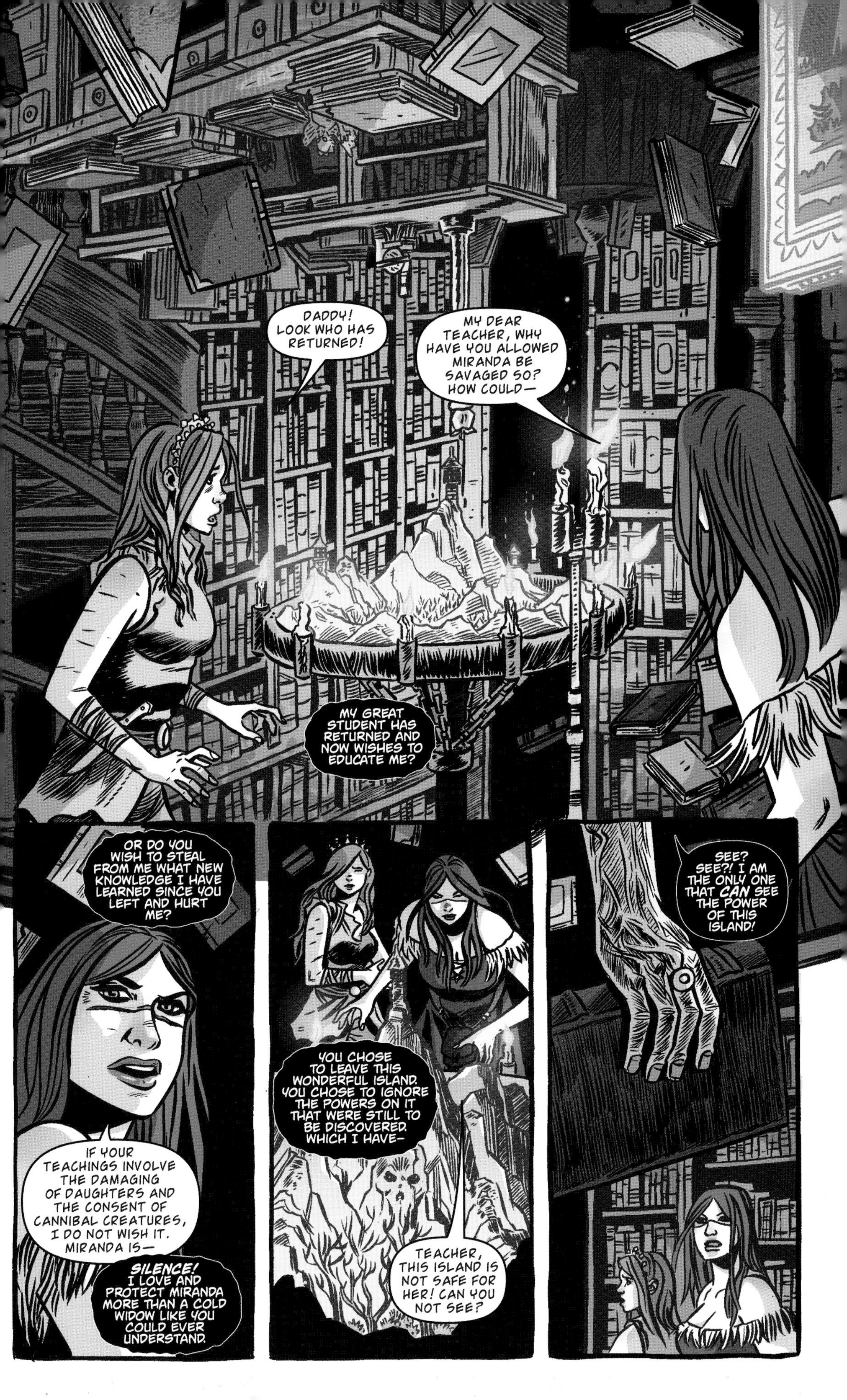
DADDY! LOOK WHO HAS RETURNED!
MY DEAR TEACHER, WHY HAVE YOU ALLOWED MIRANDA BE SAVAGED SO? HOW COULD—
MY GREAT STUDENT HAS RETURNED AND NOW WISHES TO EDUCATE ME?
OR DO YOU WISH TO STEAL FROM ME WHAT NEW KNOWLEDGE I HAVE LEARNED SINCE YOU LEFT AND HURT ME?
IF YOUR TEACHINGS INVOLVE THE DAMAGING OF DAUGHTERS AND THE CONSENT OF CANNIBAL CREATURES, I DO NOT WISH IT. MIRANDA IS—
SILENCE! I LOVE AND PROTECT MIRANDA MORE THAN A COLD WIDOW LIKE YOU COULD EVER UNDERSTAND.
YOU CHOSE TO LEAVE THIS WONDERFUL ISLAND. YOU CHOSE TO IGNORE THE POWERS ON IT THAT WERE STILL TO BE DISCOVERED. WHICH I HAVE-
TEACHER, THIS ISLAND IS NOT SAFE FOR HER! CAN YOU NOT SEE?
SEE? SEE?! I AM THE ONLY ONE THAT CAN SEE THE POWER OF THIS ISLAND!

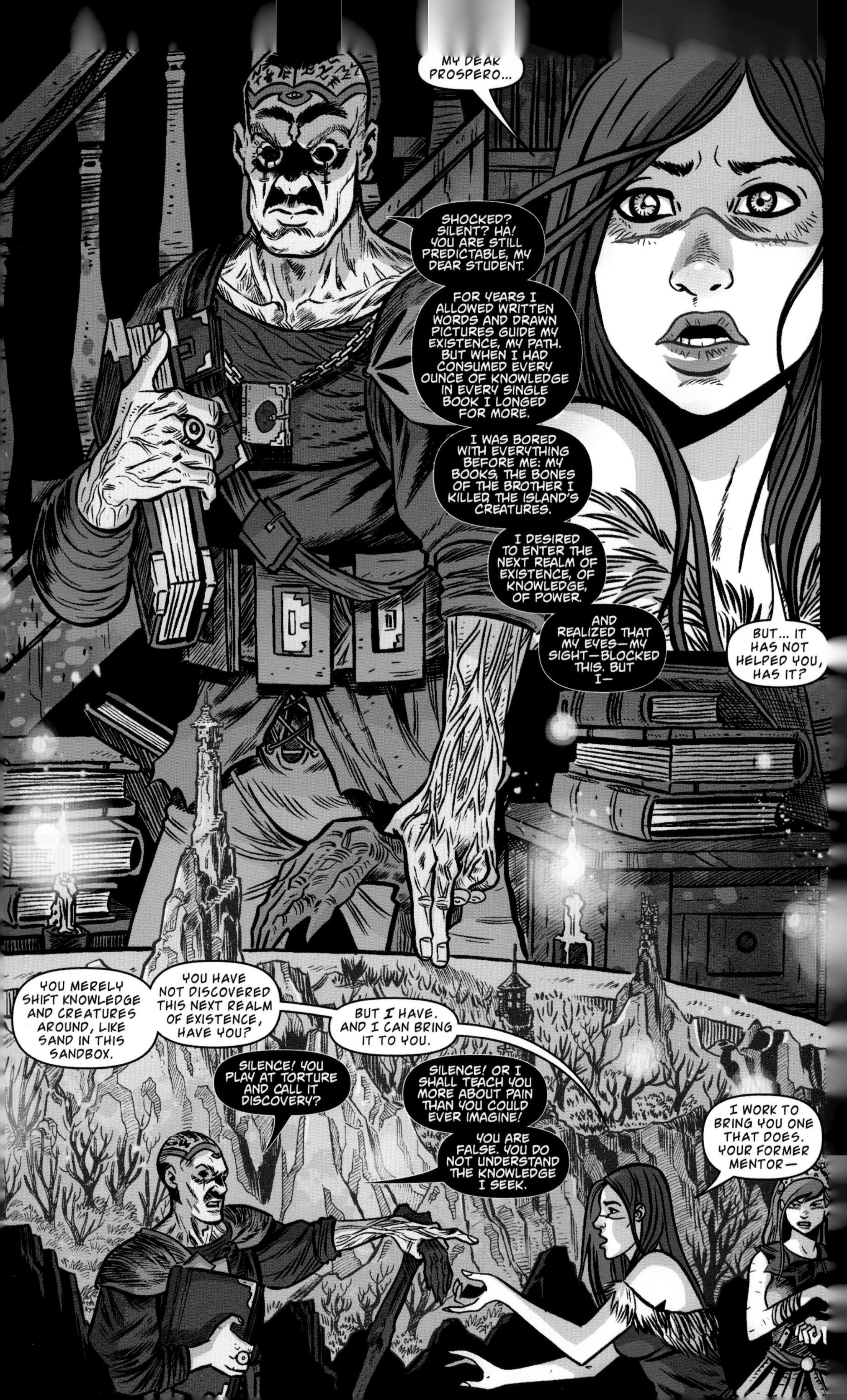
MY DEAR PROSPERO...
SHOCKED? SILENT? HA! YOU ARE STILL PREDICTABLE, MY DEAR STUDENT.
FOR YEARS I ALLOWED WRITTEN WORDS AND DRAWN PICTURES GUIDE MY EXISTENCE, MY PATH. BUT WHEN I HAD CONSUMED EVERY OUNCE OF KNOWLEDGE IN EVERY SINGLE BOOK I LONGED FOR MORE.
I WAS BORED WITH EVERYTHING BEFORE ME: MY BOOKS, THE BONES OF THE BROTHER I KILLED, THE ISLAND'S CREATURES.
I DESIRED TO ENTER THE NEXT REALM OF EXISTENCE, OF KNOWLEDGE, OF POWER.
AND REALIZED THAT MY EYES—MY SIGHT—BLOCKED THIS. BUT I—
BUT... IT HAS NOT HELPED YOU, HAS IT?
YOU MERELY SHIFT KNOWLEDGE AND CREATURES AROUND, LIKE SAND IN THIS SANDBOX.
YOU HAVE NOT DISCOVERED THIS NEXT REALM OF EXISTENCE, HAVE YOU?
BUT I HAVE. AND I CAN BRING IT TO YOU.
SILENCE! YOU PLAY AT TORTURE AND CALL IT DISCOVERY?
SILENCE! OR I SHALL TEACH YOU MORE ABOUT PAIN THAN YOU COULD EVER IMAGINE!
YOU ARE FALSE. YOU DO NOT UNDERSTAND THE KNOWLEDGE I SEEK.
I WORK TO BRING YOU ONE THAT DOES. YOUR FORMER MENTOR—

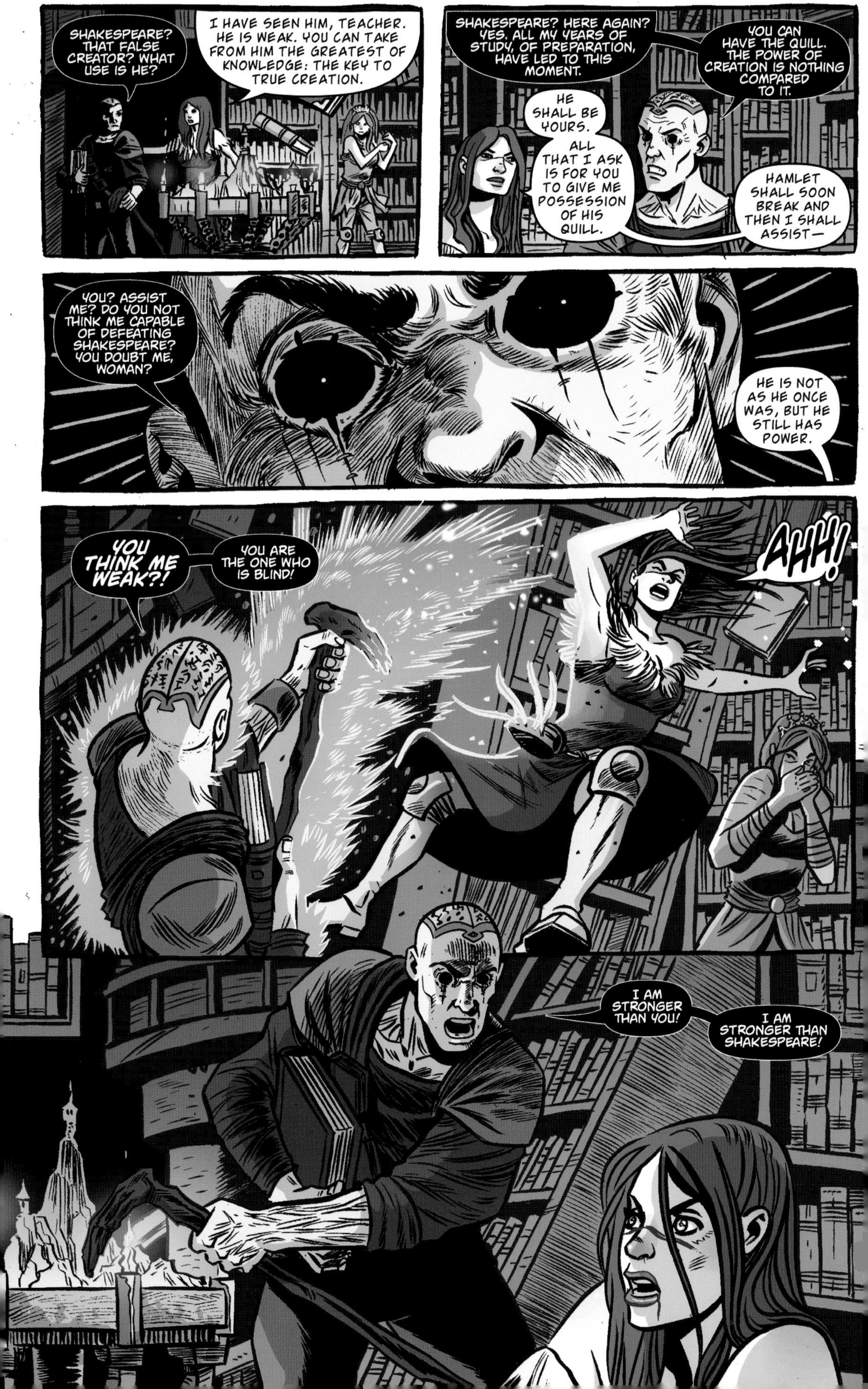
SHAKESPEARE? THAT FALSE CREATOR? WHAT USE IS HE?
I HAVE SEEN HIM, TEACHER. HE IS WEAK. YOU CAN TAKE FROM HIM THE GREATEST OF KNOWLEDGE: THE KEY TO TRUE CREATION.
SHAKESPEARE? HERE AGAIN? YES. ALL MY YEARS OF STUDY, OF PREPARATION, HAVE LED TO THIS MOMENT.
YOU CAN HAVE THE QUILL. THE POWER OF CREATION IS NOTHING COMPARED TO IT.
HE SHALL BE YOURS.
ALL THAT I ASK IS FOR YOU TO GIVE ME POSSESSION OF HIS QUILL.
HAMLET SHALL SOON BREAK AND THEN I SHALL ASSIST—
YOU? ASSIST ME? DO YOU NOT THINK ME CAPABLE OF DEFEATING SHAKESPEARE? YOU DOUBT ME, WOMAN?
HE IS NOT AS HE ONCE WAS, BUT HE STILL HAS POWER.
YOU THINK ME WEAK?!
YOU ARE THE ONE WHO IS BLIND!
AHH!
I AM STRONGER THAN YOU!
I AM STRONGER THAN SHAKESPEARE!

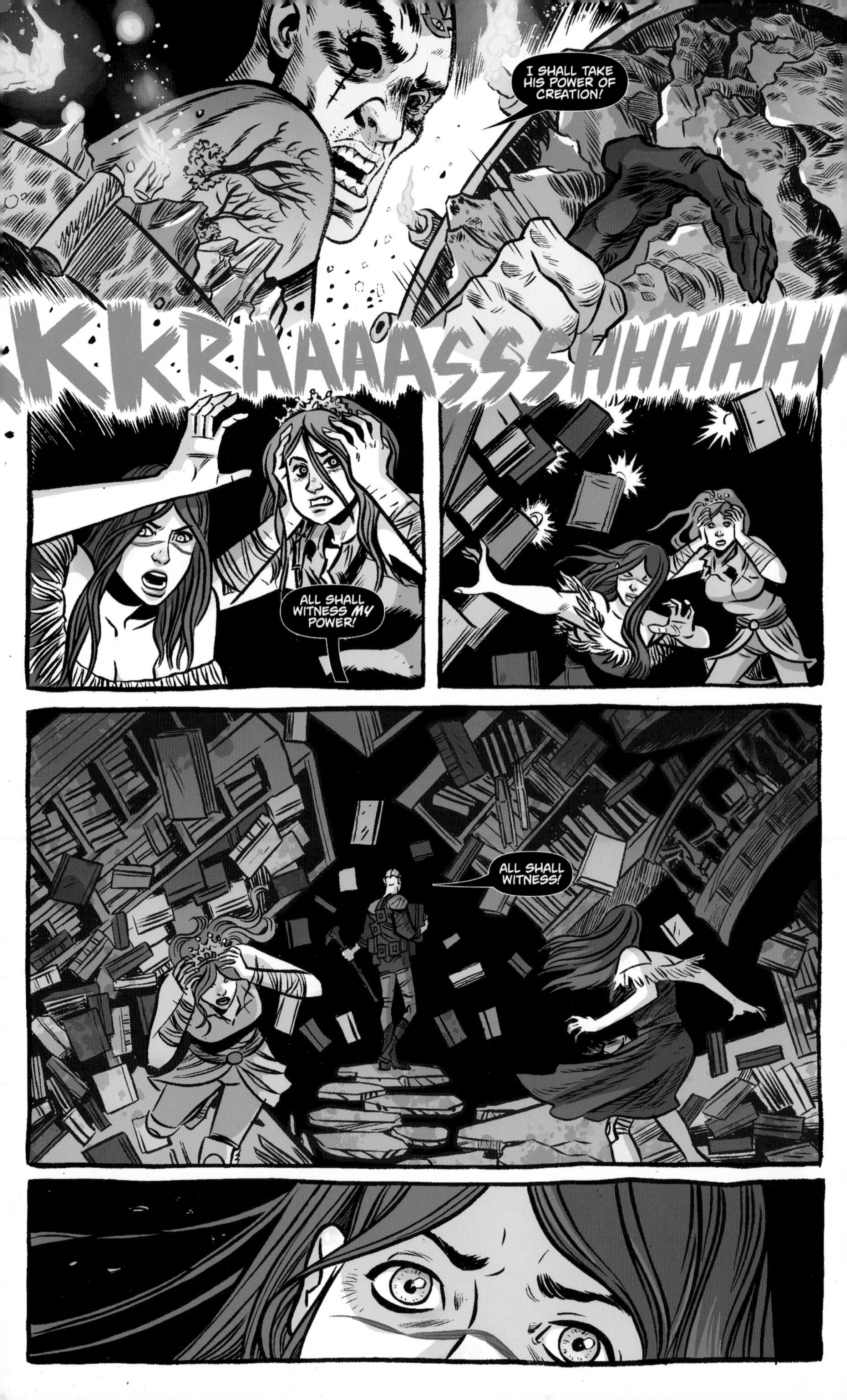
I SHALL TAKE HIS POWER OF CREATION!
KKRAAAAASSSSHHHHHH!
ALL SHALL WITNESS MY POWER!
ALL SHALL WITNESS!

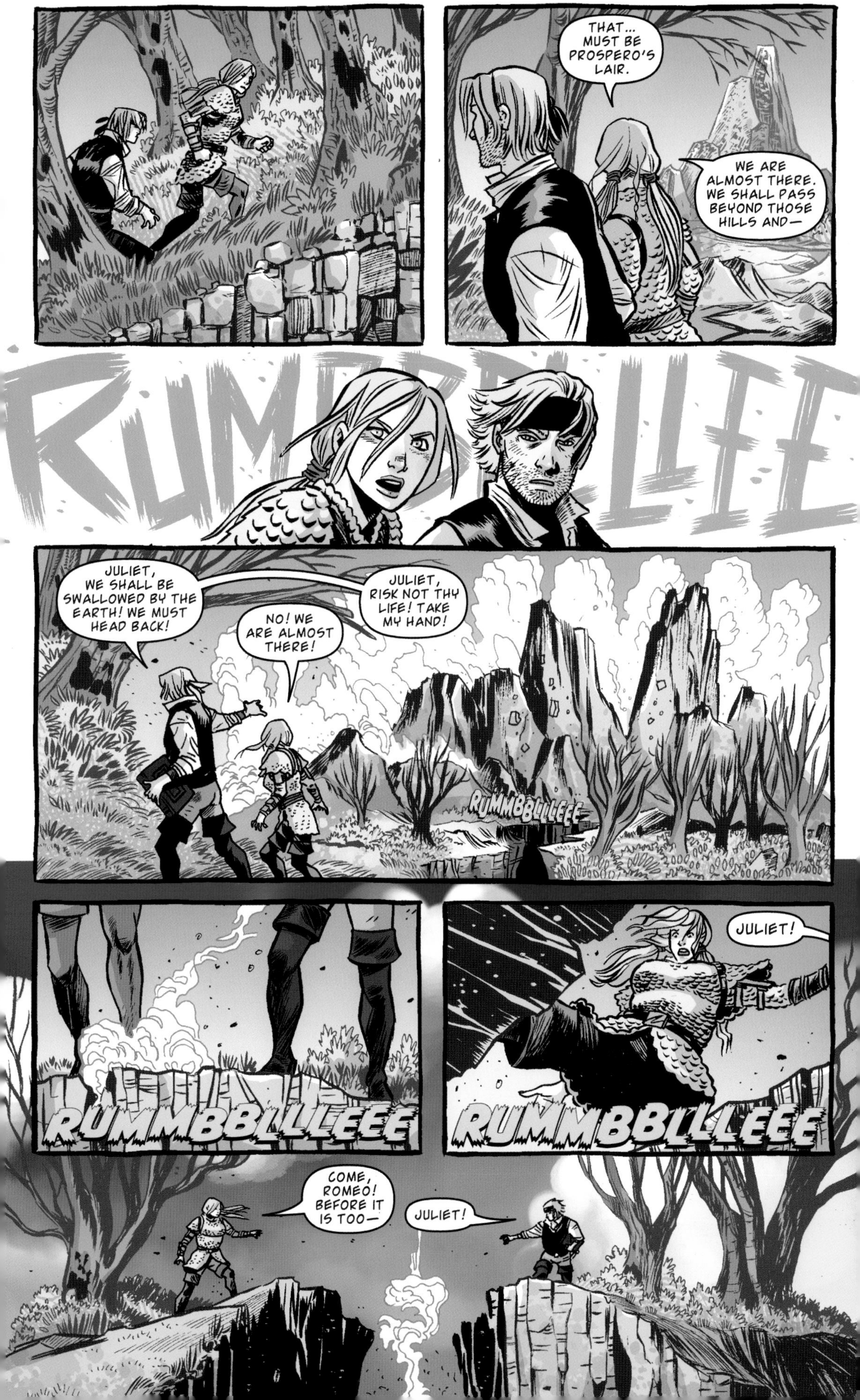
THAT... MUST BE PROSPERO'S LAIR.
WE ARE ALMOST THERE. WE SHALL PASS BEYOND THOSE HILLS AND—
JULIET, WE SHALL BE SWALLOWED BY THE EARTH! WE MUST HEAD BACK!
NO! WE ARE ALMOST THERE!
JULIET, RISK NOT THY LIFE! TAKE MY HAND!
RUMMBBLLLEEE
RUMMBBLLLEEE
JULIET!
RUMMBBLLLEEE
COME, ROMEO! BEFORE IT IS TOO—
JULIET!

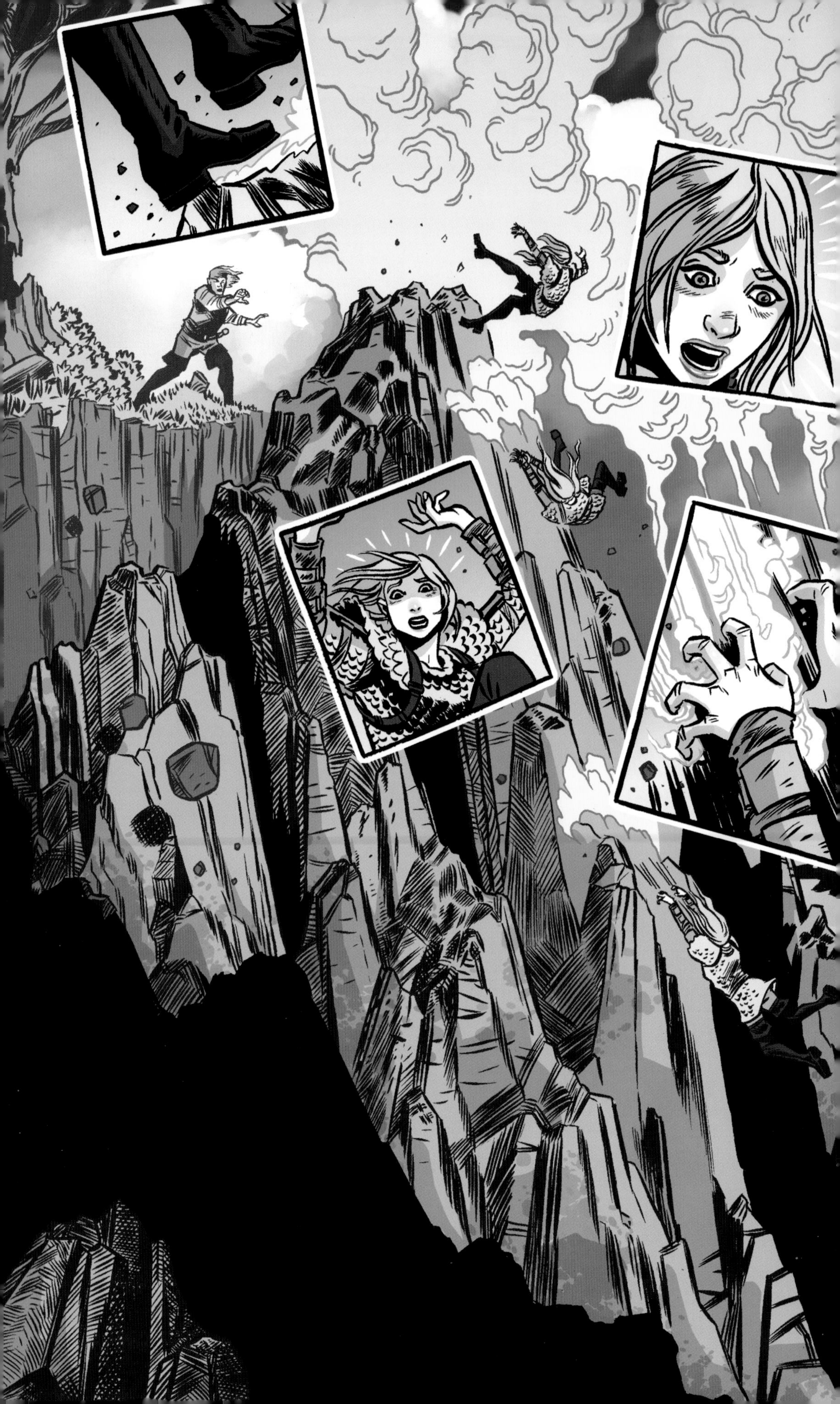

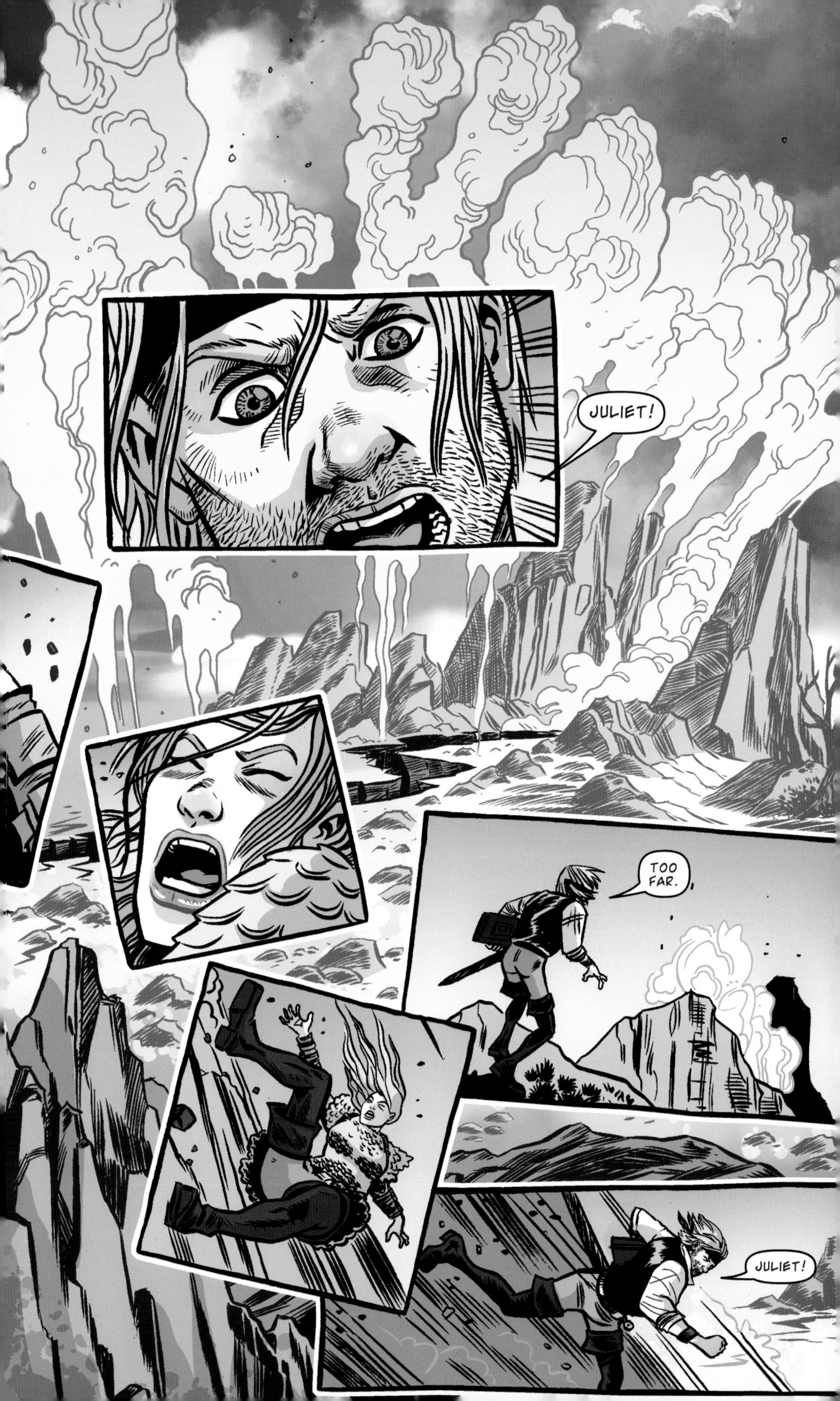
JULIET!
TOO FAR.
JULIET!

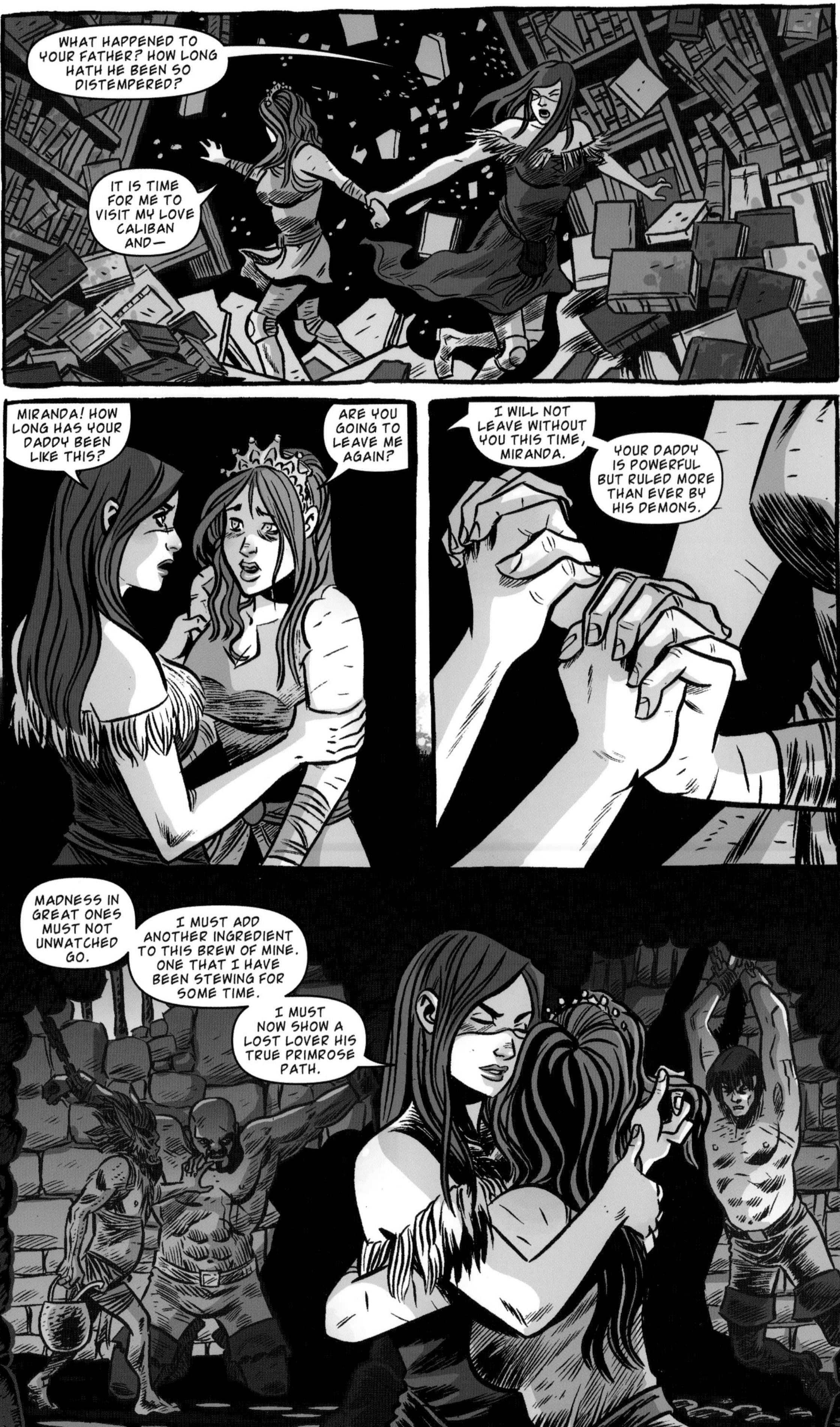
WHAT HAPPENED TO YOUR FATHER? HOW LONG HATH HE BEEN SO DISTEMPERED?
IT IS TIME FOR ME TO VISIT MY LOVE CALIBAN AND—
MIRANDA! HOW LONG HAS YOUR DADDY BEEN LIKE THIS?
ARE YOU GOING TO LEAVE ME AGAIN?
I WILL NOT LEAVE WITHOUT YOU THIS TIME, MIRANDA.
YOUR DADDY IS POWERFUL BUT RULED MORE THAN EVER BY HIS DEMONS.
MADNESS IN GREAT ONES MUST NOT UNWATCHED GO.
I MUST ADD ANOTHER INGREDIENT TO THIS BREW OF MINE. ONE THAT I HAVE BEEN STEWING FOR SOME TIME.
I MUST NOW SHOW A LOST LOVER HIS TRUE PRIMROSE PATH.

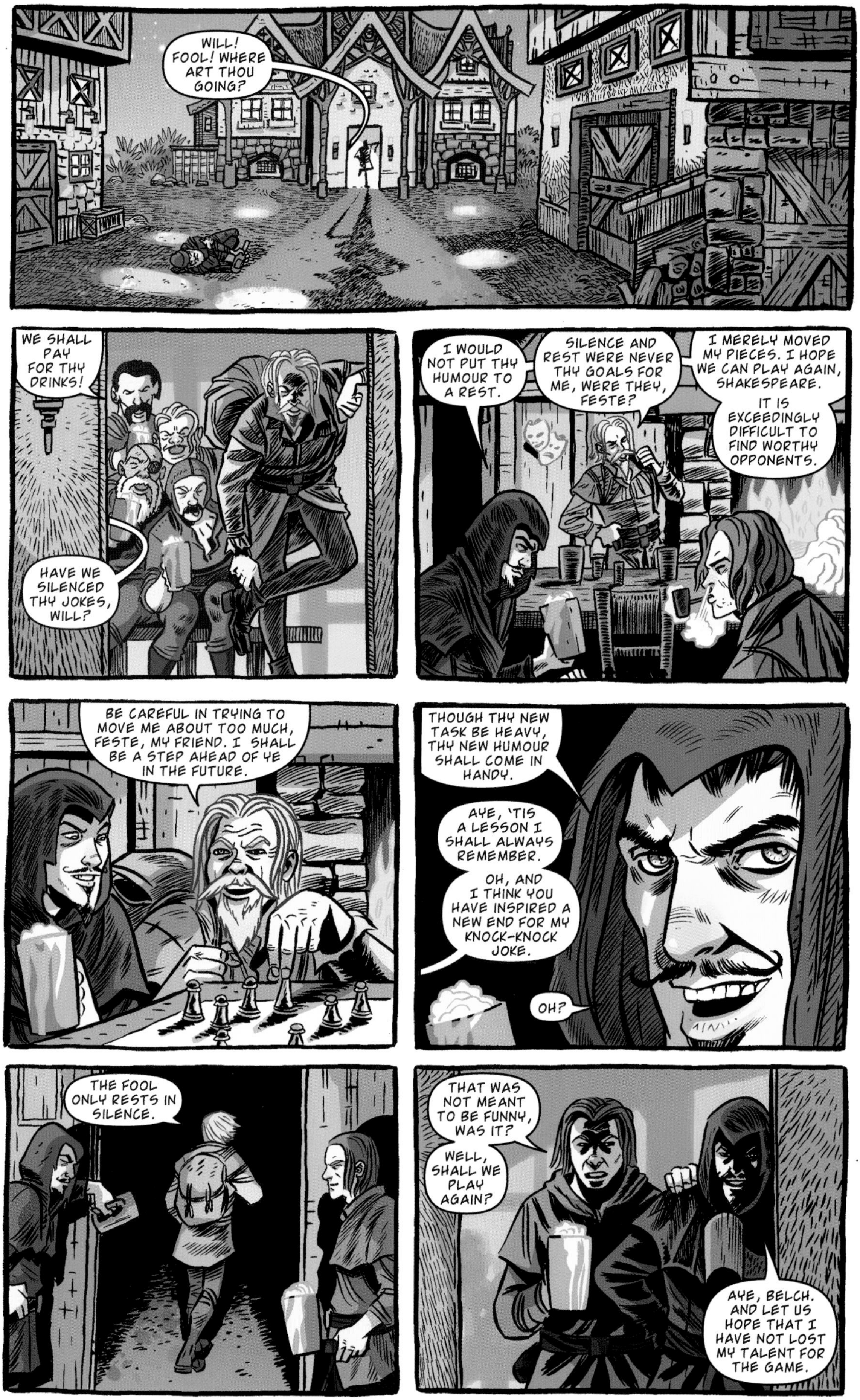
WILL! FOOL! WHERE ART THOU GOING?
WE SHALL PAY FOR THY DRINKS!
HAVE WE SILENCED THY JOKES, WILL?
I WOULD NOT PUT THY HUMOUR TO A REST.
SILENCE AND REST WERE NEVER THY GOALS FOR ME, WERE THEY, FESTE?
I MERELY MOVED MY PIECES. I HOPE WE CAN PLAY AGAIN, SHAKESPEARE.
IT IS EXCEEDINGLY DIFFICULT TO FIND WORTHY OPPONENTS.
BE CAREFUL IN TRYING TO MOVE ME ABOUT TOO MUCH, FESTE, MY FRIEND. I SHALL BE A STEP AHEAD OF YE IN THE FUTURE.
THOUGH THY NEW TASK BE HEAVY, THY NEW HUMOUR SHALL COME IN HANDY.
AYE, 'TIS A LESSON I SHALL ALWAYS REMEMBER.
OH, AND I THINK YOU HAVE INSPIRED A NEW END FOR MY KNOCK-KNOCK JOKE.
OH?
THE FOOL ONLY RESTS IN SILENCE.
THAT WAS NOT MEANT TO BE FUNNY, WAS IT?
WELL, SHALL WE PLAY AGAIN?
AYE, BELCH. AND LET US HOPE THAT I HAVE NOT LOST MY TALENT FOR THE GAME.

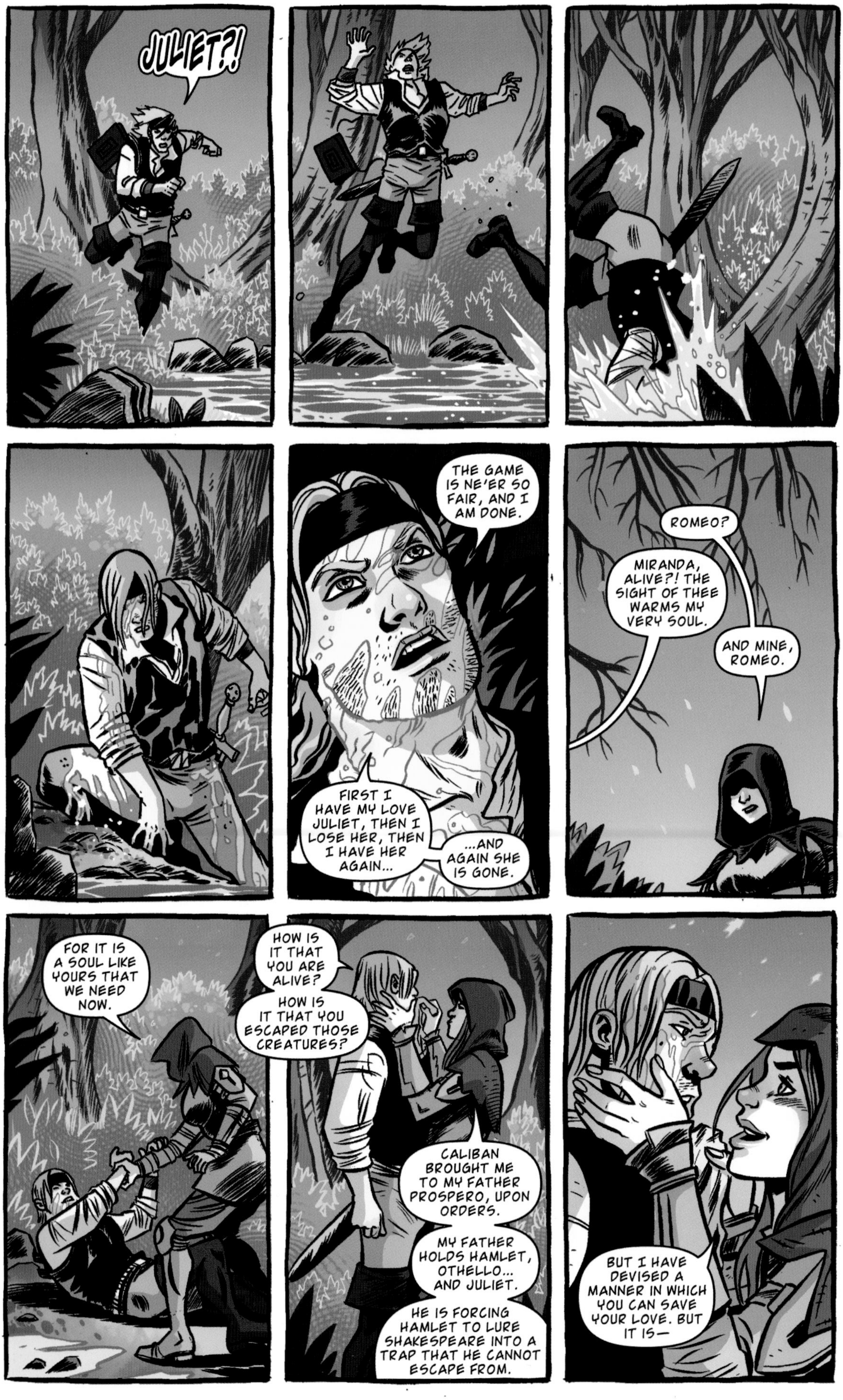
JULIET?!
THE GAME IS NE'ER SO FAIR, AND I AM DONE.
FIRST I HAVE MY LOVE JULIET, THEN I LOSE HER, THEN I HAVE HER AGAIN...
...AND AGAIN SHE IS GONE.
ROMEO?
MIRANDA, ALIVE?! THE SIGHT OF THEE WARMS MY VERY SOUL.
AND MINE, ROMEO.
FOR IT IS A SOUL LIKE YOURS THAT WE NEED NOW.
HOW IS IT THAT YOU ARE ALIVE?
HOW IS IT THAT YOU ESCAPED THOSE CREATURES?
CALIBAN BROUGHT ME TO MY FATHER PROSPERO, UPON ORDERS.
MY FATHER HOLDS HAMLET, OTHELLO... AND JULIET.
HE IS FORCING HAMLET TO LURE SHAKESPEARE INTO A TRAP THAT HE CANNOT ESCAPE FROM.
BUT I HAVE DEVISED A MANNER IN WHICH YOU CAN SAVE YOUR LOVE. BUT IT IS—

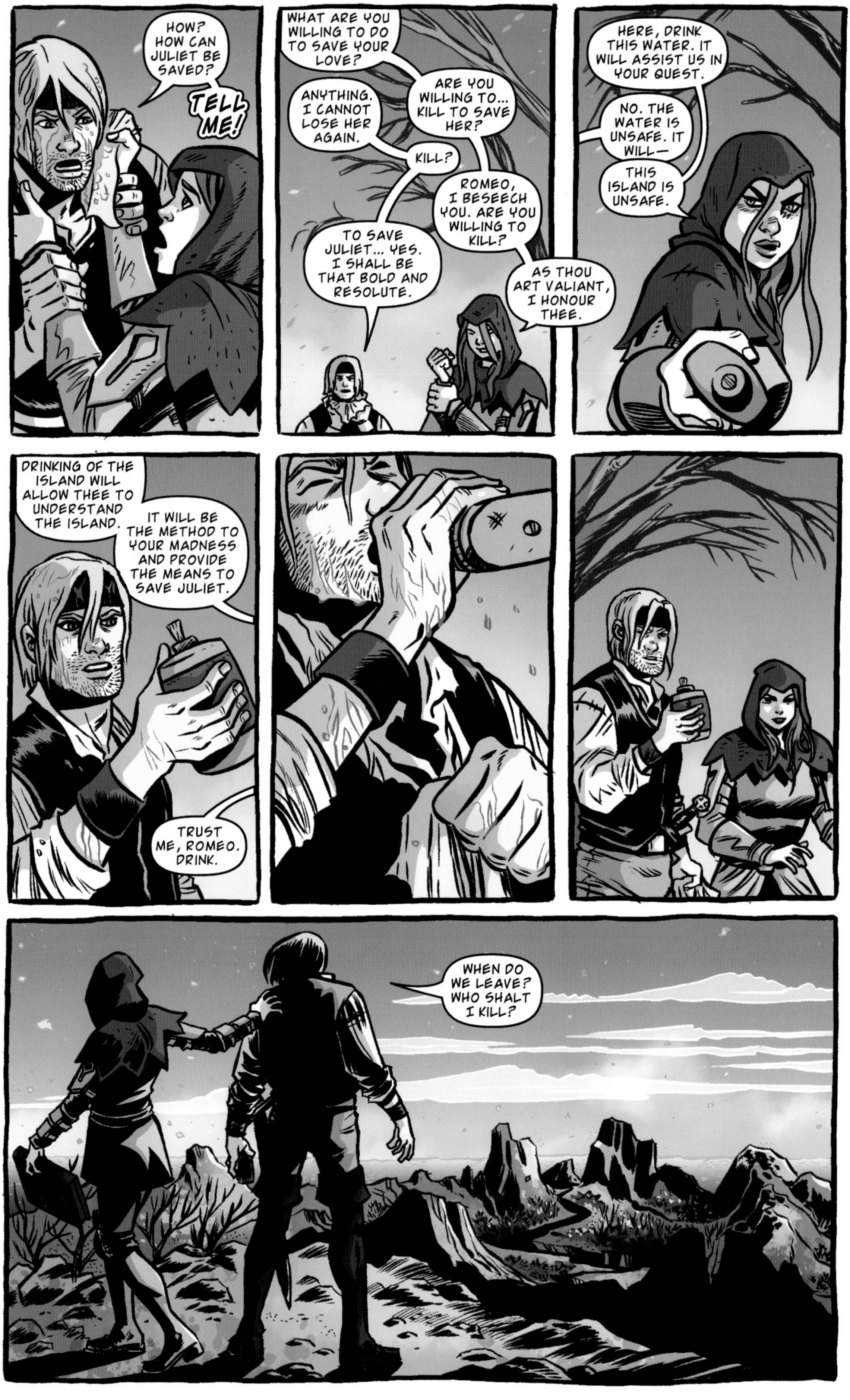
HOW? HOW CAN JULIET BE SAVED?
TELL ME!
WHAT ARE YOU WILLING TO DO TO SAVE YOUR LOVE?
ANYTHING. I CANNOT LOSE HER AGAIN.
ARE YOU WILLING TO... KILL TO SAVE HER?
KILL?
ROMEO, I BESEECH YOU. ARE YOU WILLING TO KILL?
TO SAVE JULIET... YES. I SHALL BE THAT BOLD AND RESOLUTE.
AS THOU ART VALIANT, I HONOUR THEE.
HERE, DRINK THIS WATER. IT WILL ASSIST US IN YOUR QUEST.
NO. THE WATER IS UNSAFE. IT WILL—
THIS ISLAND IS UNSAFE.
DRINKING OF THE ISLAND WILL ALLOW THEE TO UNDERSTAND THE ISLAND.
IT WILL BE THE METHOD TO YOUR MADNESS AND PROVIDE THE MEANS TO SAVE JULIET.
TRUST ME, ROMEO. DRINK.
WHEN DO WE LEAVE? WHO SHALT I KILL?

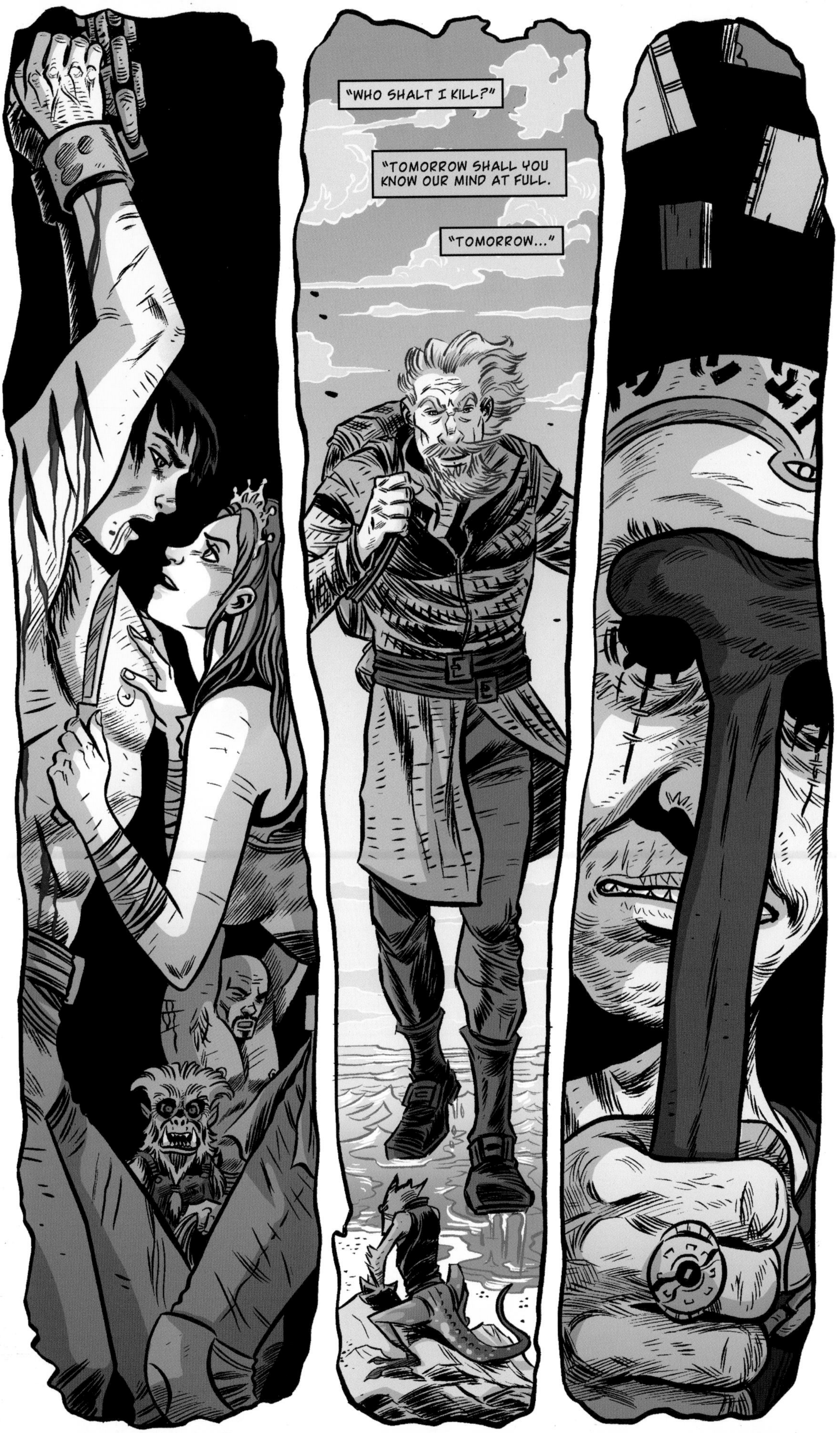
"WHO SHALT I KILL?"
"TOMORROW SHALL YOU KNOW OUR MIND AT FULL.
"TOMORROW..."

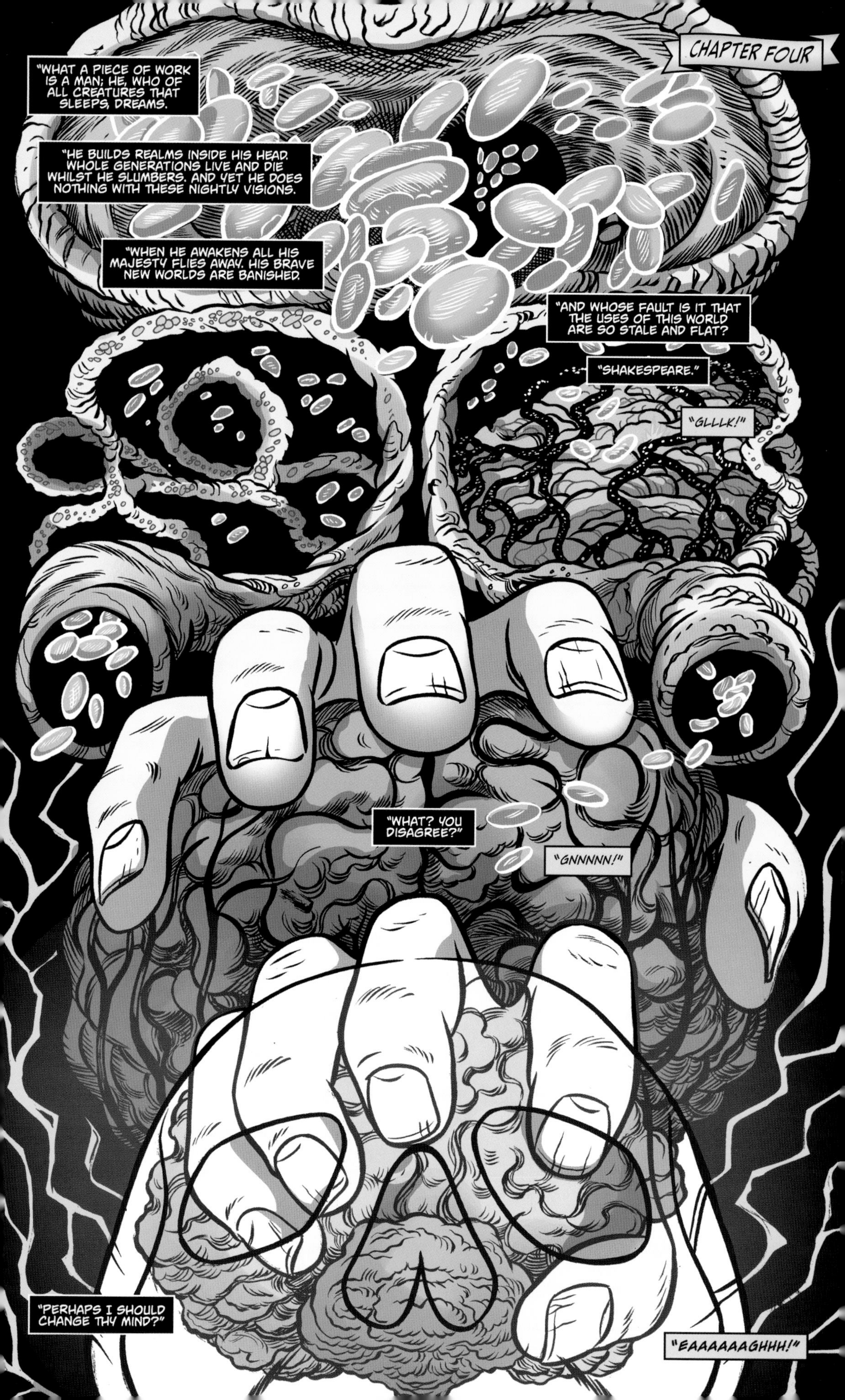
CHAPTER FOUR
"WHAT A PIECE OF WORK IS A MAN; HE, WHO OF ALL CREATURES THAT SLEEPS, DREAMS.
"HE BUILDS REALMS INSIDE HIS HEAD. WHOLE GENERATIONS LIVE AND DIE WHILST HE SLUMBERS. AND YET HE DOES NOTHING WITH THESE NIGHTLY VISIONS.
"WHEN HE AWAKENS ALL HIS MAJESTY FLIES AWAY. HIS BRAVE NEW WORLDS ARE BANISHED.
"AND WHOSE FAULT IS IT THAT THE USES OF THIS WORLD ARE SO STALE AND FLAT?
"SHAKESPEARE."
"GLLLK!"
"WHAT? YOU DISAGREE?"
"GNNNNN!"
"PERHAPS I SHOULD CHANGE THY MIND?"
"EAAAAAAGHHH!"

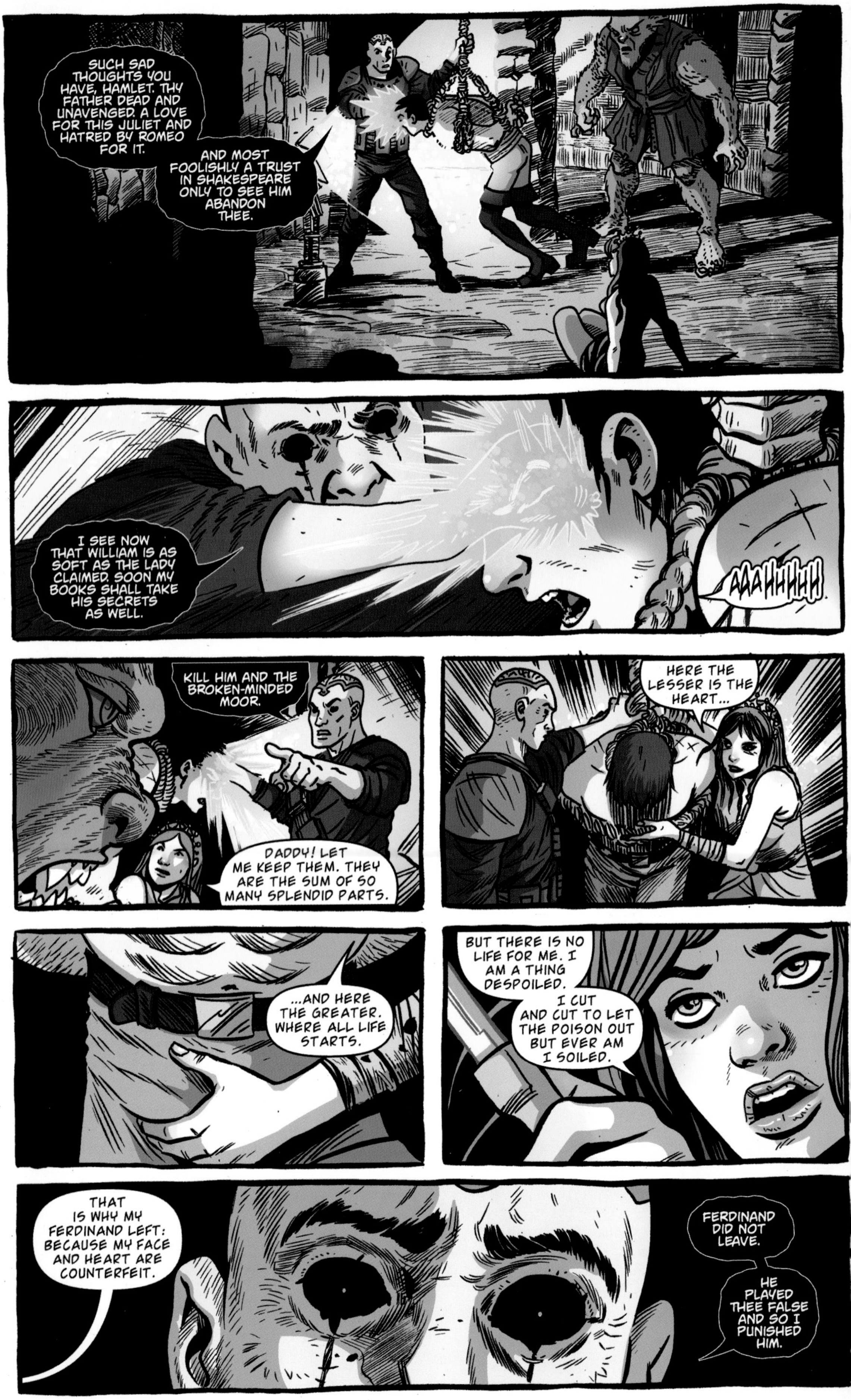
SUCH SAD THOUGHTS YOU HAVE, HAMLET. THY FATHER DEAD AND UNAVENGED. A LOVE FOR THIS JULIET AND HATRED BY ROMEO FOR IT.
AND MOST FOOLISHLY A TRUST IN SHAKESPEARE ONLY TO SEE HIM ABANDON THEE.
I SEE NOW THAT WILLIAM IS AS SOFT AS THE LADY CLAIMED. SOON MY BOOKS SHALL TAKE HIS SECRETS AS WELL.
AAAHHHHH
KILL HIM AND THE BROKEN-MINDED MOOR.
DADDY! LET ME KEEP THEM. THEY ARE THE SUM OF SO MANY SPLENDID PARTS.
HERE THE LESSER IS THE HEART...
...AND HERE THE GREATER. WHERE ALL LIFE STARTS.
BUT THERE IS NO LIFE FOR ME. I AM A THING DESPOILED.
I CUT AND CUT TO LET THE POISON OUT BUT EVER AM I SOILED.
THAT IS WHY MY FERDINAND LEFT: BECAUSE MY FACE AND HEART ARE COUNTERFEIT.
FERDINAND DID NOT LEAVE.
HE PLAYED THEE FALSE AND SO I PUNISHED HIM.

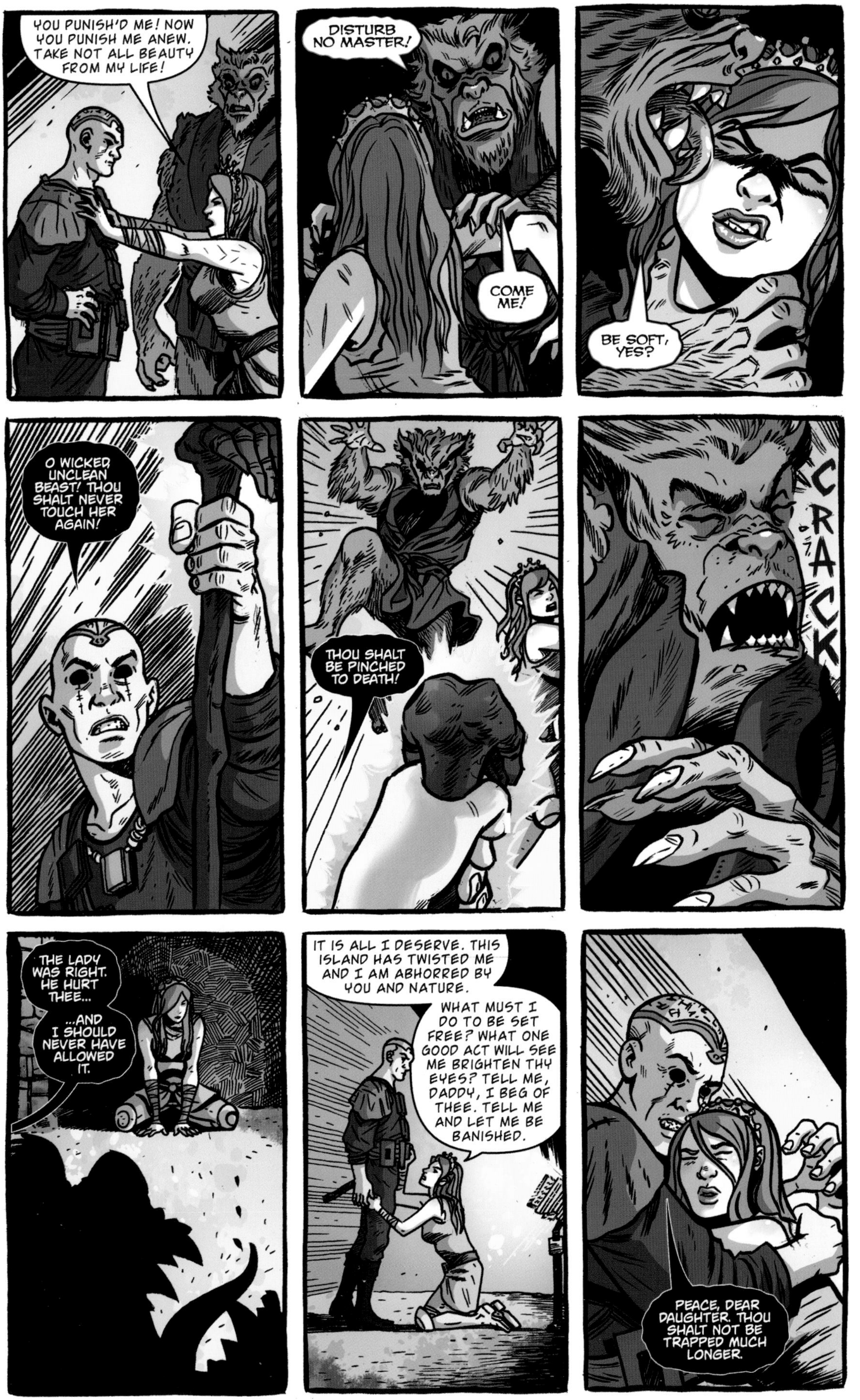
YOU PUNISH'D ME! NOW YOU PUNISH ME ANEW. TAKE NOT ALL BEAUTY FROM MY LIFE!
DISTURB NO MASTER!
COME ME!
BE SOFT, YES?
O WICKED, UNCLEAN BEAST! THOU SHALT NEVER TOUCH HER AGAIN!
THOU SHALT BE PINCHED TO DEATH!
CRACK
THE LADY WAS RIGHT. HE HURT THEE...
...AND I SHOULD NEVER HAVE ALLOWED IT.
IT IS ALL I DESERVE. THIS ISLAND HAS TWISTED ME AND I AM ABHORRED BY YOU AND NATURE.
WHAT MUST I DO TO BE SET FREE? WHAT ONE GOOD ACT WILL SEE ME BRIGHTEN THY EYES? TELL ME, DADDY, I BEG OF THEE. TELL ME AND LET ME BE BANISHED.
PEACE, DEAR DAUGHTER. THOU SHALT NOT BE TRAPPED MUCH LONGER.

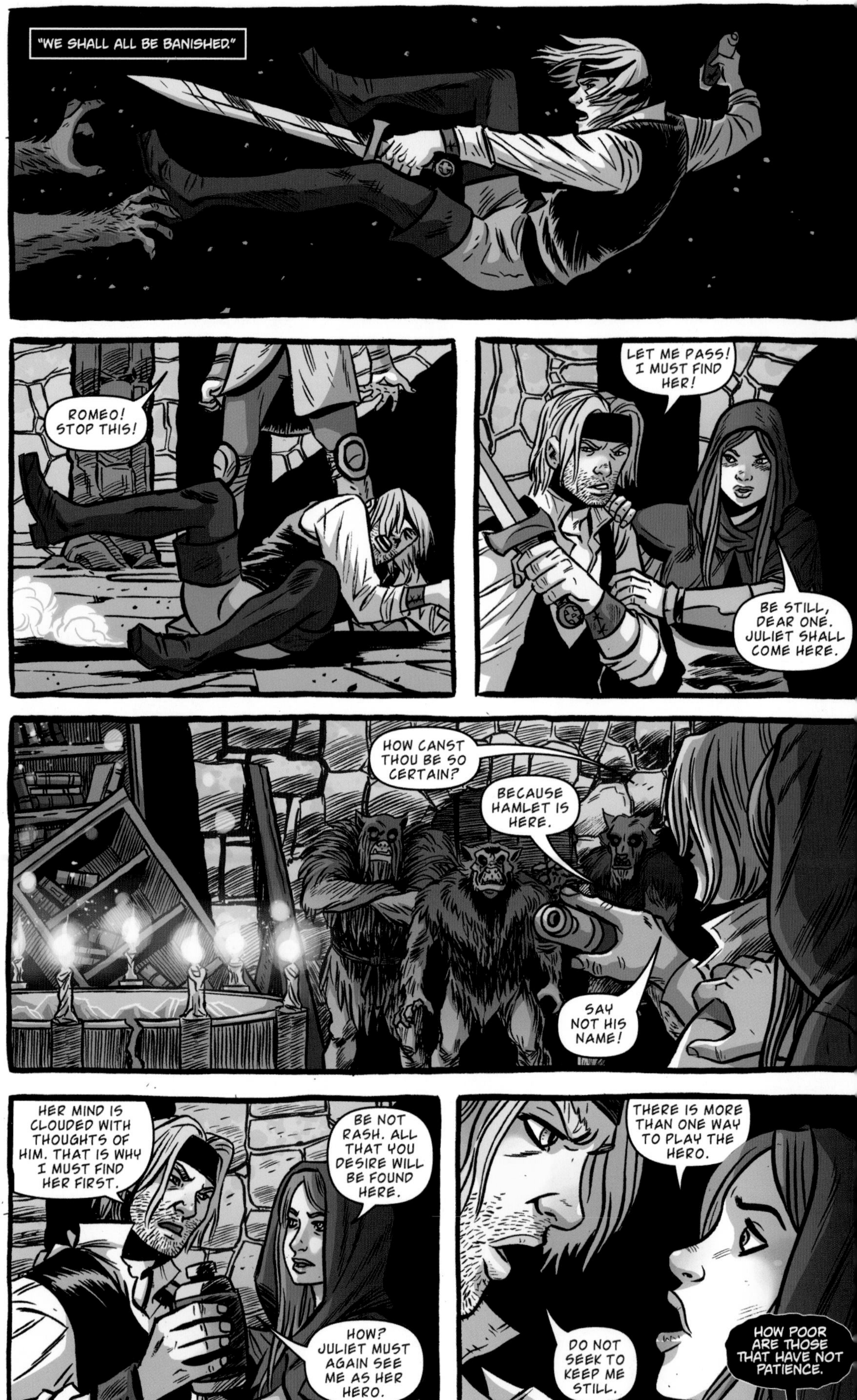
"WE SHALL ALL BE BANISHED."
ROMEO! STOP THIS!
LET ME PASS! I MUST FIND HER!
BE STILL, DEAR ONE. JULIET SHALL COME HERE.
HOW CANST THOU BE SO CERTAIN?
BECAUSE HAMLET IS HERE.
SAY NOT HIS NAME!
HER MIND IS CLOUDED WITH THOUGHTS OF HIM. THAT IS WHY I MUST FIND HER FIRST.
BE NOT RASH. ALL THAT YOU DESIRE WILL BE FOUND HERE.
HOW? JULIET MUST AGAIN SEE ME AS HER HERO.
THERE IS MORE THAN ONE WAY TO PLAY THE HERO.
DO NOT SEEK TO KEEP ME STILL.
HOW POOR ARE THOSE THAT HAVE NOT PATIENCE.

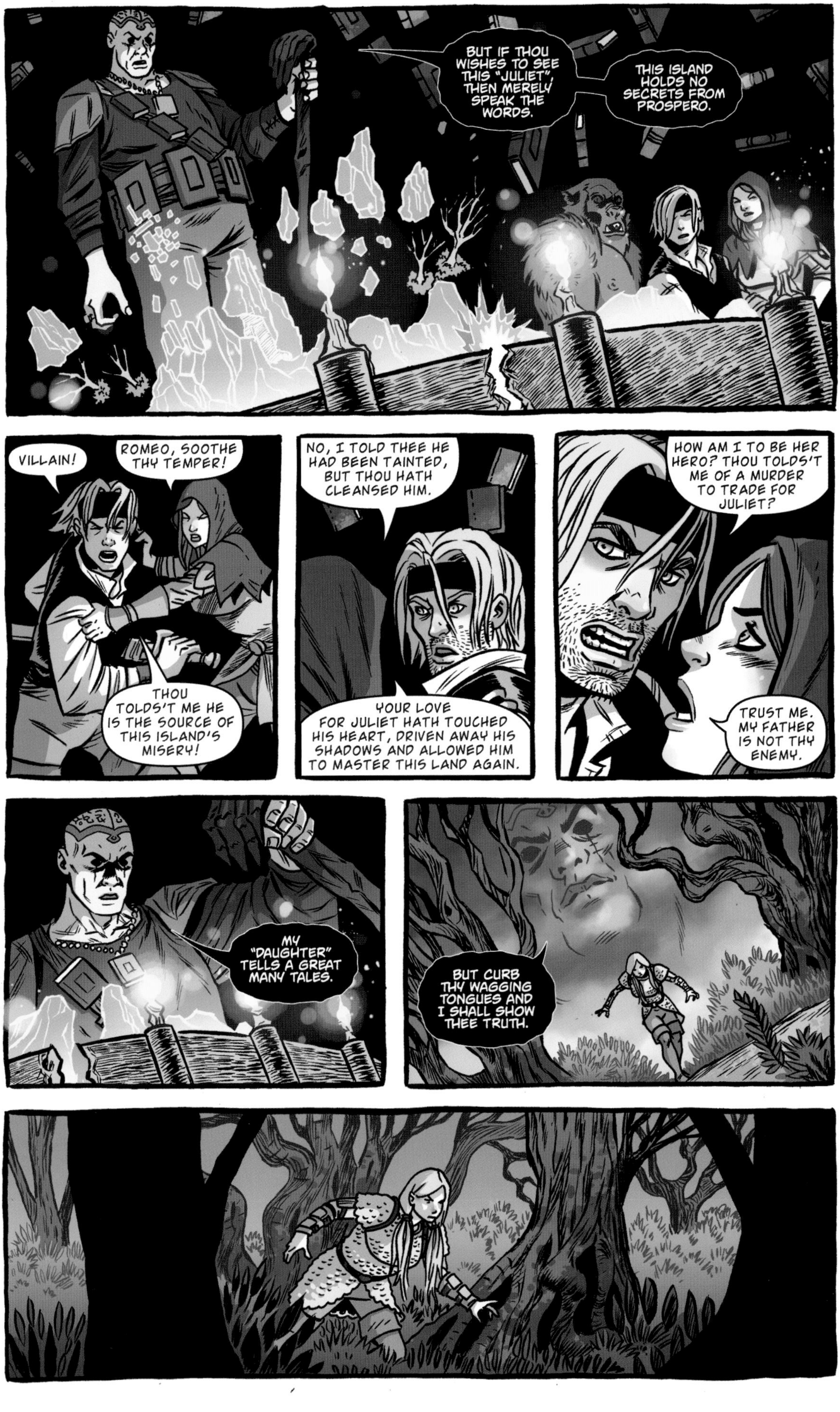
BUT IF THOU WISHES TO SEE THIS "JULIET", THEN MERELY SPEAK THE WORDS.
THIS ISLAND HOLDS NO SECRETS FROM PROSPERO.
VILLAIN!
ROMEO, SOOTHE THY TEMPER!
THOU TOLDS'T ME HE IS THE SOURCE OF THIS ISLAND'S MISERY!
NO, I TOLD THEE HE HAD BEEN TAINTED, BUT THOU HATH CLEANSED HIM.
YOUR LOVE FOR JULIET HATH TOUCHED HIS HEART, DRIVEN AWAY HIS SHADOWS AND ALLOWED HIM TO MASTER THIS LAND AGAIN.
HOW AM I TO BE HER HERO? THOU TOLDS'T ME OF A MURDER TO TRADE FOR JULIET?
TRUST ME. MY FATHER IS NOT THY ENEMY.
MY "DAUGHTER" TELLS A GREAT MANY TALES.
BUT CURB THY WAGGING TONGUES AND I SHALL SHOW THEE TRUTH.

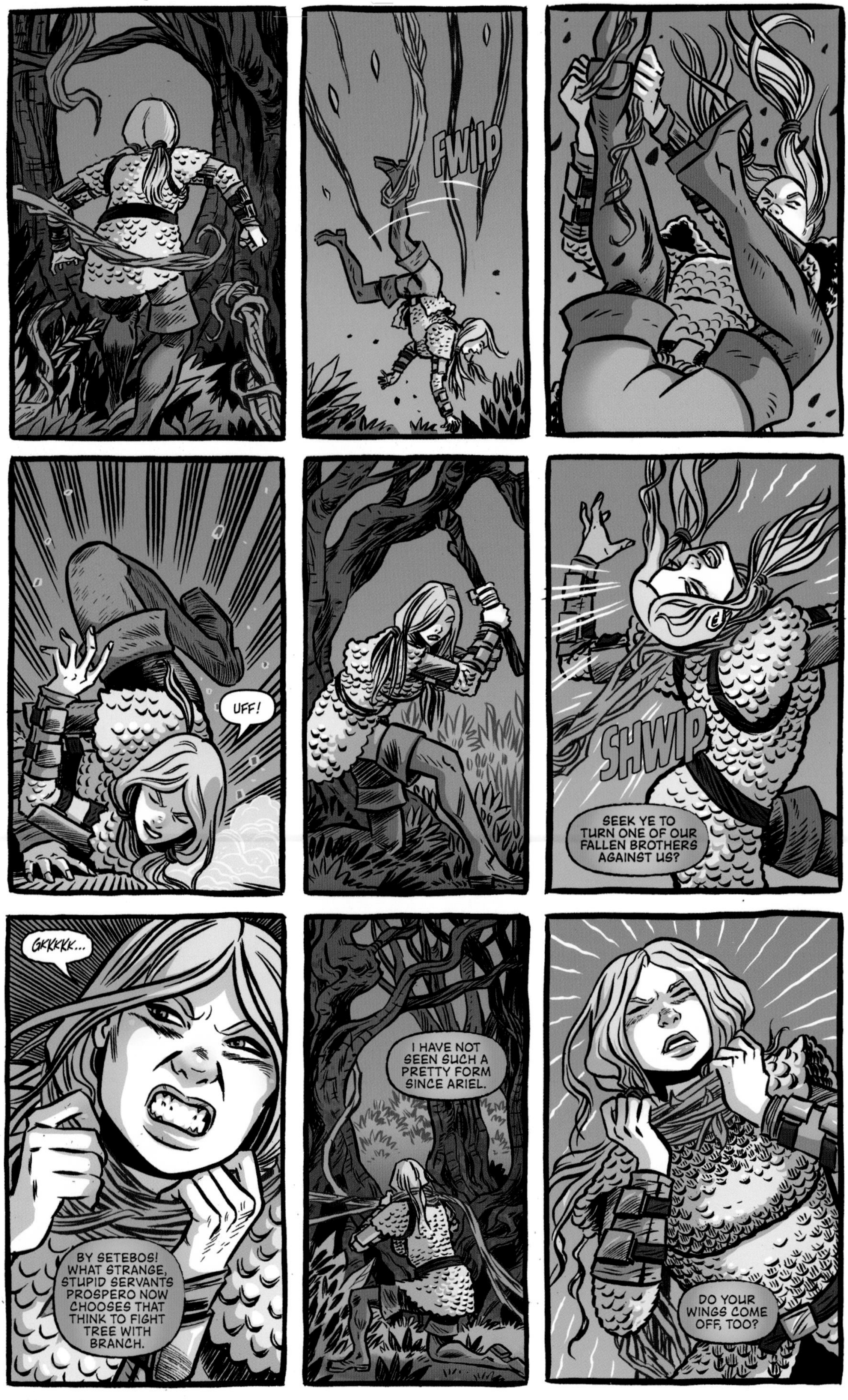
FWIP
UFF!
SHWIP
SEEK YE TO TURN ONE OF OUR FALLEN BROTHERS AGAINST US?
GKKKKK...
BY SETEBOS! WHAT STRANGE, STUPID SERVANTS PROSPERO NOW CHOOSES THAT THINK TO FIGHT TREE WITH BRANCH.
I HAVE NOT SEEN SUCH A PRETTY FORM SINCE ARIEL.
DO YOUR WINGS COME OFF, TOO?

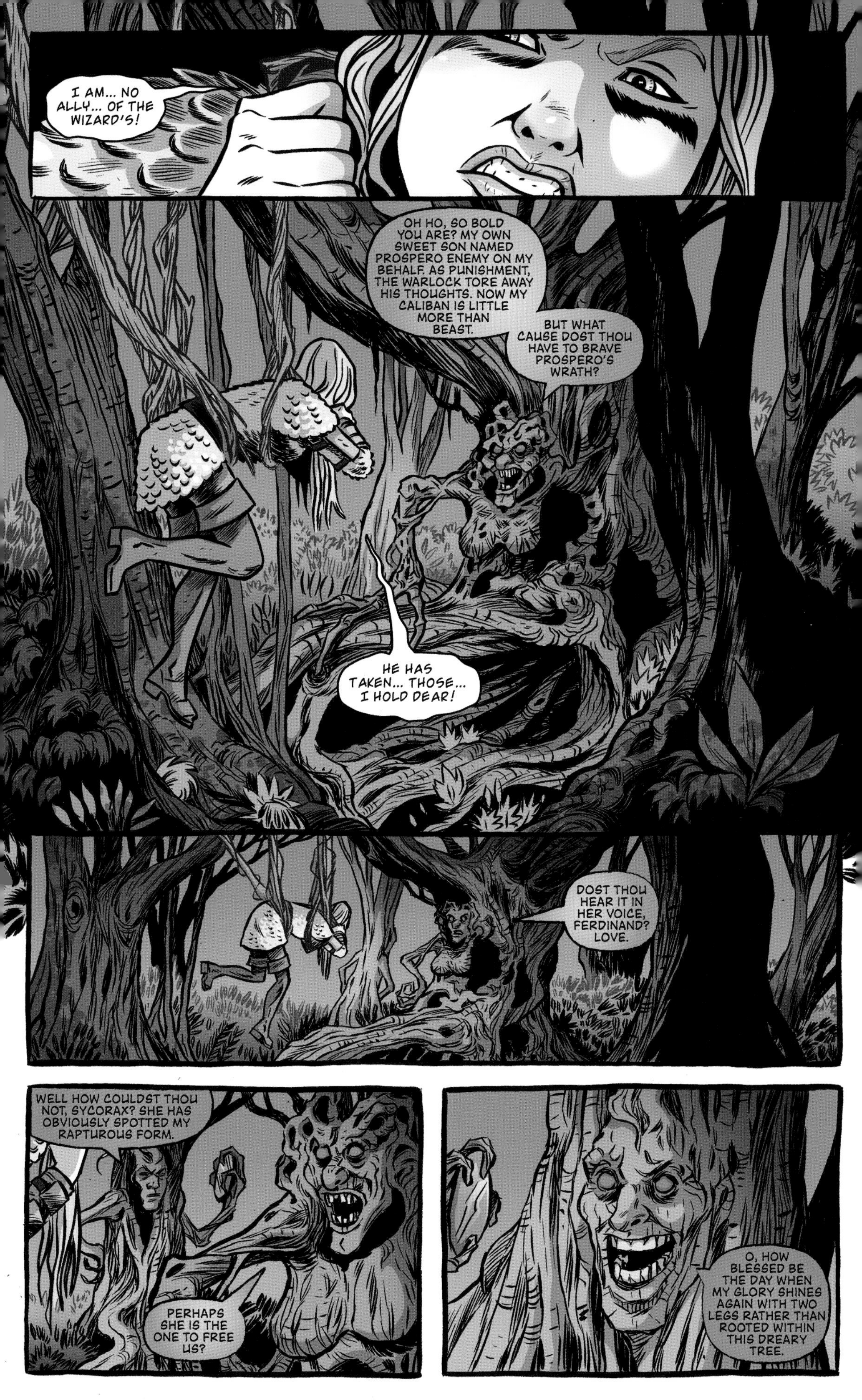
I AM... NO ALLY... OF THE WIZARD'S!
OH HO, SO BOLD YOU ARE? MY OWN SWEET SON NAMED PROSPERO ENEMY ON MY BEHALF. AS PUNISHMENT, THE WARLOCK TORE AWAY HIS THOUGHTS. NOW MY CALIBAN IS LITTLE MORE THAN BEAST.
BUT WHAT CAUSE DOST THOU HAVE TO BRAVE PROSPERO'S WRATH?
HE HAS TAKEN... THOSE... I HOLD DEAR!
DOST THOU HEAR IT IN HER VOICE, FERDINAND? LOVE.
WELL HOW COULDST THOU NOT, SYCORAX? SHE HAS OBVIOUSLY SPOTTED MY RAPTUROUS FORM.
PERHAPS SHE IS THE ONE TO FREE US?
O, HOW BLESSED BE THE DAY WHEN MY GLORY SHINES AGAIN WITH TWO LEGS RATHER THAN ROOTED WITHIN THIS DREARY TREE.

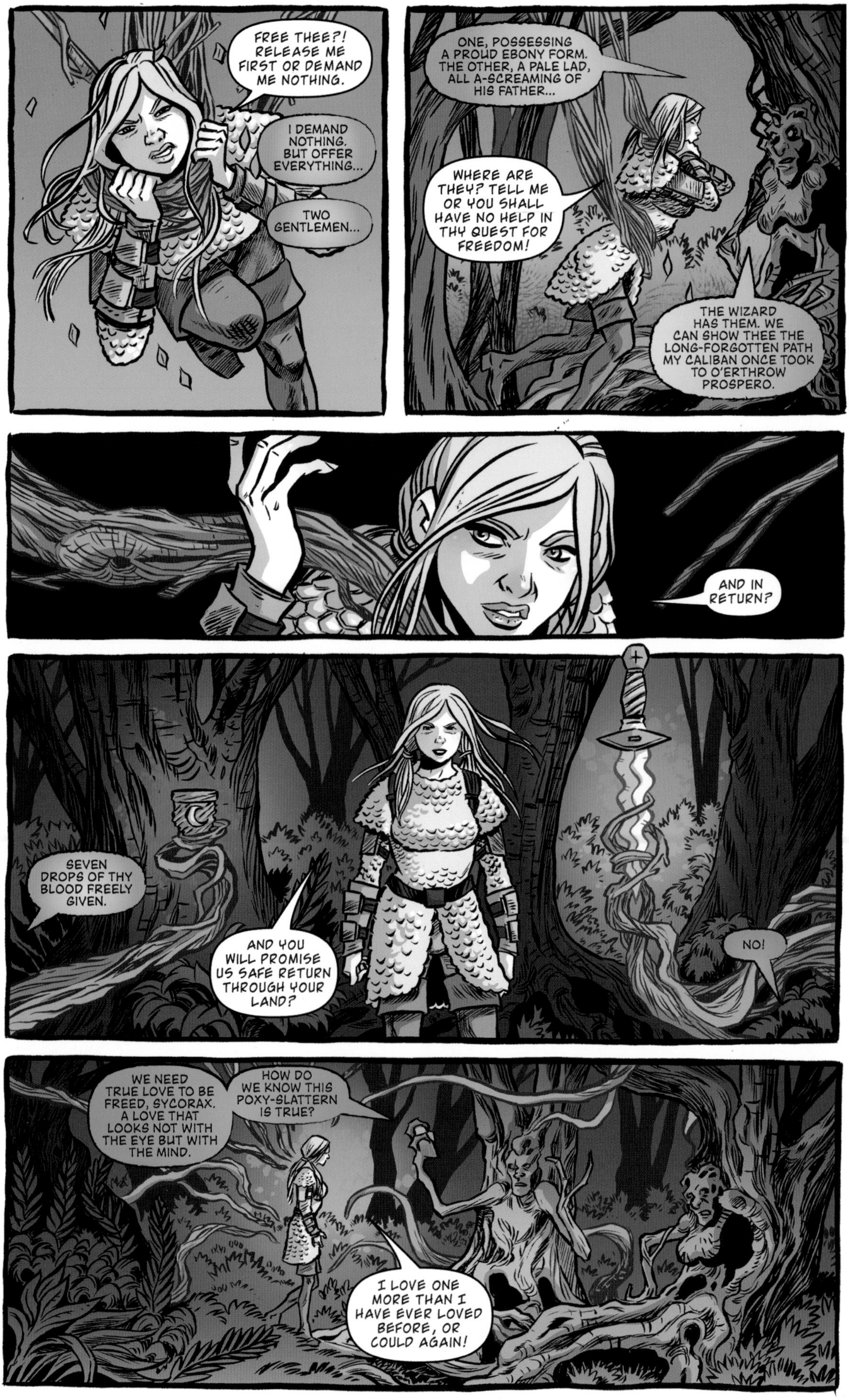
FREE THEE?! RELEASE ME FIRST OR DEMAND ME NOTHING.
I DEMAND NOTHING. BUT OFFER EVERYTHING...
TWO GENTLEMEN...
ONE, POSSESSING A PROUD EBONY FORM. THE OTHER, A PALE LAD, ALL A-SCREAMING OF HIS FATHER...
WHERE ARE THEY? TELL ME OR YOU SHALL HAVE NO HELP IN THY QUEST FOR FREEDOM!
THE WIZARD HAS THEM. WE CAN SHOW THEE THE LONG-FORGOTTEN PATH MY CALIBAN ONCE TOOK TO O'ERTHROW PROSPERO.
AND IN RETURN?
SEVEN DROPS OF THY BLOOD FREELY GIVEN.
AND YOU WILL PROMISE US SAFE RETURN THROUGH YOUR LAND?
NO!
WE NEED TRUE LOVE TO BE FREED, SYCORAX. A LOVE THAT LOOKS NOT WITH THE EYE BUT WITH THE MIND.
HOW DO WE KNOW THIS POXY-SLATTERN IS TRUE?
I LOVE ONE MORE THAN I HAVE EVER LOVED BEFORE, OR COULD AGAIN!

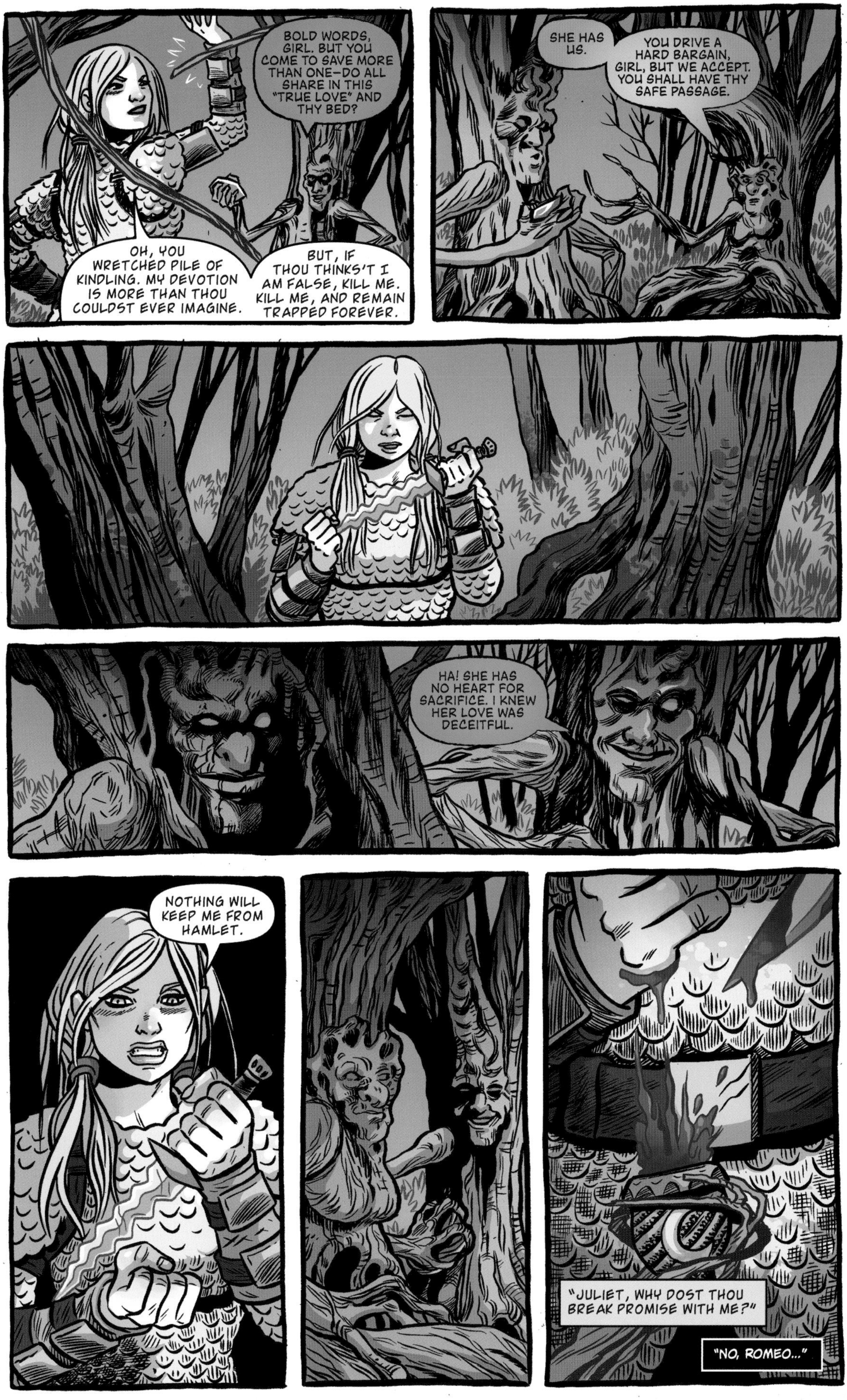
BOLD WORDS, GIRL. BUT YOU COME TO SAVE MORE THAN ONE—DO ALL SHARE IN THIS "TRUE LOVE" AND THY BED?
OH, YOU WRETCHED PILE OF KINDLING. MY DEVOTION IS MORE THAN THOU COULDST EVER IMAGINE.
BUT, IF THOU THINKS'T I AM FALSE, KILL ME. KILL ME, AND REMAIN TRAPPED FOREVER.
SHE HAS US.
YOU DRIVE A HARD BARGAIN, GIRL, BUT WE ACCEPT. YOU SHALL HAVE THY SAFE PASSAGE.
HA! SHE HAS NO HEART FOR SACRIFICE. I KNEW HER LOVE WAS DECEITFUL.
NOTHING WILL KEEP ME FROM HAMLET.
"JULIET, WHY DOST THOU BREAK PROMISE WITH ME?"
"NO, ROMEO..."

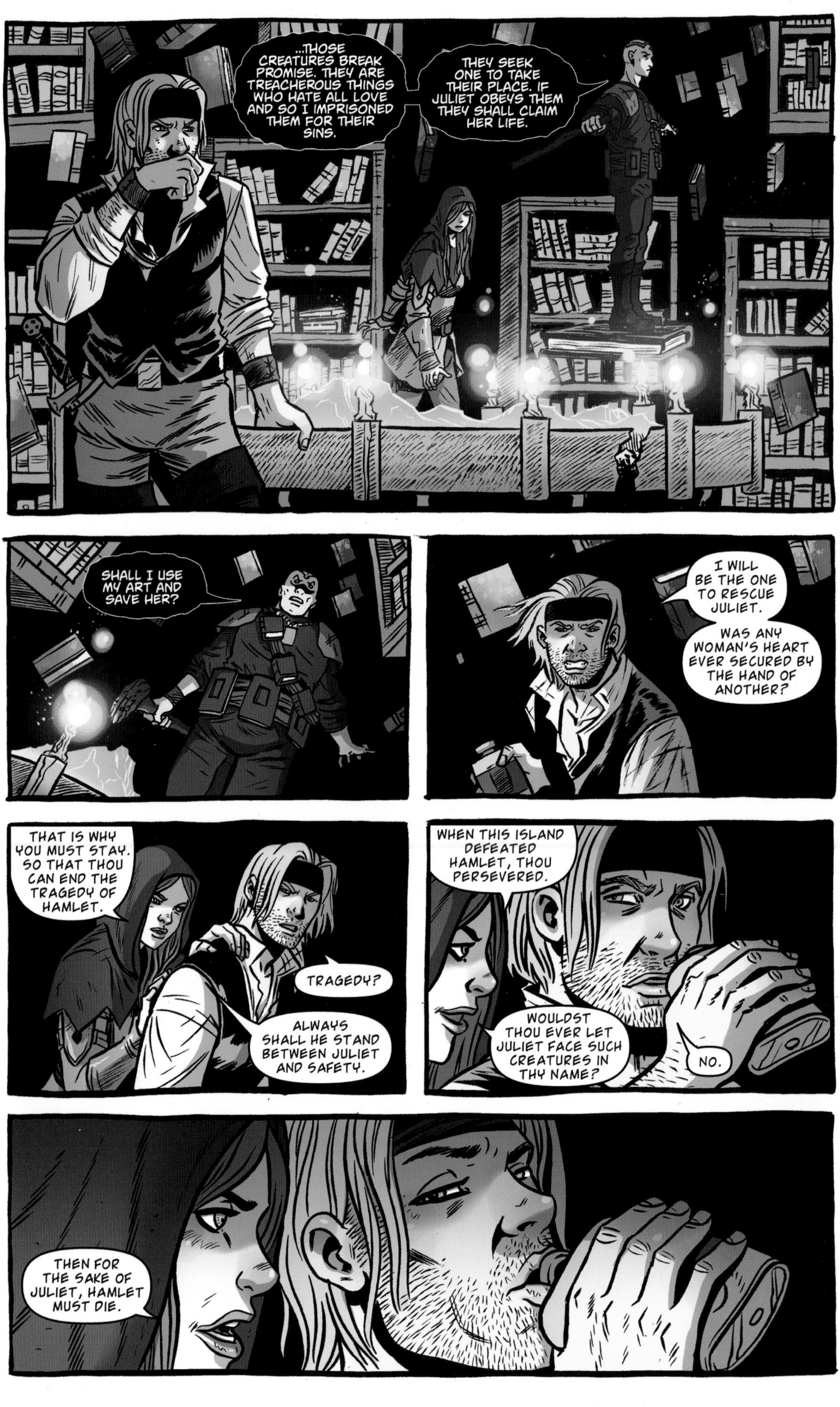
...THOSE CREATURES BREAK PROMISE. THEY ARE TREACHEROUS THINGS WHO HATE ALL LOVE AND SO I IMPRISONED THEM FOR THEIR SINS.
THEY SEEK ONE TO TAKE THEIR PLACE. IF JULIET OBEYS THEM THEY SHALL CLAIM HER LIFE.
SHALL I USE MY ART AND SAVE HER?
I WILL BE THE ONE TO RESCUE JULIET.
WAS ANY WOMAN'S HEART EVER SECURED BY THE HAND OF ANOTHER?
THAT IS WHY YOU MUST STAY. SO THAT THOU CAN END THE TRAGEDY OF HAMLET.
TRAGEDY?
ALWAYS SHALL HE STAND BETWEEN JULIET AND SAFETY.
WHEN THIS ISLAND DEFEATED HAMLET, THOU PERSEVERED.
WOULDST THOU EVER LET JULIET FACE SUCH CREATURES IN THY NAME?
NO.
THEN FOR THE SAKE OF JULIET, HAMLET MUST DIE.

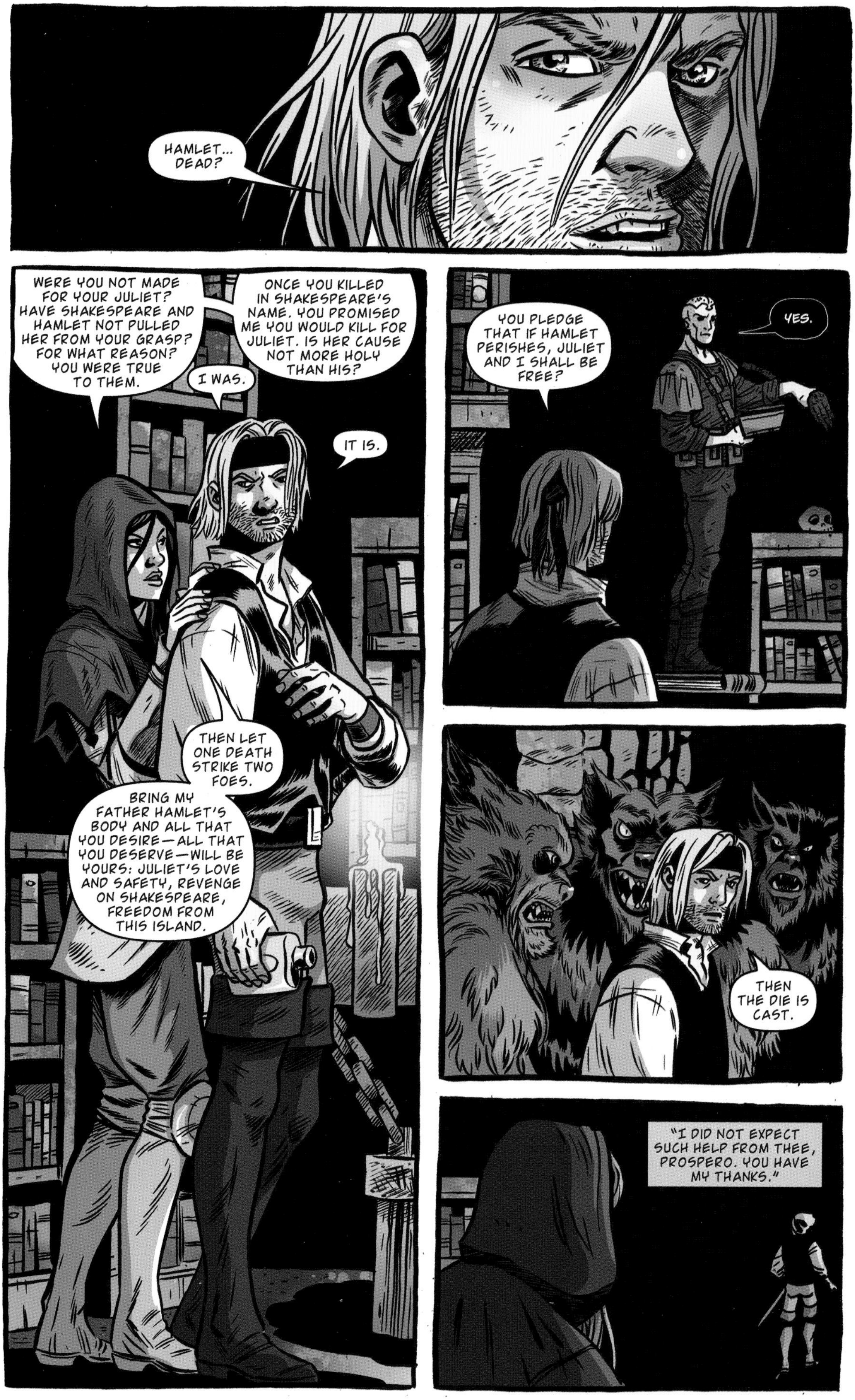
HAMLET... DEAD?
WERE YOU NOT MADE FOR YOUR JULIET? HAVE SHAKESPEARE AND HAMLET NOT PULLED HER FROM YOUR GRASP? FOR WHAT REASON? YOU WERE TRUE TO THEM.
I WAS.
ONCE YOU KILLED IN SHAKESPEARE'S NAME. YOU PROMISED ME YOU WOULD KILL FOR JULIET. IS HER CAUSE NOT MORE HOLY THAN HIS?
IT IS.
THEN LET ONE DEATH STRIKE TWO FOES.
BRING MY FATHER HAMLET'S BODY AND ALL THAT YOU DESIRE—ALL THAT YOU DESERVE—WILL BE YOURS: JULIET'S LOVE AND SAFETY, REVENGE ON SHAKESPEARE, FREEDOM FROM THIS ISLAND.
YOU PLEDGE THAT IF HAMLET PERISHES, JULIET AND I SHALL BE FREE?
YES.
THEN THE DIE IS CAST.
"I DID NOT EXPECT SUCH HELP FROM THEE, PROSPERO. YOU HAVE MY THANKS."

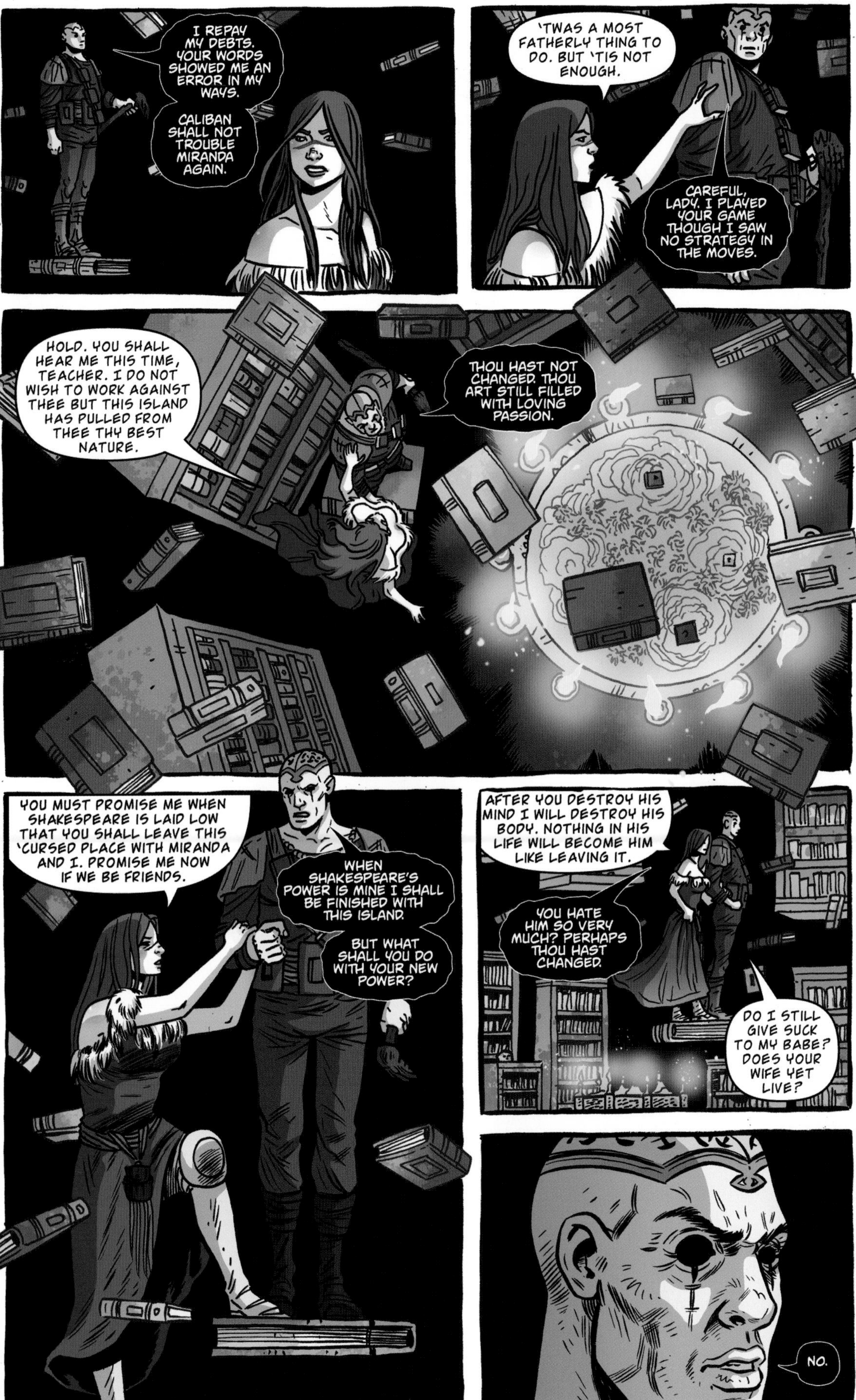
I REPAY MY DEBTS. YOUR WORDS SHOWED ME AN ERROR IN MY WAYS.
CALIBAN SHALL NOT TROUBLE MIRANDA AGAIN.
'TWAS A MOST FATHERLY THING TO DO. BUT 'TIS NOT ENOUGH.
CAREFUL, LADY. I PLAYED YOUR GAME THOUGH I SAW NO STRATEGY IN THE MOVES.
HOLD. YOU SHALL HEAR ME THIS TIME, TEACHER. I DO NOT WISH TO WORK AGAINST THEE BUT THIS ISLAND HAS PULLED FROM THEE THY BEST NATURE.
THOU HAST NOT CHANGED. THOU ART STILL FILLED WITH LOVING PASSION.
YOU MUST PROMISE ME WHEN SHAKESPEARE IS LAID LOW THAT YOU SHALL LEAVE THIS 'CURSED PLACE WITH MIRANDA AND I. PROMISE ME NOW IF WE BE FRIENDS.
WHEN SHAKESPEARE'S POWER IS MINE I SHALL BE FINISHED WITH THIS ISLAND.
BUT WHAT SHALL YOU DO WITH YOUR NEW POWER?
AFTER YOU DESTROY HIS MIND I WILL DESTROY HIS BODY. NOTHING IN HIS LIFE WILL BECOME HIM LIKE LEAVING IT.
YOU HATE HIM SO VERY MUCH? PERHAPS THOU HAST CHANGED.
DO I STILL GIVE SUCK TO MY BABE? DOES YOUR WIFE YET LIVE?
NO.

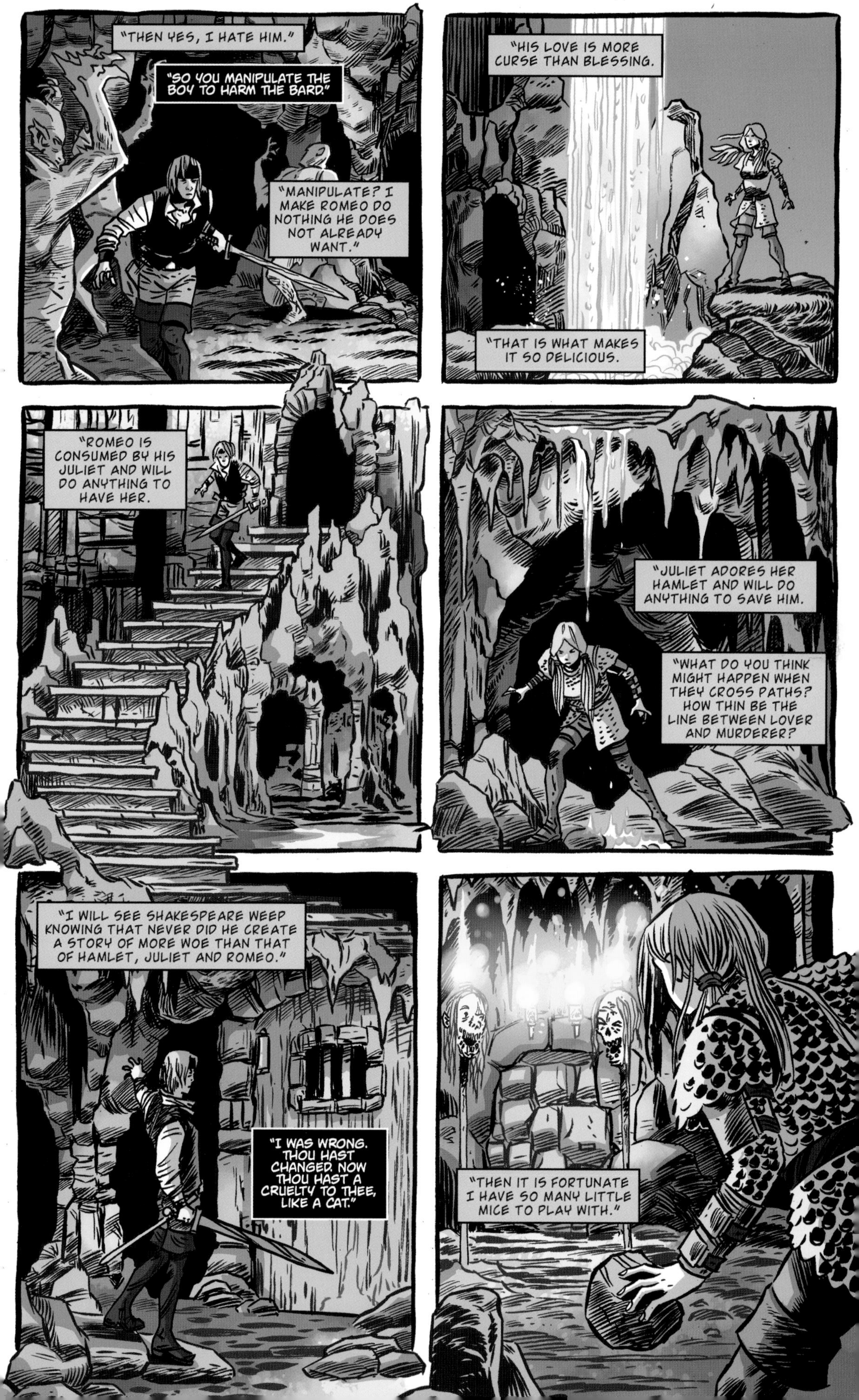
"THEN YES, I HATE HIM."
"SO YOU MANIPULATE THE BOY TO HARM THE BARD."
"MANIPULATE? I MAKE ROMEO DO NOTHING HE DOES NOT ALREADY WANT."
"HIS LOVE IS MORE CURSE THAN BLESSING.
"THAT IS WHAT MAKES IT SO DELICIOUS.
"ROMEO IS CONSUMED BY HIS JULIET AND WILL DO ANYTHING TO HAVE HER.
"JULIET ADORES HER HAMLET AND WILL DO ANYTHING TO SAVE HIM.
"WHAT DO YOU THINK MIGHT HAPPEN WHEN THEY CROSS PATHS? HOW THIN BE THE LINE BETWEEN LOVER AND MURDERER?
"I WILL SEE SHAKESPEARE WEEP KNOWING THAT NEVER DID HE CREATE A STORY OF MORE WOE THAN THAT OF HAMLET, JULIET AND ROMEO."
"I WAS WRONG. THOU HAST CHANGED. NOW THOU HAST A CRUELTY TO THEE, LIKE A CAT."
"THEN IT IS FORTUNATE I HAVE SO MANY LITTLE MICE TO PLAY WITH."

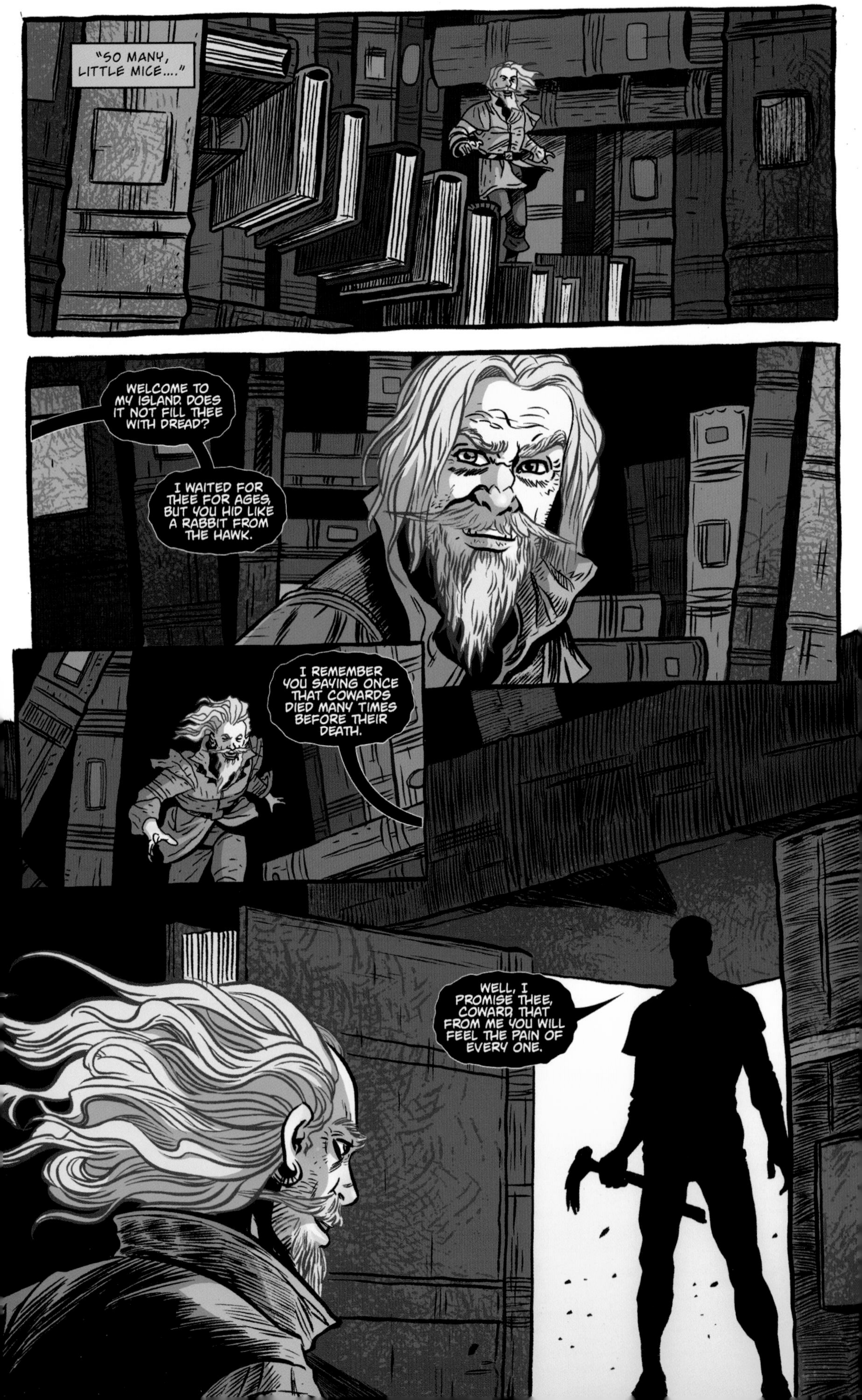
"SO MANY, LITTLE MICE...."
WELCOME TO MY ISLAND. DOES IT NOT FILL THEE WITH DREAD?
I WAITED FOR THEE FOR AGES, BUT YOU HID LIKE A RABBIT FROM THE HAWK.
I REMEMBER YOU SAYING ONCE THAT COWARDS DIED MANY TIMES BEFORE THEIR DEATH.
WELL, I PROMISE THEE, COWARD, THAT FROM ME YOU WILL FEEL THE PAIN OF EVERY ONE.

WELL, *THAT* WAS QUITE DRAMATIC...

WELL MET, WILLIAM. I THOUGHT YOU HAD LOST ALL YOUR LEVITY.

IT WILL SERVE AS A WARM COMPANION FOR YOU IN THE GRAVE.

IS THAT WHAT THIS IS ALL ABOUT THEN? PUTTING ME IN MY GRAVE? I THOUGHT YOU HAD BEEN DEVOTING ALL YOUR ENERGY TO BUILDING YOUR OWN LITTLE WORLD.

FROM THE LOOKS OF THINGS IT IS PROBABLY JUST AS WELL THAT I DECIDED AGAINST LETTING YOU DESIGN VERONA.

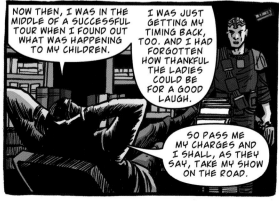

NOW THEN, I WAS IN THE MIDDLE OF A SUCCESSFUL TOUR WHEN I FOUND OUT WHAT WAS HAPPENING TO MY CHILDREN.

I WAS JUST GETTING MY TIMING BACK, TOO. AND I HAD FORGOTTEN HOW THANKFUL THE LADIES COULD BE FOR A GOOD LAUGH.

SO PASS ME MY CHARGES AND I SHALL, AS THEY SAY, TAKE MY SHOW ON THE ROAD.

YOU THINK TO ORDER ME? HERE?

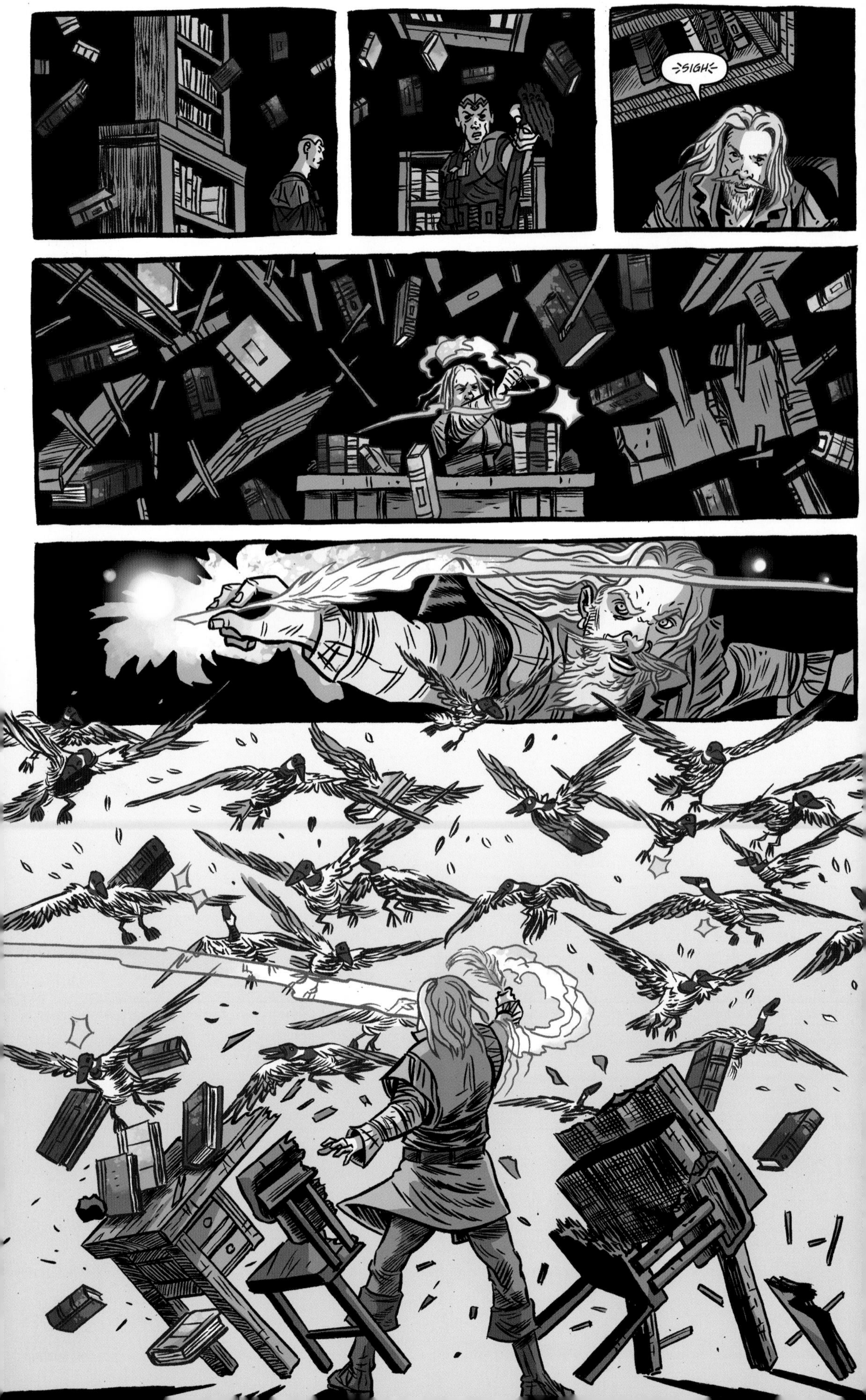
SIGH

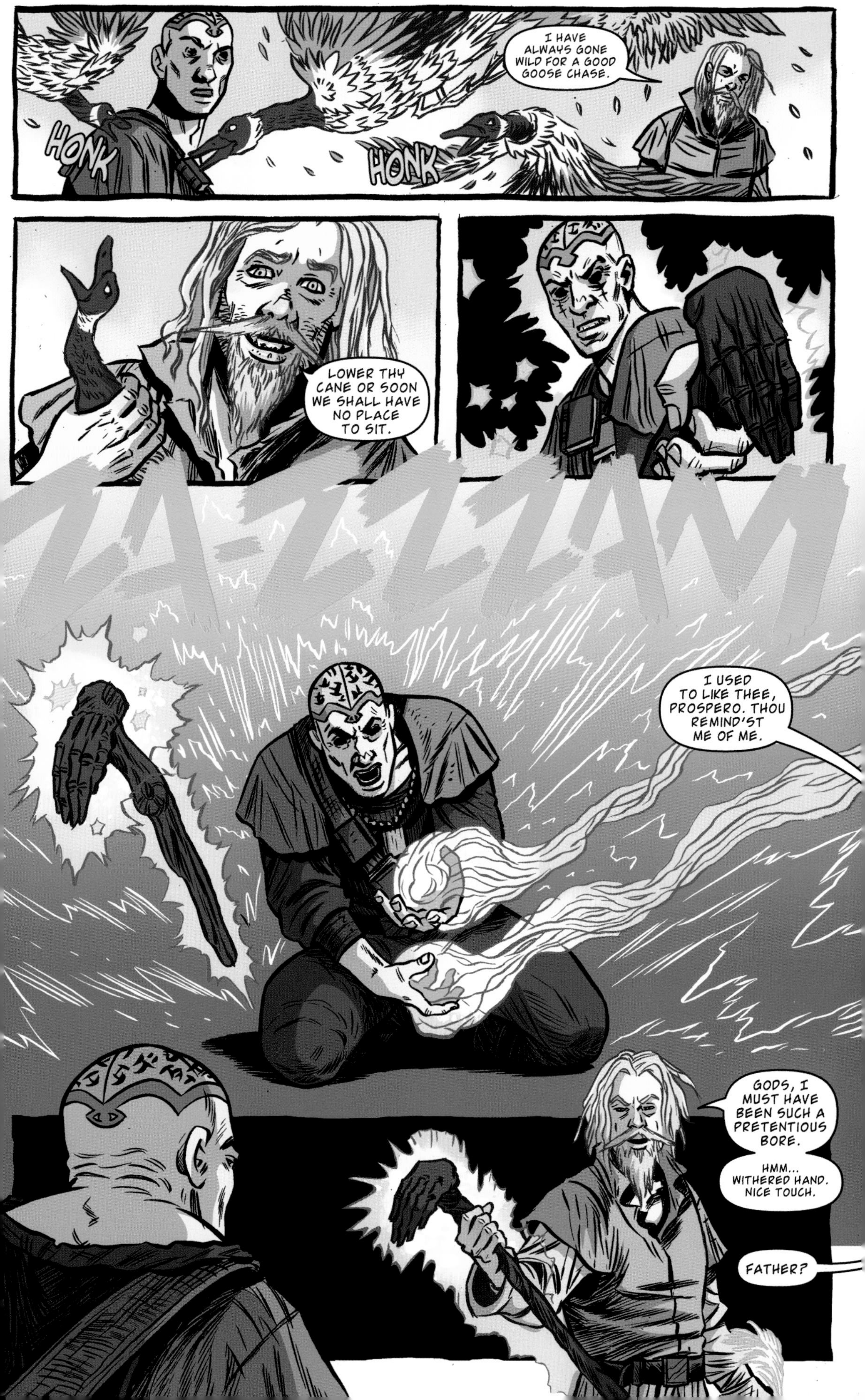
HONK
HONK
I HAVE ALWAYS GONE WILD FOR A GOOD GOOSE CHASE.
LOWER THY CANE OR SOON WE SHALL HAVE NO PLACE TO SIT.
ZA-ZZZAM
I USED TO LIKE THEE, PROSPERO. THOU REMIND'ST ME OF ME.
GODS, I MUST HAVE BEEN SUCH A PRETENTIOUS BORE.
HMM... WITHERED HAND. NICE TOUCH.
FATHER?

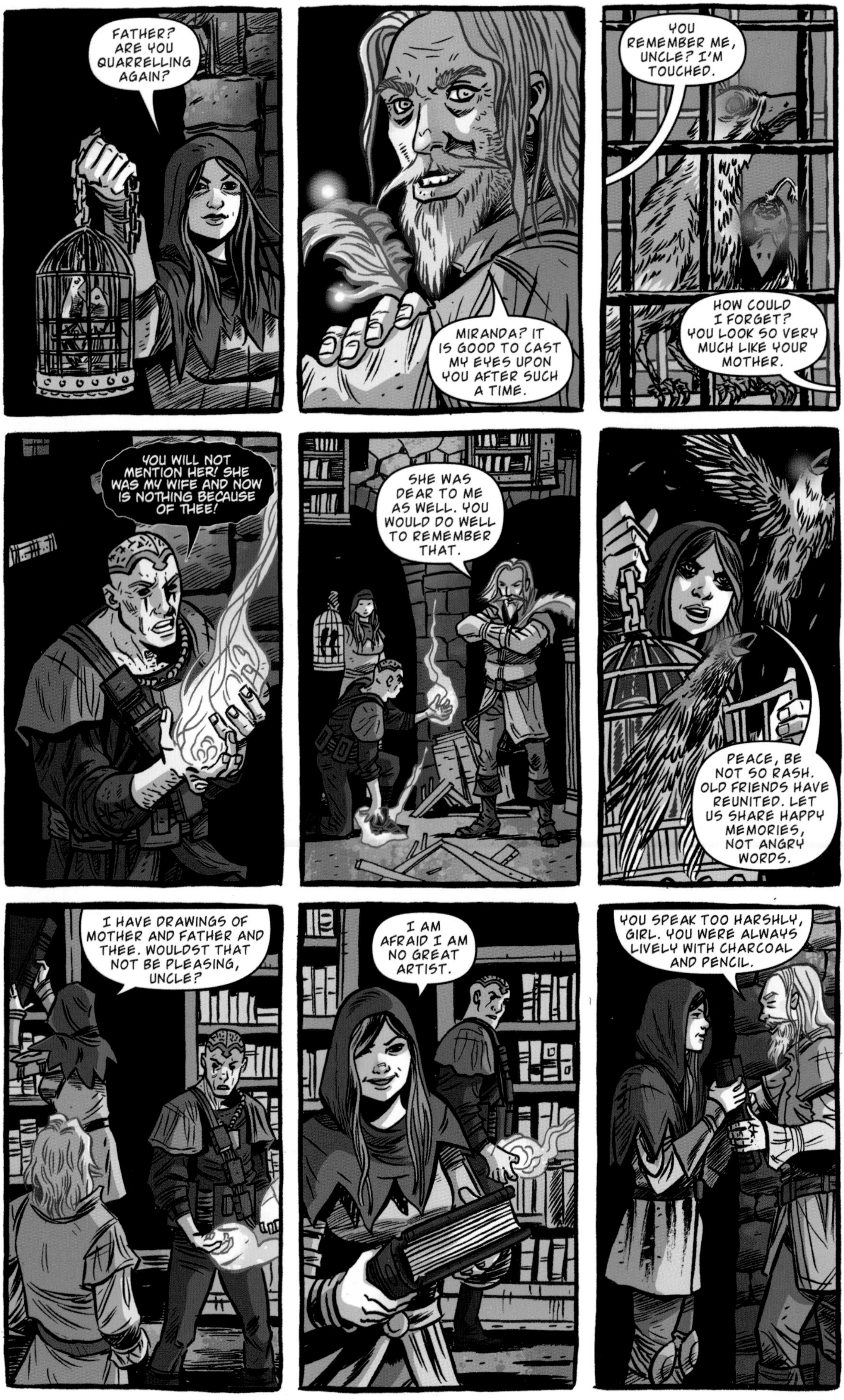
FATHER? ARE YOU QUARRELLING AGAIN?
MIRANDA? IT IS GOOD TO CAST MY EYES UPON YOU AFTER SUCH A TIME.
YOU REMEMBER ME, UNCLE? I'M TOUCHED.
HOW COULD I FORGET? YOU LOOK SO VERY MUCH LIKE YOUR MOTHER.
YOU WILL NOT MENTION HER! SHE WAS MY WIFE AND NOW IS NOTHING BECAUSE OF THEE!
SHE WAS DEAR TO ME AS WELL. YOU WOULD DO WELL TO REMEMBER THAT.
PEACE, BE NOT SO RASH. OLD FRIENDS HAVE REUNITED. LET US SHARE HAPPY MEMORIES, NOT ANGRY WORDS.
I HAVE DRAWINGS OF MOTHER AND FATHER AND THEE. WOULDST THAT NOT BE PLEASING, UNCLE?
I AM AFRAID I AM NO GREAT ARTIST.
YOU SPEAK TOO HARSHLY, GIRL. YOU WERE ALWAYS LIVELY WITH CHARCOAL AND PENCIL.

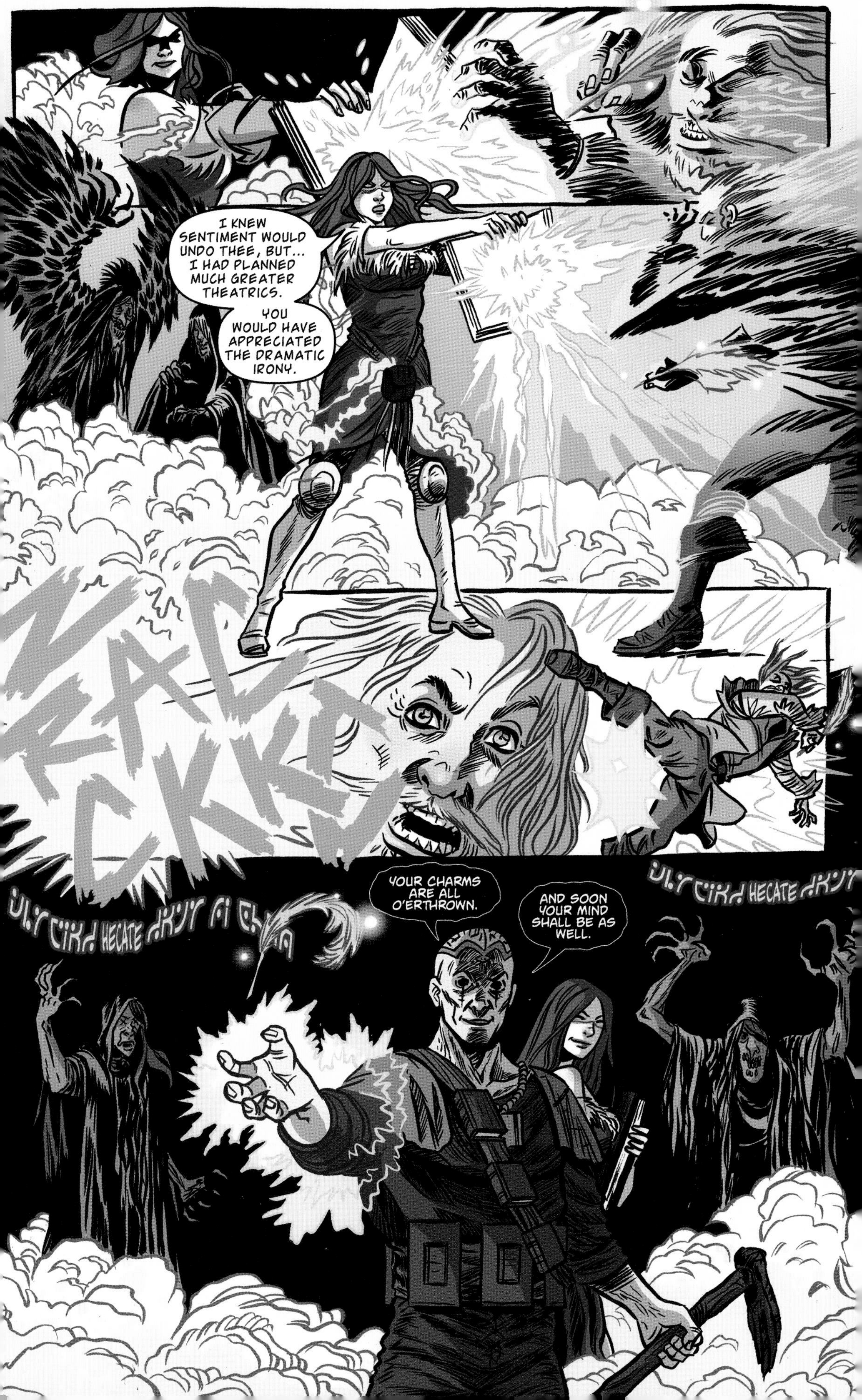
I KNEW SENTIMENT WOULD UNDO THEE, BUT... I HAD PLANNED MUCH GREATER THEATRICS.
YOU WOULD HAVE APPRECIATED THE DRAMATIC IRONY.
YOUR CHARMS ARE ALL O'ERTHROWN.
AND SOON YOUR MIND SHALL BE AS WELL.

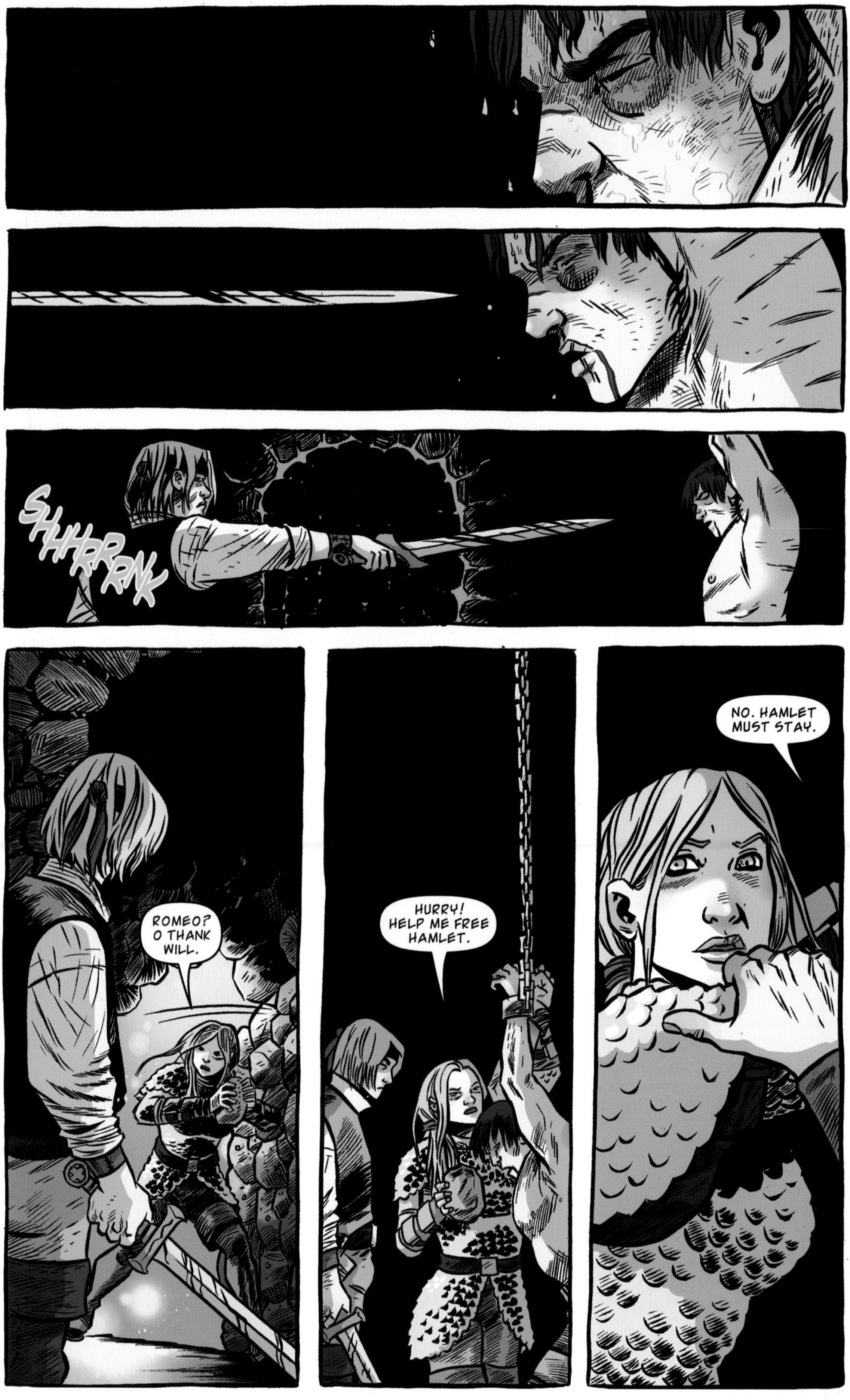
SHHHRRRNK
ROMEO? O THANK WILL.
HURRY! HELP ME FREE HAMLET.
NO. HAMLET MUST STAY.

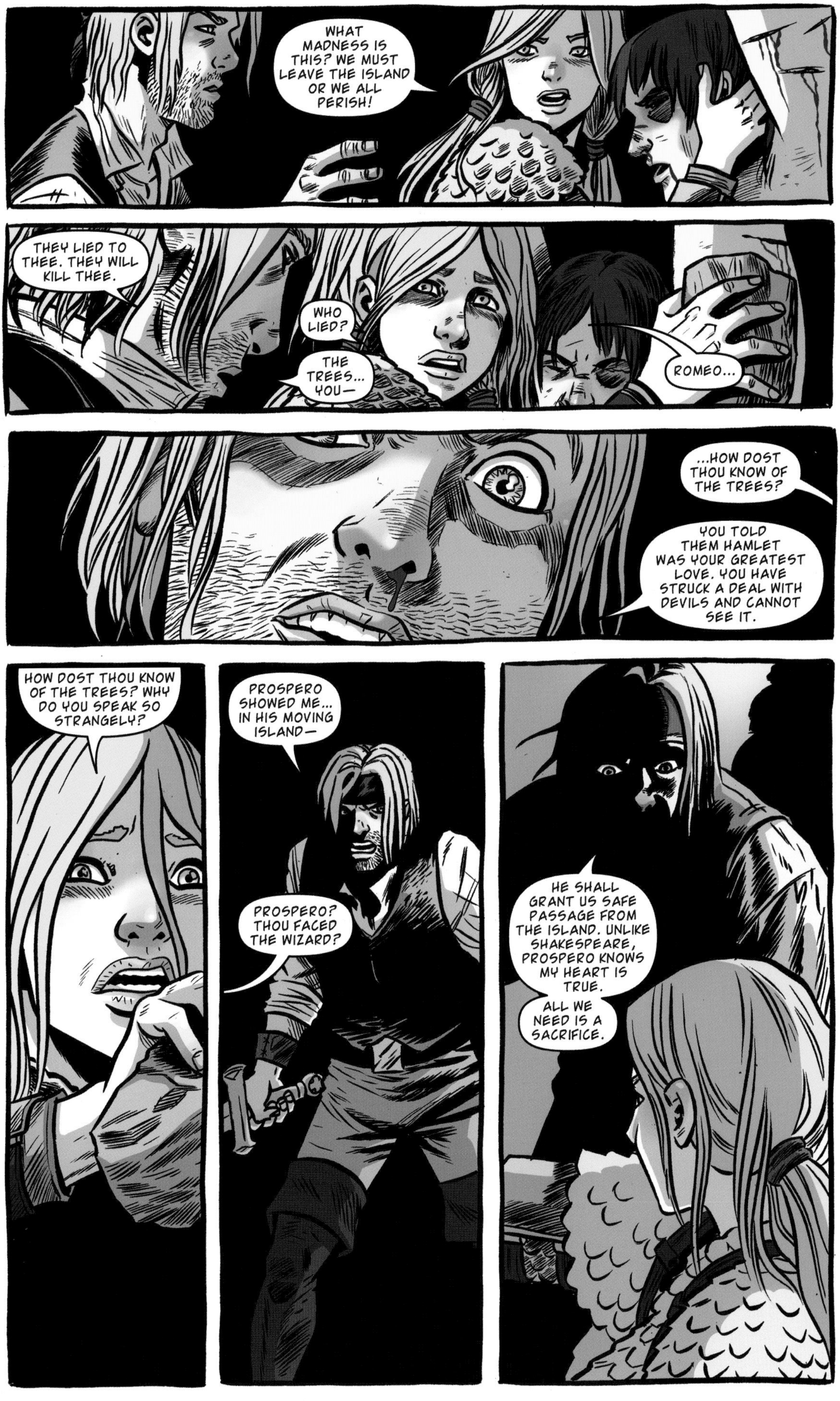

WHAT MADNESS IS THIS? WE MUST LEAVE THE ISLAND OR WE ALL PERISH!
THEY LIED TO THEE. THEY WILL KILL THEE.
WHO LIED?
THE TREES... YOU—
ROMEO...
...HOW DOST THOU KNOW OF THE TREES?
YOU TOLD THEM HAMLET WAS YOUR GREATEST LOVE. YOU HAVE STRUCK A DEAL WITH DEVILS AND CANNOT SEE IT.
HOW DOST THOU KNOW OF THE TREES? WHY DO YOU SPEAK SO STRANGELY?
PROSPERO SHOWED ME... IN HIS MOVING ISLAND—
PROSPERO? THOU FACED THE WIZARD?
HE SHALL GRANT US SAFE PASSAGE FROM THE ISLAND. UNLIKE SHAKESPEARE, PROSPERO KNOWS MY HEART IS TRUE.
ALL WE NEED IS A SACRIFICE.

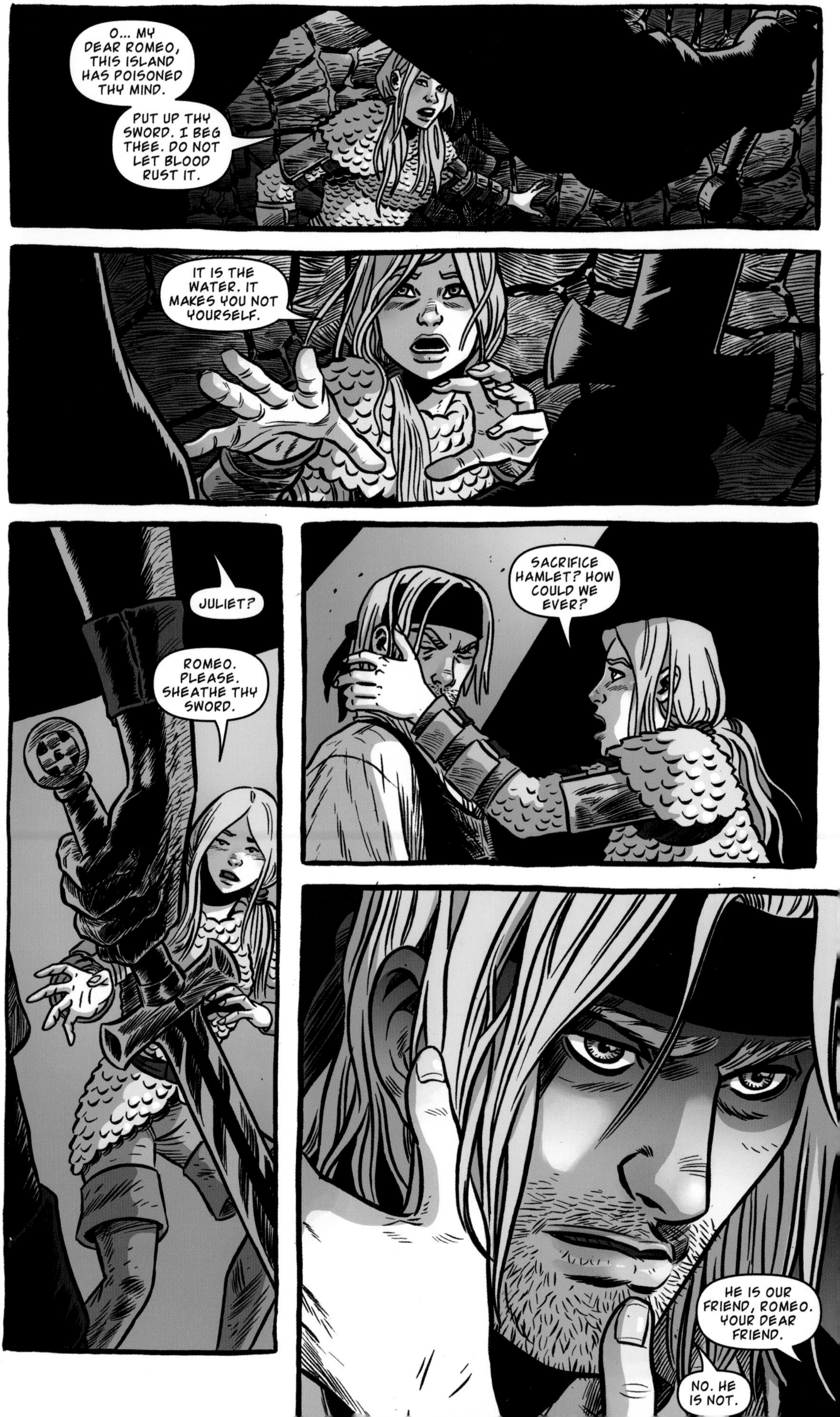
O... MY DEAR ROMEO, THIS ISLAND HAS POISONED THY MIND.
PUT UP THY SWORD. I BEG THEE. DO NOT LET BLOOD RUST IT.
IT IS THE WATER. IT MAKES YOU NOT YOURSELF.
JULIET?
ROMEO. PLEASE. SHEATHE THY SWORD.
SACRIFICE HAMLET? HOW COULD WE EVER?
HE IS OUR FRIEND, ROMEO. YOUR DEAR FRIEND.
NO. HE IS NOT.

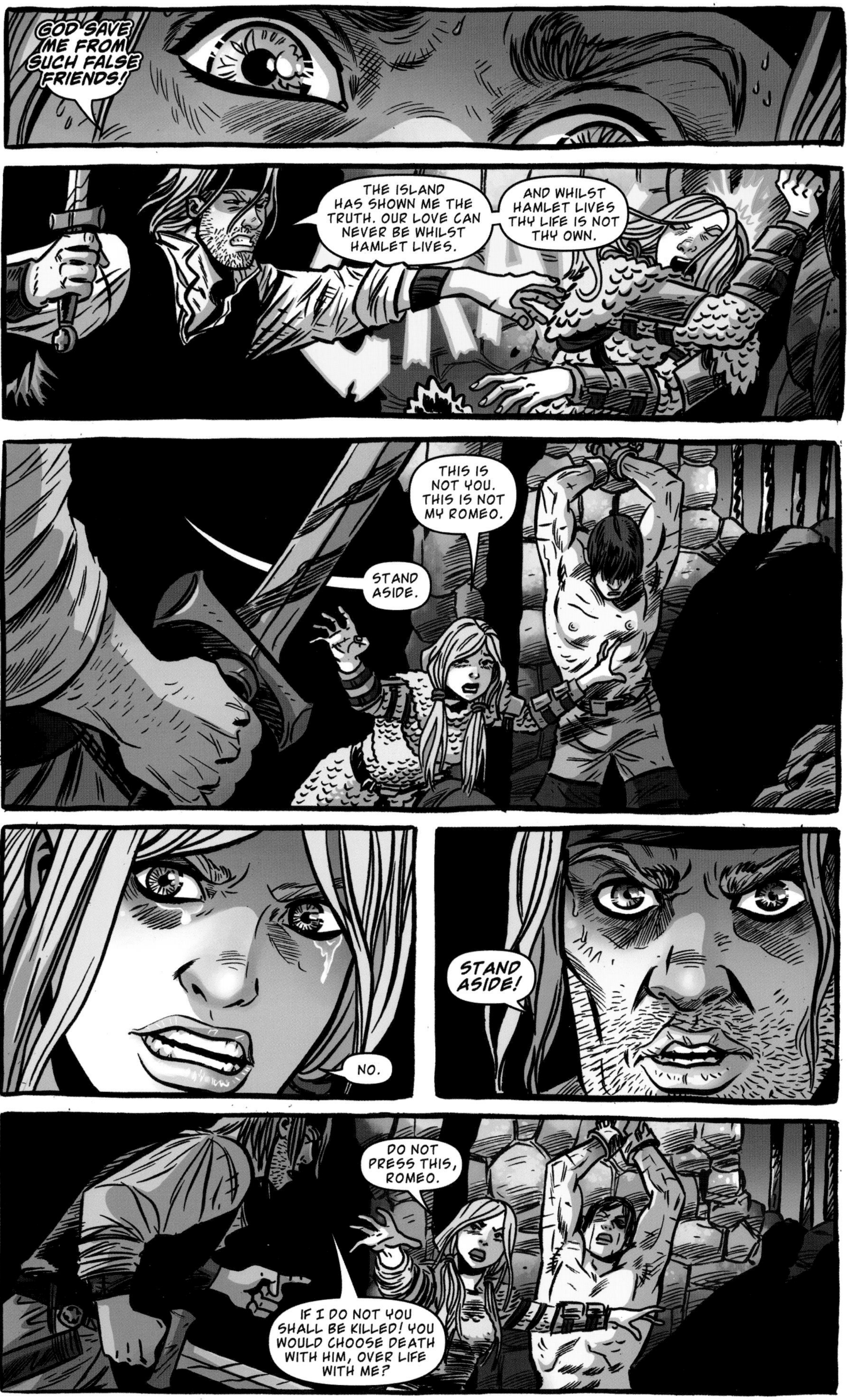
GOD SAVE ME FROM SUCH FALSE FRIENDS!
THE ISLAND HAS SHOWN ME THE TRUTH. OUR LOVE CAN NEVER BE WHILST HAMLET LIVES.
AND WHILST HAMLET LIVES THY LIFE IS NOT THY OWN.
THIS IS NOT YOU. THIS IS NOT MY ROMEO.
STAND ASIDE.
NO.
STAND ASIDE!
DO NOT PRESS THIS, ROMEO.
IF I DO NOT YOU SHALL BE KILLED! YOU WOULD CHOOSE DEATH WITH HIM, OVER LIFE WITH ME?

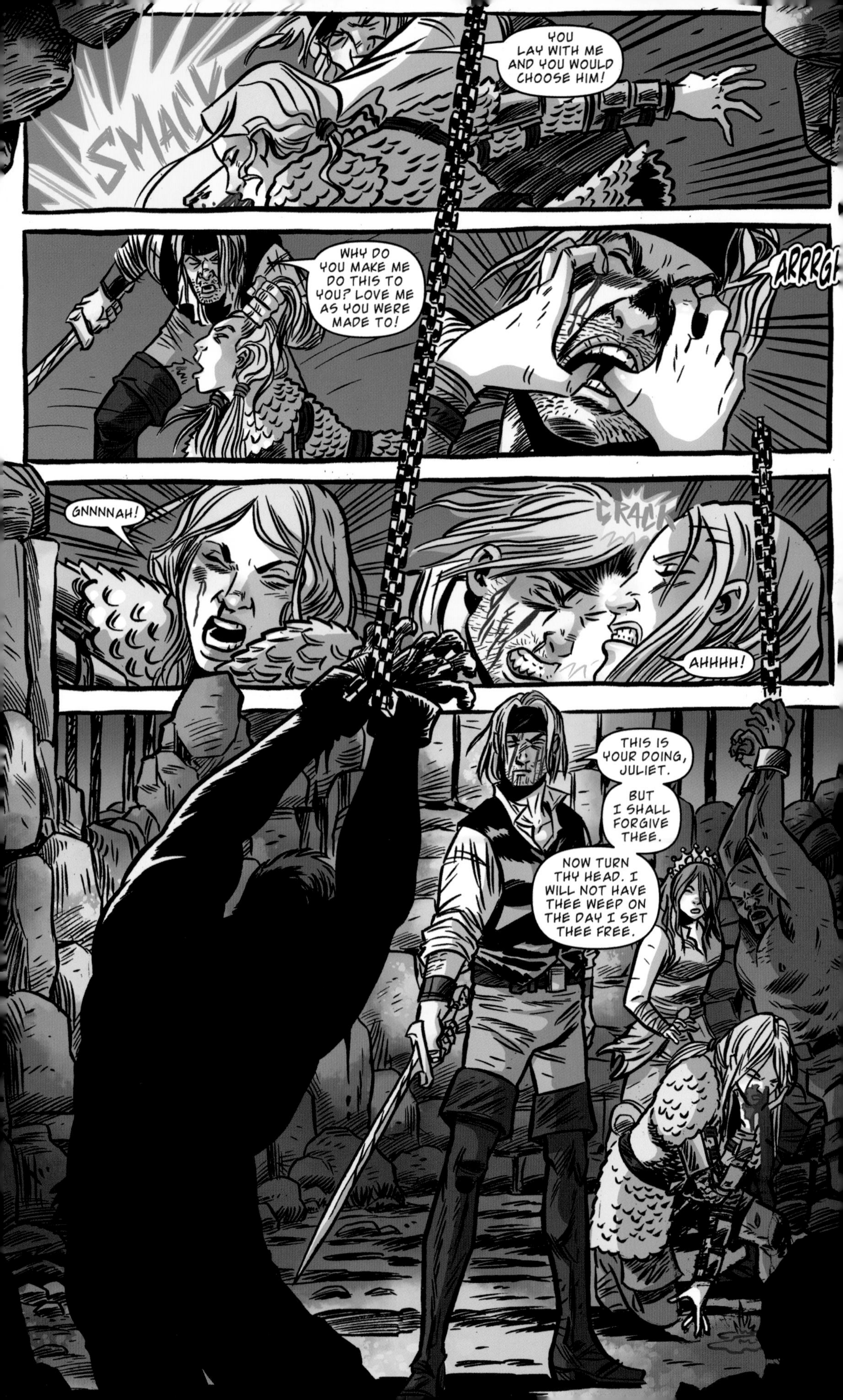
SMACK
YOU LAY WITH ME AND YOU WOULD CHOOSE HIM!
WHY DO YOU MAKE ME DO THIS TO YOU? LOVE ME AS YOU WERE MADE TO!
ARRRG!
GNNNNAH!
CRACK
AHHHH!
THIS IS YOUR DOING, JULIET.
BUT I SHALL FORGIVE THEE.
NOW TURN THY HEAD. I WILL NOT HAVE THEE WEEP ON THE DAY I SET THEE FREE.

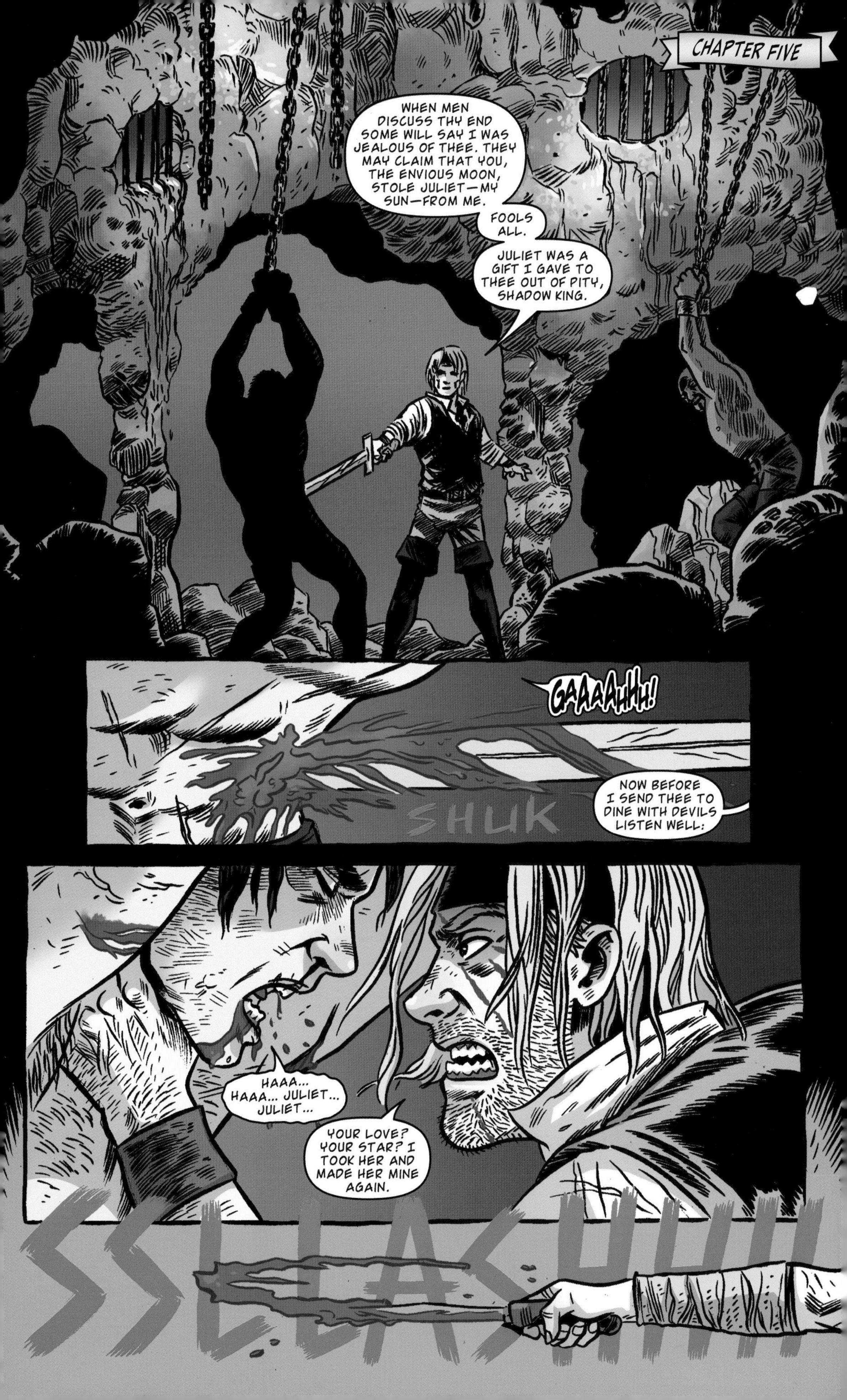
CHAPTER FIVE
WHEN MEN DISCUSS THY END SOME WILL SAY I WAS JEALOUS OF THEE. THEY MAY CLAIM THAT YOU, THE ENVIOUS MOON, STOLE JULIET—MY SUN—FROM ME.
FOOLS ALL.
JULIET WAS A GIFT I GAVE TO THEE OUT OF PITY, SHADOW KING.
GAAAAHH!
SHUK
NOW BEFORE I SEND THEE TO DINE WITH DEVILS LISTEN WELL:
HAAA... HAAA... JULIET... JULIET...
YOUR LOVE? YOUR STAR? I TOOK HER AND MADE HER MINE AGAIN.
SSLLASHHH

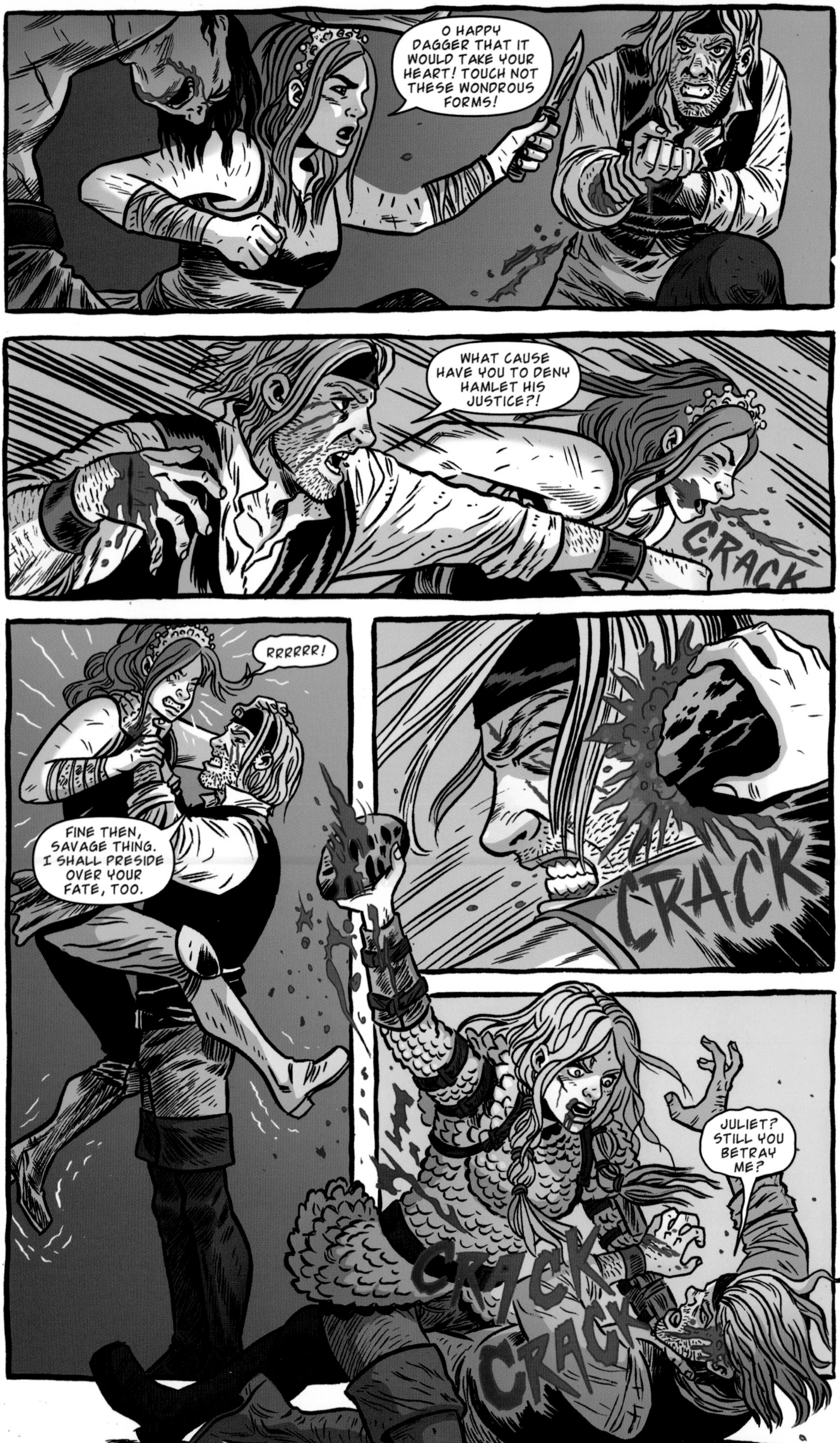
O HAPPY DAGGER THAT IT WOULD TAKE YOUR HEART! TOUCH NOT THESE WONDROUS FORMS!
WHAT CAUSE HAVE YOU TO DENY HAMLET HIS JUSTICE?!
CRACK
RRRRRR!
FINE THEN, SAVAGE THING. I SHALL PRESIDE OVER YOUR FATE, TOO.
CRACK
JULIET? STILL YOU BETRAY ME?
CRACK
CRACK

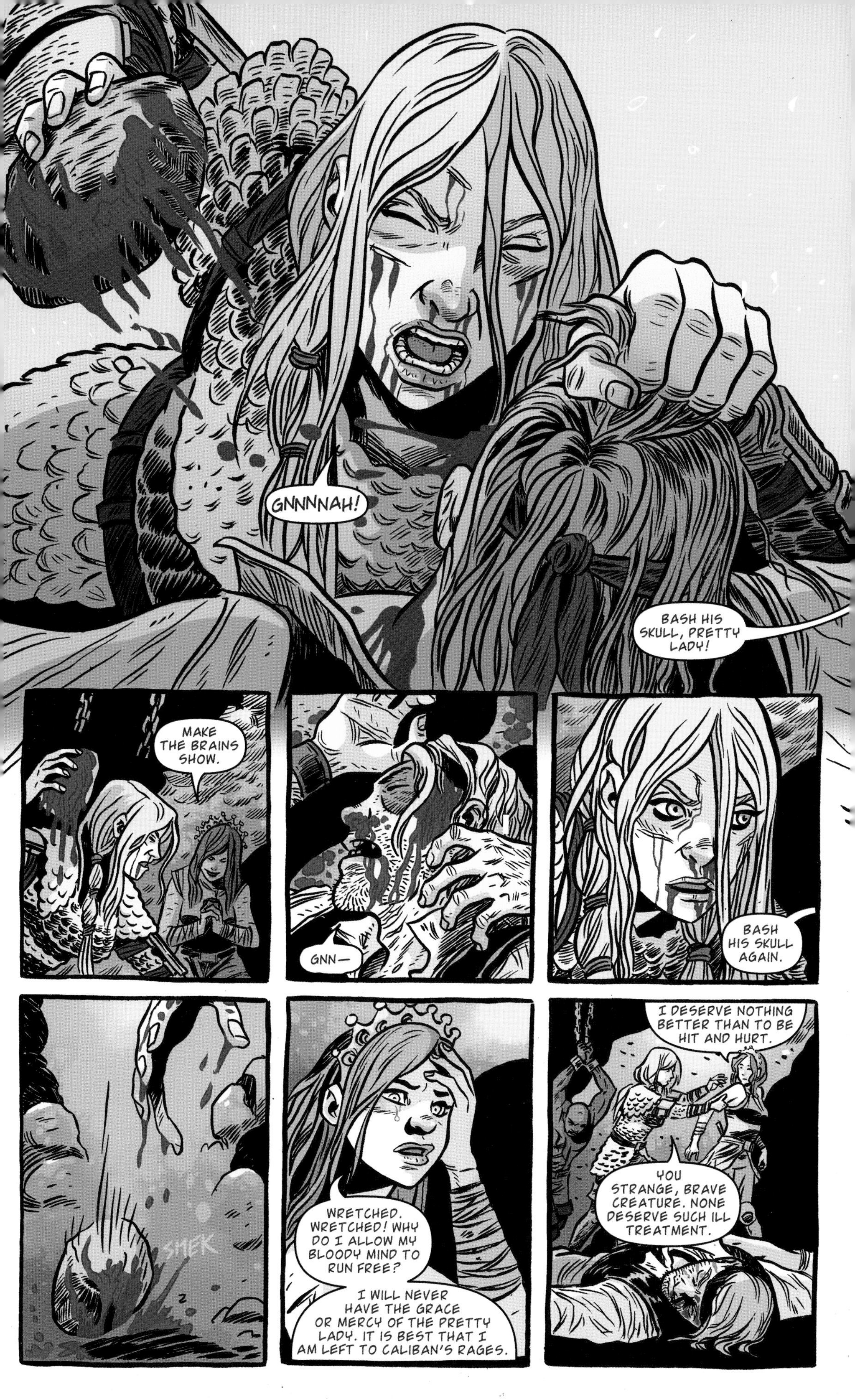
GNNNNAH!
BASH HIS SKULL, PRETTY LADY!
MAKE THE BRAINS SHOW.
GNN—
BASH HIS SKULL AGAIN.
SMEK
WRETCHED. WRETCHED! WHY DO I ALLOW MY BLOODY MIND TO RUN FREE?
I WILL NEVER HAVE THE GRACE OR MERCY OF THE PRETTY LADY. IT IS BEST THAT I AM LEFT TO CALIBAN'S RAGES.
I DESERVE NOTHING BETTER THAN TO BE HIT AND HURT.
YOU STRANGE, BRAVE CREATURE. NONE DESERVE SUCH ILL TREATMENT.

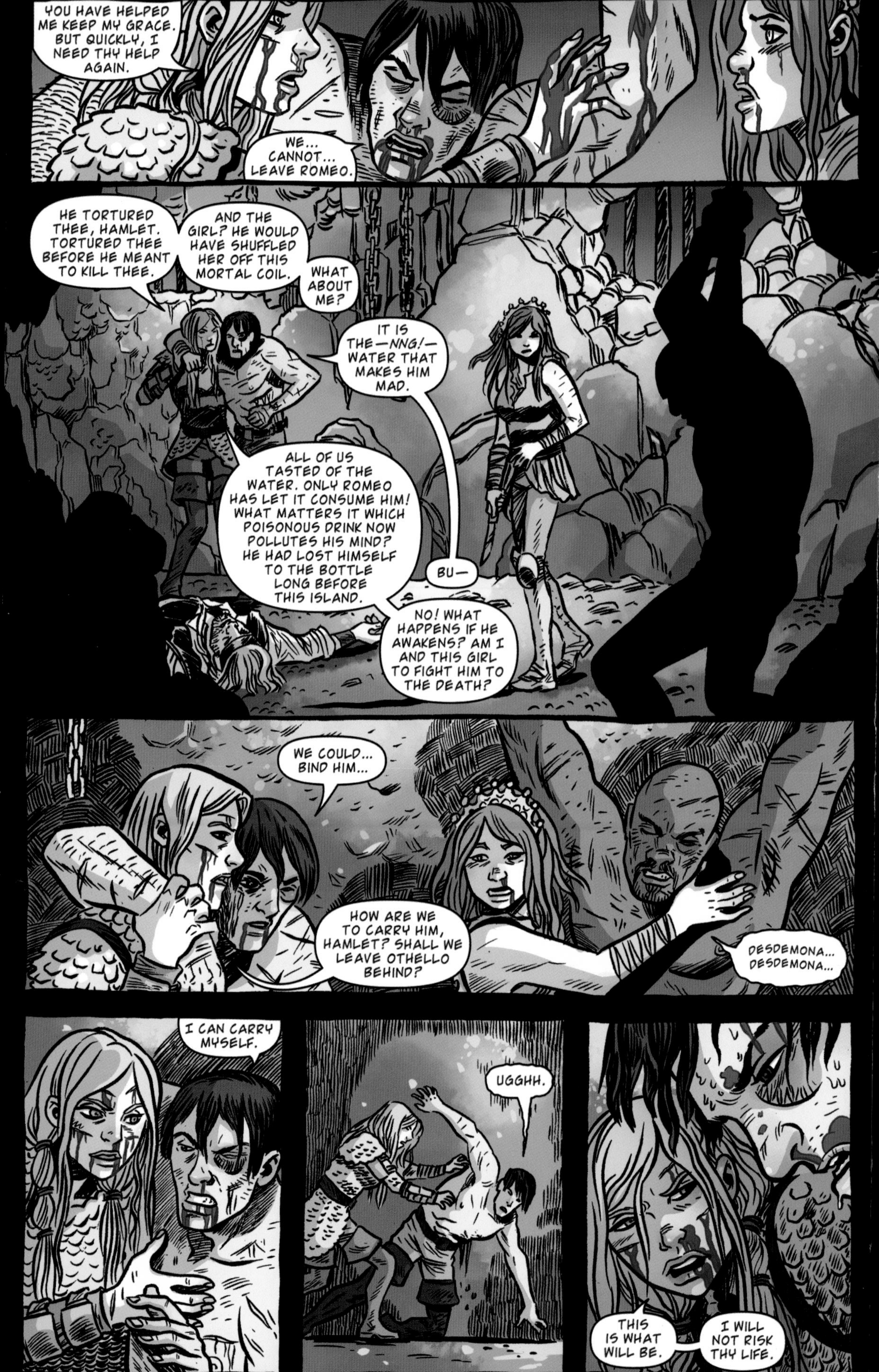
YOU HAVE HELPED ME KEEP MY GRACE. BUT QUICKLY, I NEED THY HELP AGAIN.
WE... CANNOT... LEAVE ROMEO.
HE TORTURED THEE, HAMLET. TORTURED THEE BEFORE HE MEANT TO KILL THEE.
AND THE GIRL? HE WOULD HAVE SHUFFLED HER OFF THIS MORTAL COIL.
WHAT ABOUT ME?
IT IS THE—*NNG!*—WATER THAT MAKES HIM MAD.
ALL OF US TASTED OF THE WATER. ONLY ROMEO HAS LET IT CONSUME HIM! WHAT MATTERS IT WHICH POISONOUS DRINK NOW POLLUTES HIS MIND? HE HAD LOST HIMSELF TO THE BOTTLE LONG BEFORE THIS ISLAND.
BU—
NO! WHAT HAPPENS IF HE AWAKENS? AM I AND THIS GIRL TO FIGHT HIM TO THE DEATH?
WE COULD... BIND HIM...
HOW ARE WE TO CARRY HIM, HAMLET? SHALL WE LEAVE OTHELLO BEHIND?
DESDEMONA... DESDEMONA...
I CAN CARRY MYSELF.
UGGHH.
THIS IS WHAT WILL BE.
I WILL NOT RISK THY LIFE.

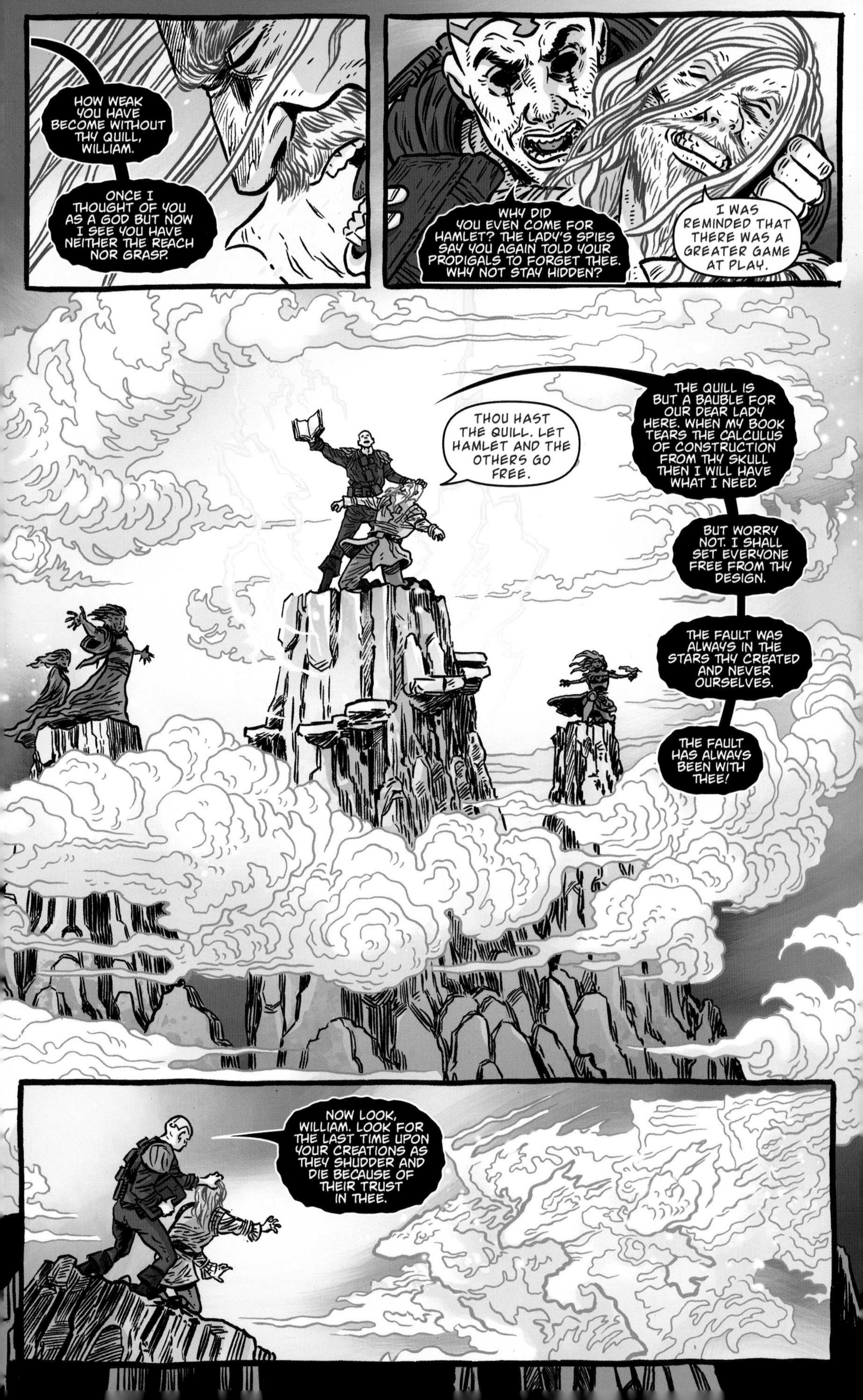
HOW WEAK YOU HAVE BECOME WITHOUT THY QUILL, WILLIAM.
ONCE I THOUGHT OF YOU AS A GOD BUT NOW I SEE YOU HAVE NEITHER THE REACH NOR GRASP.
WHY DID YOU EVEN COME FOR HAMLET? THE LADY'S SPIES SAY YOU AGAIN TOLD YOUR PRODIGALS TO FORGET THEE. WHY NOT STAY HIDDEN?
I WAS REMINDED THAT THERE WAS A GREATER GAME AT PLAY.
THOU HAST THE QUILL. LET HAMLET AND THE OTHERS GO FREE.
THE QUILL IS BUT A BAUBLE FOR OUR DEAR LADY HERE. WHEN MY BOOK TEARS THE CALCULUS OF CONSTRUCTION FROM THY SKULL THEN I WILL HAVE WHAT I NEED.
BUT WORRY NOT. I SHALL SET EVERYONE FREE FROM THY DESIGN.
THE FAULT WAS ALWAYS IN THE STARS THY CREATED AND NEVER OURSELVES.
THE FAULT HAS ALWAYS BEEN WITH THEE!
NOW LOOK, WILLIAM. LOOK FOR THE LAST TIME UPON YOUR CREATIONS AS THEY SHUDDER AND DIE BECAUSE OF THEIR TRUST IN THEE.

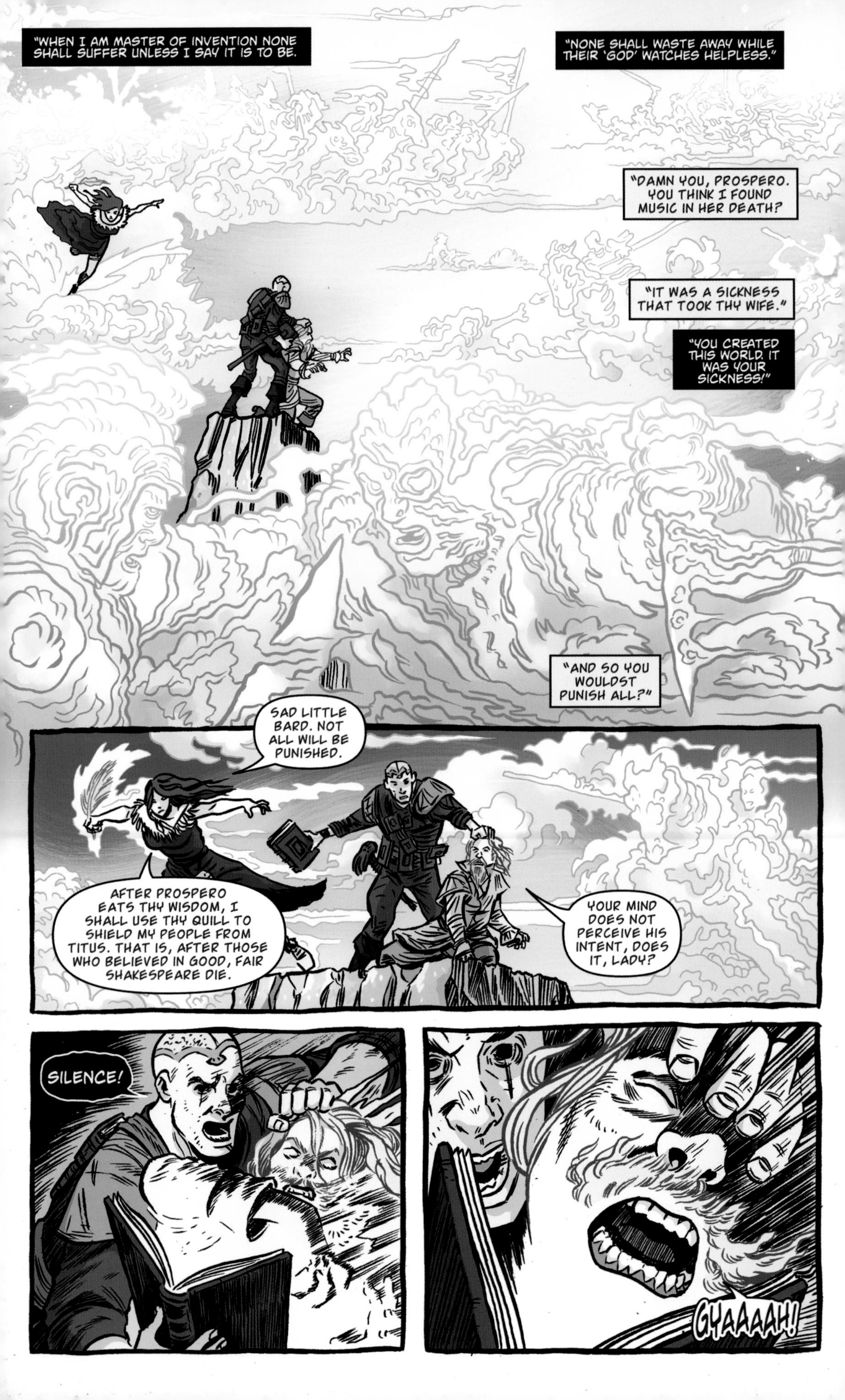
"WHEN I AM MASTER OF INVENTION NONE SHALL SUFFER UNLESS I SAY IT IS TO BE.
"NONE SHALL WASTE AWAY WHILE THEIR 'GOD' WATCHES HELPLESS."
"DAMN YOU, PROSPERO. YOU THINK I FOUND MUSIC IN HER DEATH?
"IT WAS A SICKNESS THAT TOOK THY WIFE."
"YOU CREATED THIS WORLD. IT WAS YOUR SICKNESS!"
"AND SO YOU WOULDST PUNISH ALL?"
SAD LITTLE BARD. NOT ALL WILL BE PUNISHED.
AFTER PROSPERO EATS THY WISDOM, I SHALL USE THY QUILL TO SHIELD MY PEOPLE FROM TITUS. THAT IS, AFTER THOSE WHO BELIEVED IN GOOD, FAIR SHAKESPEARE DIE.
YOUR MIND DOES NOT PERCEIVE HIS INTENT, DOES IT, LADY?
SILENCE!
GYAAAAH!

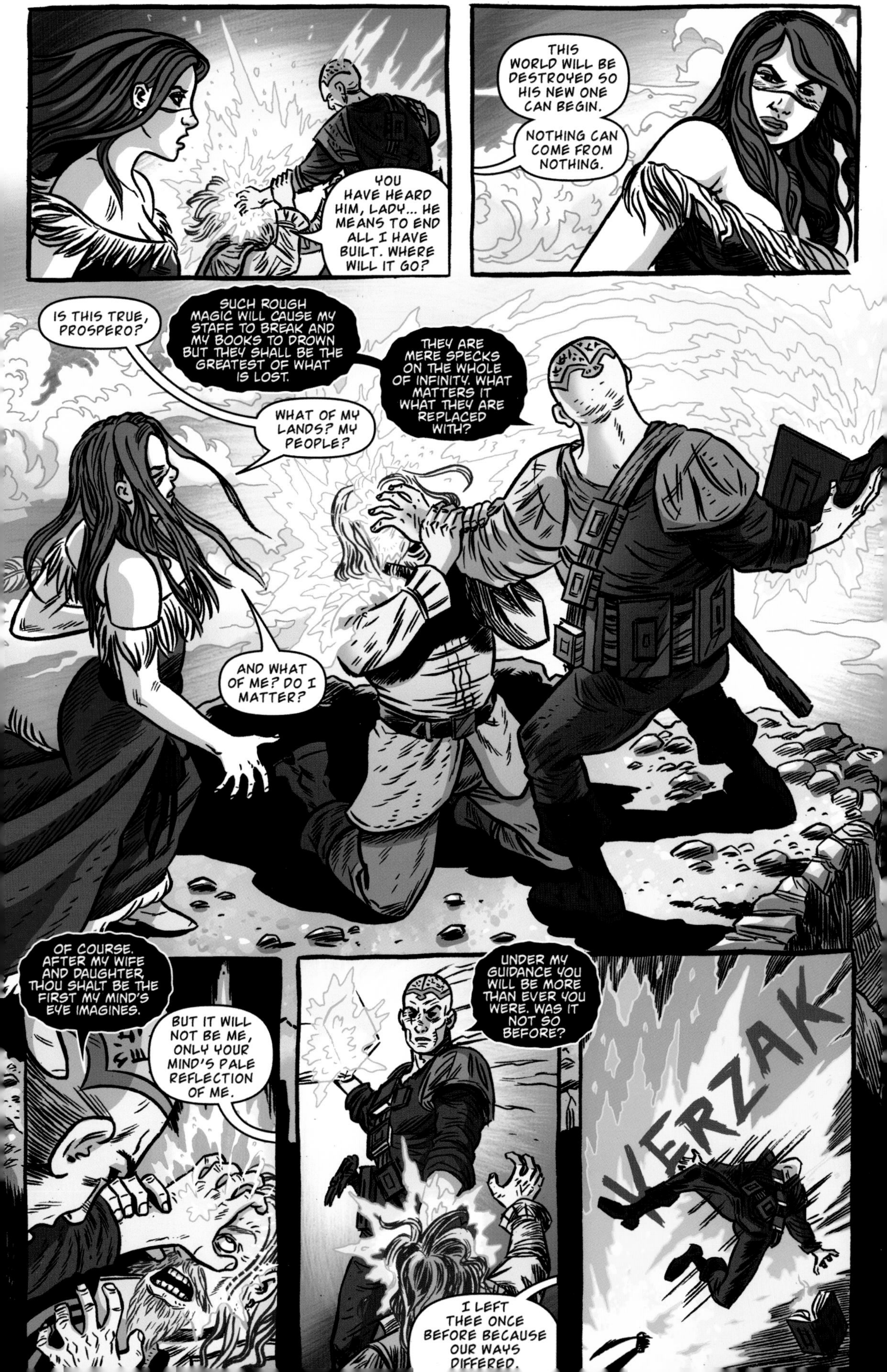
YOU HAVE HEARD HIM, LADY... HE MEANS TO END ALL I HAVE BUILT. WHERE WILL IT GO?
THIS WORLD WILL BE DESTROYED SO HIS NEW ONE CAN BEGIN.
NOTHING CAN COME FROM NOTHING.
IS THIS TRUE, PROSPERO?
SUCH ROUGH MAGIC WILL CAUSE MY STAFF TO BREAK AND MY BOOKS TO DROWN BUT THEY SHALL BE THE GREATEST OF WHAT IS LOST.
THEY ARE MERE SPECKS ON THE WHOLE OF INFINITY. WHAT MATTERS IT WHAT THEY ARE REPLACED WITH?
WHAT OF MY LANDS? MY PEOPLE?
AND WHAT OF ME? DO I MATTER?
OF COURSE. AFTER MY WIFE AND DAUGHTER, THOU SHALT BE THE FIRST MY MIND'S EYE IMAGINES.
BUT IT WILL NOT BE ME, ONLY YOUR MIND'S PALE REFLECTION OF ME.
UNDER MY GUIDANCE YOU WILL BE MORE THAN EVER YOU WERE. WAS IT NOT SO BEFORE?
I LEFT THEE ONCE BEFORE BECAUSE OUR WAYS DIFFERED.
VERZAK

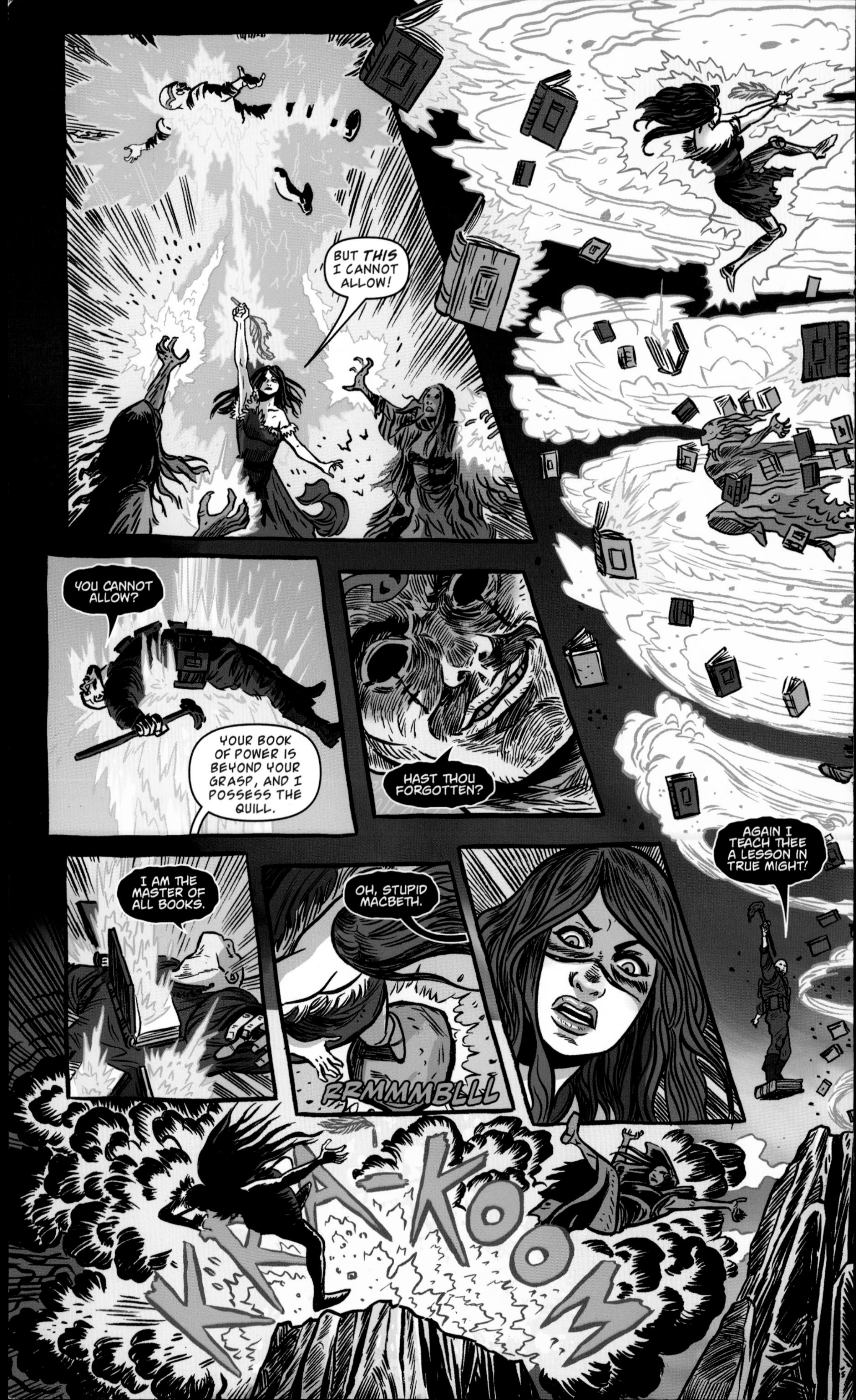
BUT THIS I CANNOT ALLOW!
YOU CANNOT ALLOW?
YOUR BOOK OF POWER IS BEYOND YOUR GRASP, AND I POSSESS THE QUILL.
HAST THOU FORGOTTEN?
AGAIN I TEACH THEE A LESSON IN TRUE MIGHT!
I AM THE MASTER OF ALL BOOKS.
OH, STUPID MACBETH.
RRMMMBLLL
KA-KOOM

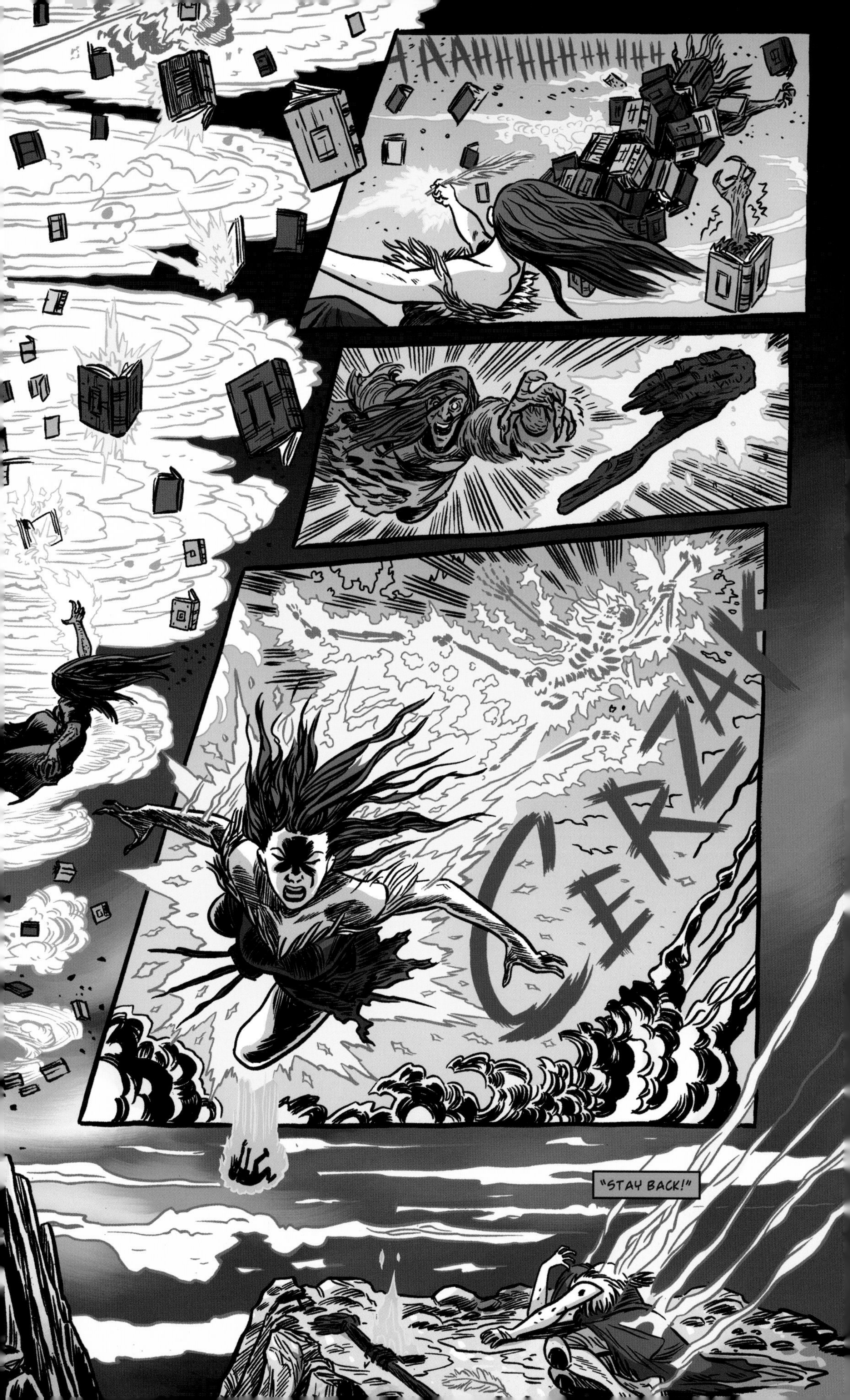
AAAHHHHHHHHHHH
CERZAK
"STAY BACK!"

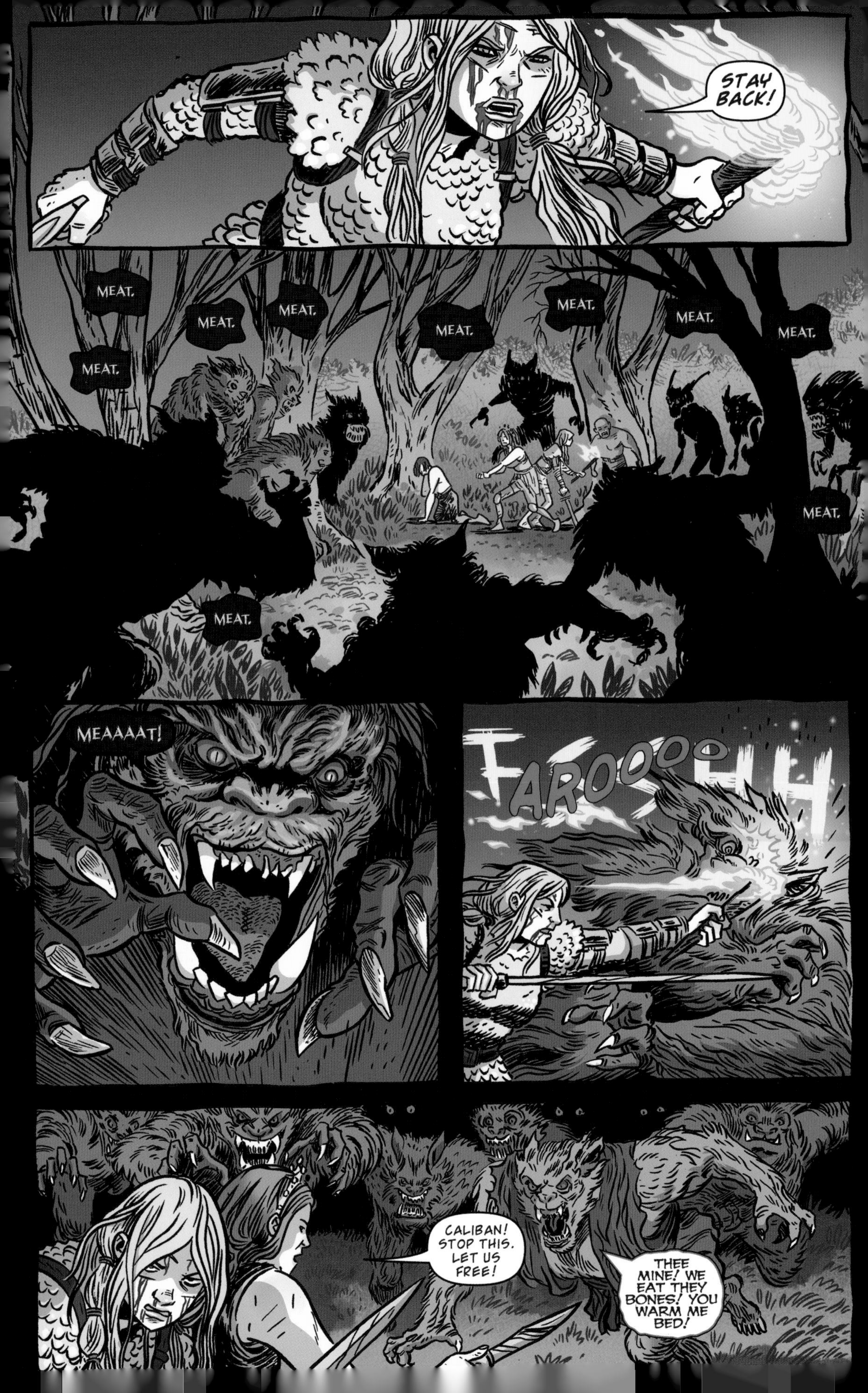
STAY BACK!
MEAT.
MEAT.
MEAT.
MEAT.
MEAT.
MEAT.
MEAT.
MEAT.
MEAT.
MEAT.
MEAAAAT!
FAROOOOSHH
CALIBAN! STOP THIS. LET US FREE!
THEE MINE! WE EAT THEY BONES! YOU WARM ME BED!

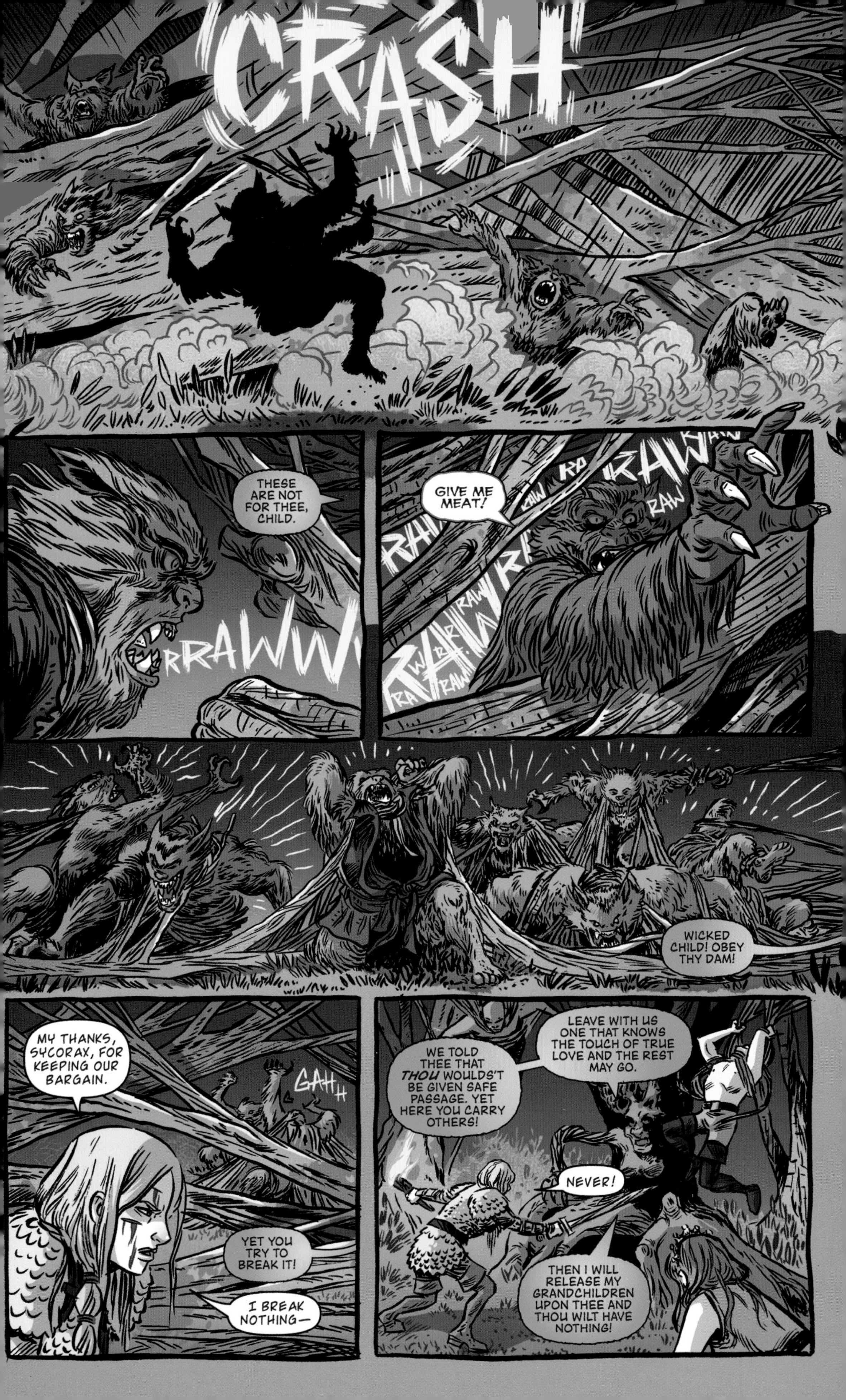
CRASH
THESE ARE NOT FOR THEE, CHILD.
RRAWW
GIVE ME MEAT!
RAW RA RAW RAW RAW
WICKED CHILD! OBEY THY DAM!
MY THANKS, SYCORAX, FOR KEEPING OUR BARGAIN.
GAHH
YET YOU TRY TO BREAK IT!
I BREAK NOTHING—
WE TOLD THEE THAT *THOU* WOULDS'T BE GIVEN SAFE PASSAGE. YET HERE YOU CARRY OTHERS!
LEAVE WITH US ONE THAT KNOWS THE TOUCH OF TRUE LOVE AND THE REST MAY GO.
NEVER!
THEN I WILL RELEASE MY GRANDCHILDREN UPON THEE AND THOU WILT HAVE NOTHING!

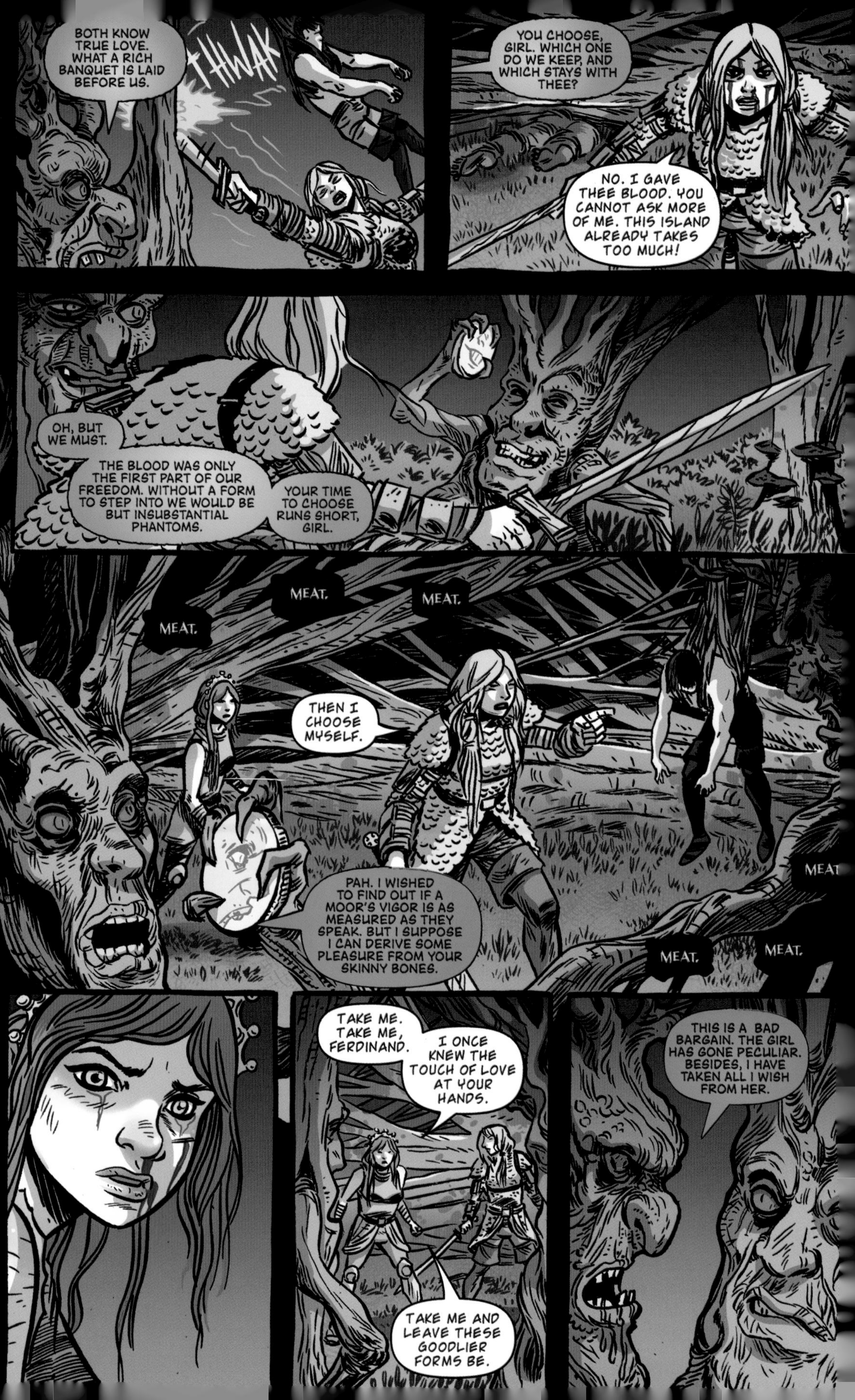
BOTH KNOW TRUE LOVE. WHAT A RICH BANQUET IS LAID BEFORE US.
THWAK
YOU CHOOSE, GIRL. WHICH ONE DO WE KEEP, AND WHICH STAYS WITH THEE?
NO. I GAVE THEE BLOOD. YOU CANNOT ASK MORE OF ME. THIS ISLAND ALREADY TAKES TOO MUCH!
OH, BUT WE MUST.
THE BLOOD WAS ONLY THE FIRST PART OF OUR FREEDOM. WITHOUT A FORM TO STEP INTO WE WOULD BE BUT INSUBSTANTIAL PHANTOMS.
YOUR TIME TO CHOOSE RUNS SHORT, GIRL.
MEAT.
MEAT.
MEAT.
THEN I CHOOSE MYSELF.
MEAT.
PAH. I WISHED TO FIND OUT IF A MOOR'S VIGOR IS AS MEASURED AS THEY SPEAK. BUT I SUPPOSE I CAN DERIVE SOME PLEASURE FROM YOUR SKINNY BONES.
MEAT.
MEAT.
TAKE ME. TAKE ME, FERDINAND.
I ONCE KNEW THE TOUCH OF LOVE AT YOUR HANDS.
TAKE ME AND LEAVE THESE GOODLIER FORMS BE.
THIS IS A BAD BARGAIN. THE GIRL HAS GONE PECULIAR. BESIDES, I HAVE TAKEN ALL I WISH FROM HER.

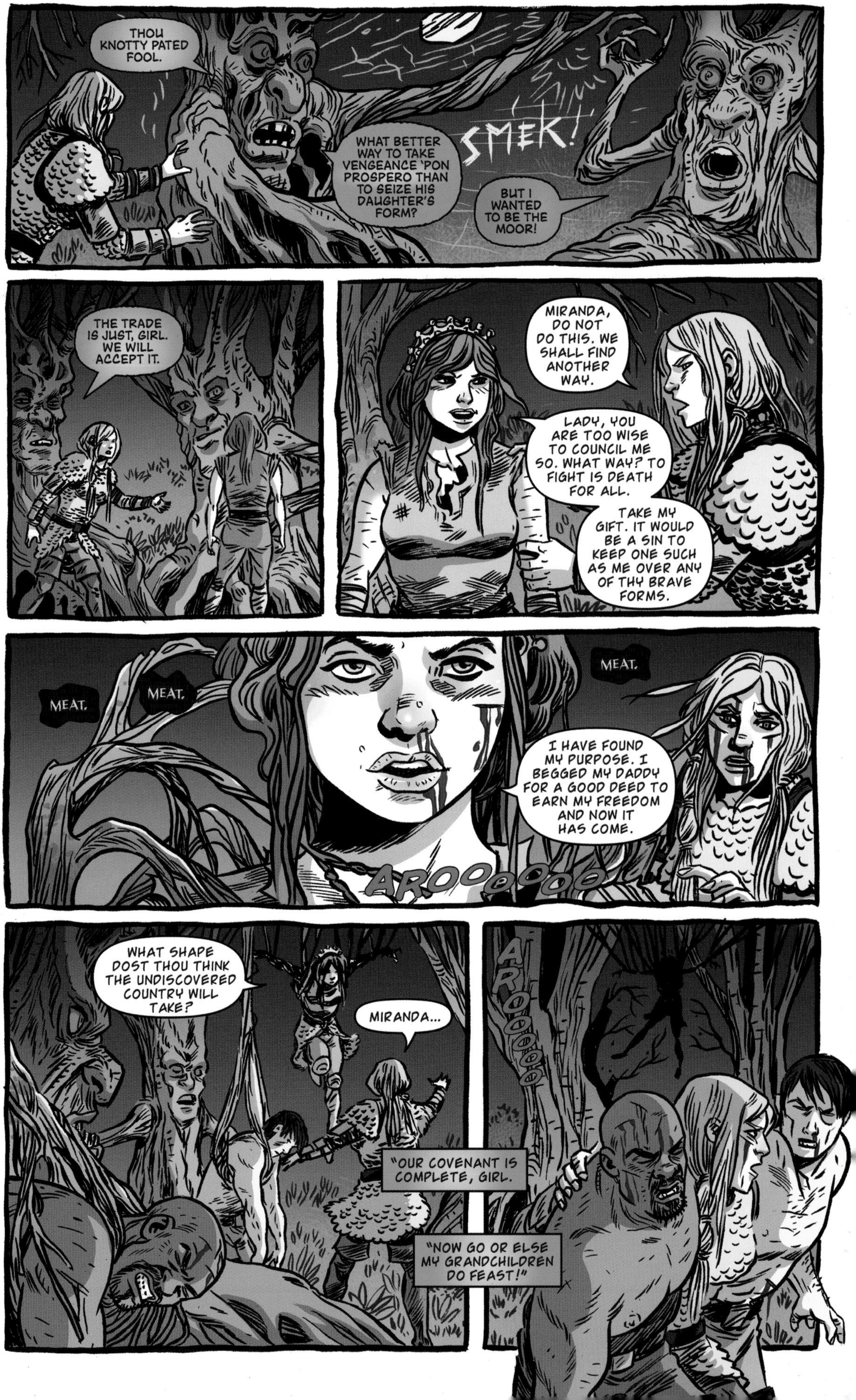
THOU KNOTTY PATED FOOL.
WHAT BETTER WAY TO TAKE VENGEANCE 'PON PROSPERO THAN TO SEIZE HIS DAUGHTER'S FORM?
SMEK!
BUT I WANTED TO BE THE MOOR!
THE TRADE IS JUST, GIRL. WE WILL ACCEPT IT.
MIRANDA, DO NOT DO THIS. WE SHALL FIND ANOTHER WAY.
LADY, YOU ARE TOO WISE TO COUNCIL ME SO. WHAT WAY? TO FIGHT IS DEATH FOR ALL.
TAKE MY GIFT. IT WOULD BE A SIN TO KEEP ONE SUCH AS ME OVER ANY OF THY BRAVE FORMS.
MEAT.
MEAT.
MEAT.
I HAVE FOUND MY PURPOSE. I BEGGED MY DADDY FOR A GOOD DEED TO EARN MY FREEDOM AND NOW IT HAS COME.
AROOOOOOO
WHAT SHAPE DOST THOU THINK THE UNDISCOVERED COUNTRY WILL TAKE?
MIRANDA...
AROOOOOO
"OUR COVENANT IS COMPLETE, GIRL.
"NOW GO OR ELSE MY GRANDCHILDREN DO FEAST!"

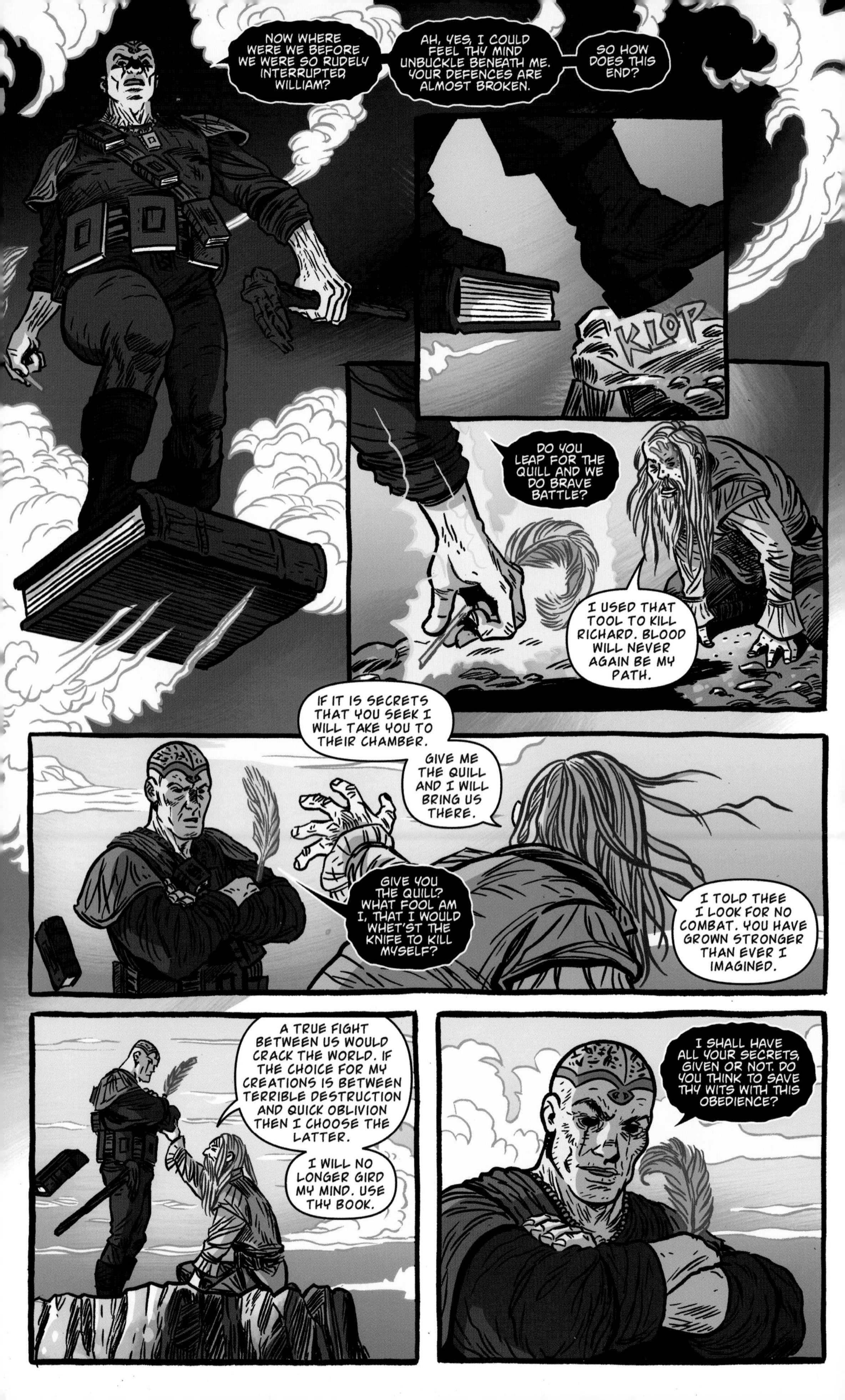
NOW WHERE WERE WE BEFORE WE WERE SO RUDELY INTERRUPTED, WILLIAM?
AH, YES, I COULD FEEL THY MIND UNBUCKLE BENEATH ME. YOUR DEFENCES ARE ALMOST BROKEN.
SO HOW DOES THIS END?
KLOP
DO YOU LEAP FOR THE QUILL AND WE DO BRAVE BATTLE?
I USED THAT TOOL TO KILL RICHARD. BLOOD WILL NEVER AGAIN BE MY PATH.
IF IT IS SECRETS THAT YOU SEEK I WILL TAKE YOU TO THEIR CHAMBER.
GIVE ME THE QUILL AND I WILL BRING US THERE.
GIVE YOU THE QUILL? WHAT FOOL AM I, THAT I WOULD WHET'ST THE KNIFE TO KILL MYSELF?
I TOLD THEE I LOOK FOR NO COMBAT. YOU HAVE GROWN STRONGER THAN EVER I IMAGINED.
A TRUE FIGHT BETWEEN US WOULD CRACK THE WORLD. IF THE CHOICE FOR MY CREATIONS IS BETWEEN TERRIBLE DESTRUCTION AND QUICK OBLIVION THEN I CHOOSE THE LATTER.
I WILL NO LONGER GIRD MY MIND. USE THY BOOK.
I SHALL HAVE ALL YOUR SECRETS, GIVEN OR NOT. DO YOU THINK TO SAVE THY WITS WITH THIS OBEDIENCE?

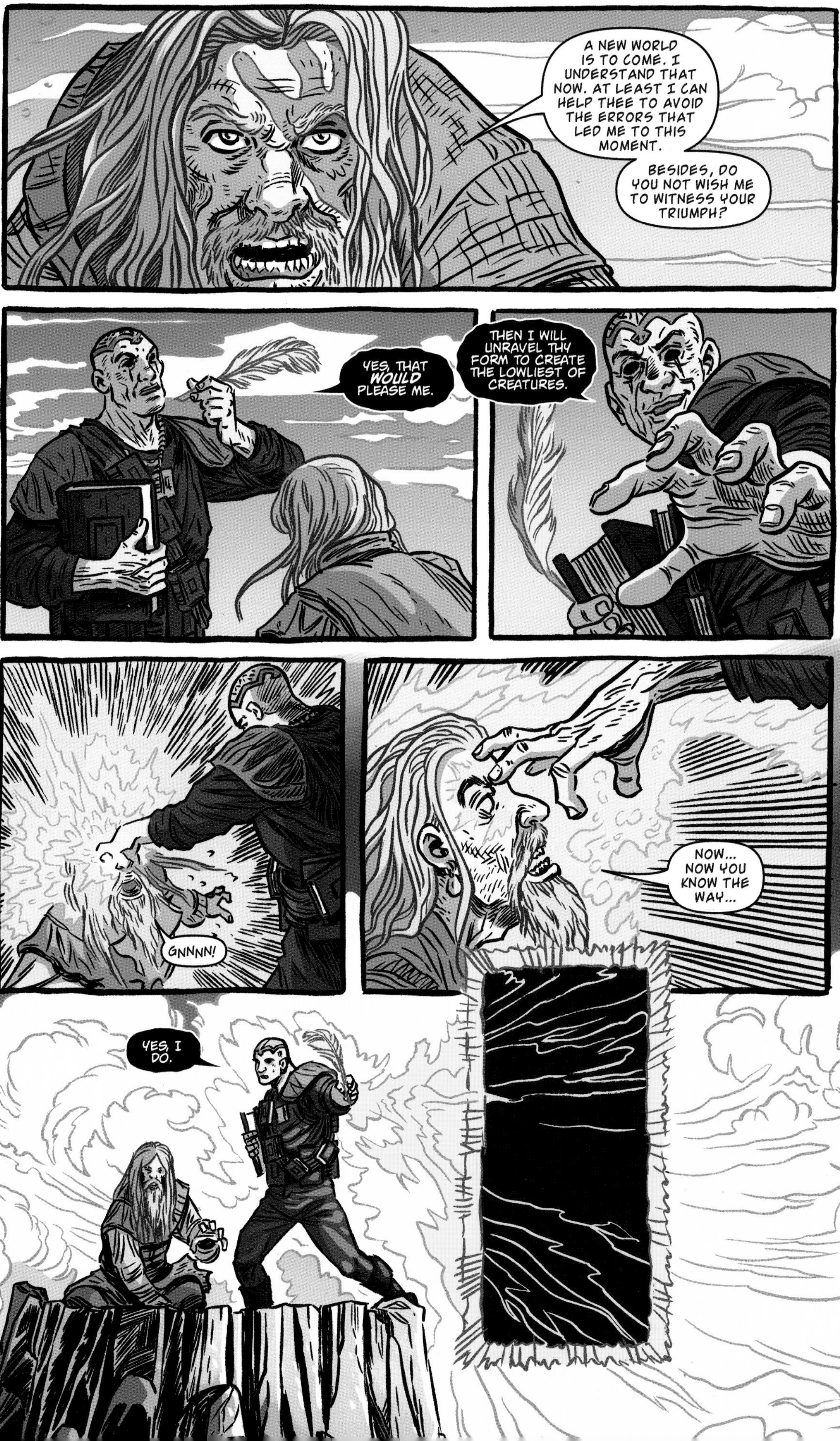
A NEW WORLD IS TO COME. I UNDERSTAND THAT NOW. AT LEAST I CAN HELP THEE TO AVOID THE ERRORS THAT LED ME TO THIS MOMENT.
BESIDES, DO YOU NOT WISH ME TO WITNESS YOUR TRIUMPH?
YES, THAT WOULD PLEASE ME.
THEN I WILL UNRAVEL THY FORM TO CREATE THE LOWLIEST OF CREATURES.
GNNNN!
NOW... NOW YOU KNOW THE WAY...
YES, I DO.

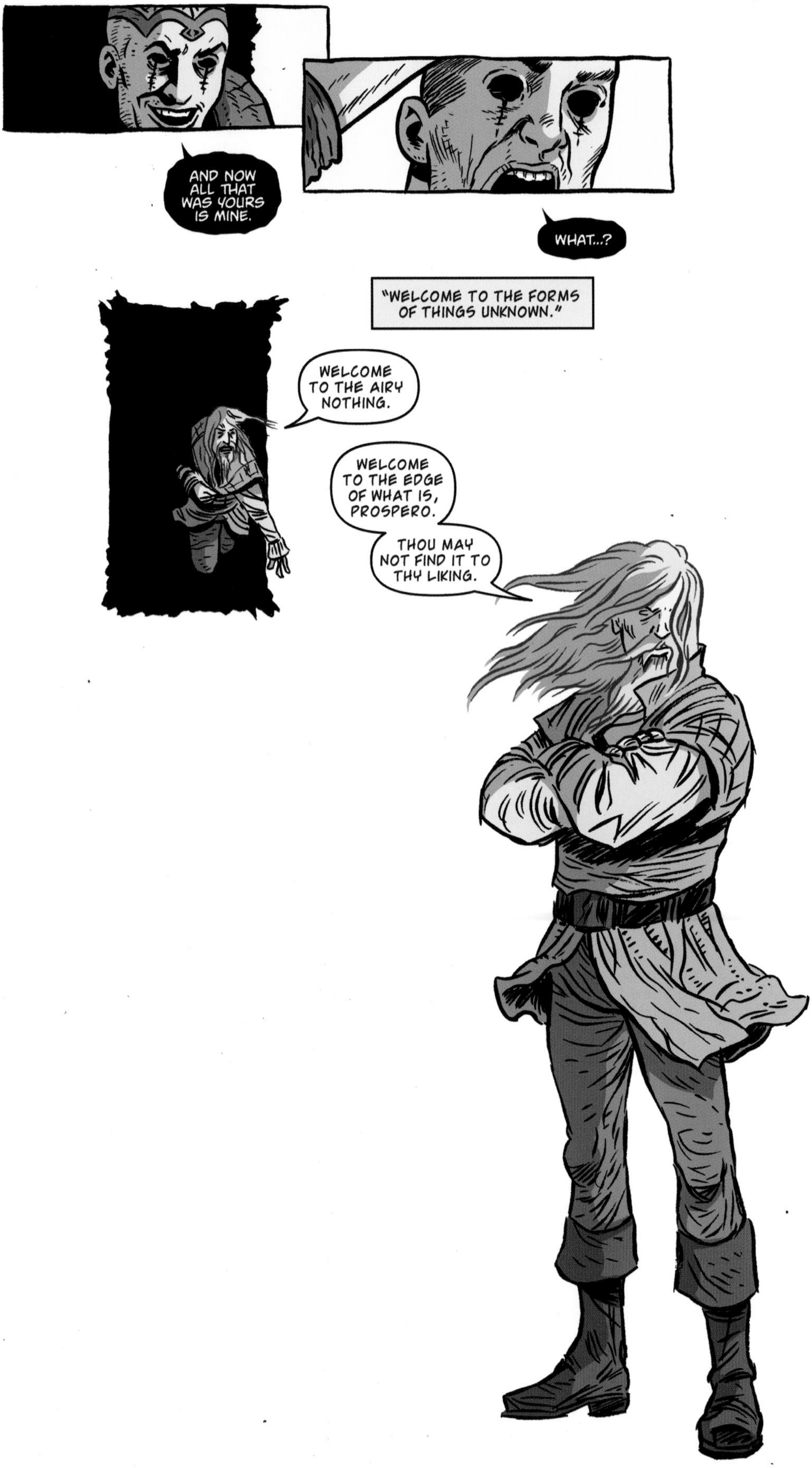

AND NOW ALL THAT WAS YOURS IS MINE.
WHAT...?
"WELCOME TO THE FORMS OF THINGS UNKNOWN."
WELCOME TO THE AIRY NOTHING.
WELCOME TO THE EDGE OF WHAT IS, PROSPERO.
THOU MAY NOT FIND IT TO THY LIKING.

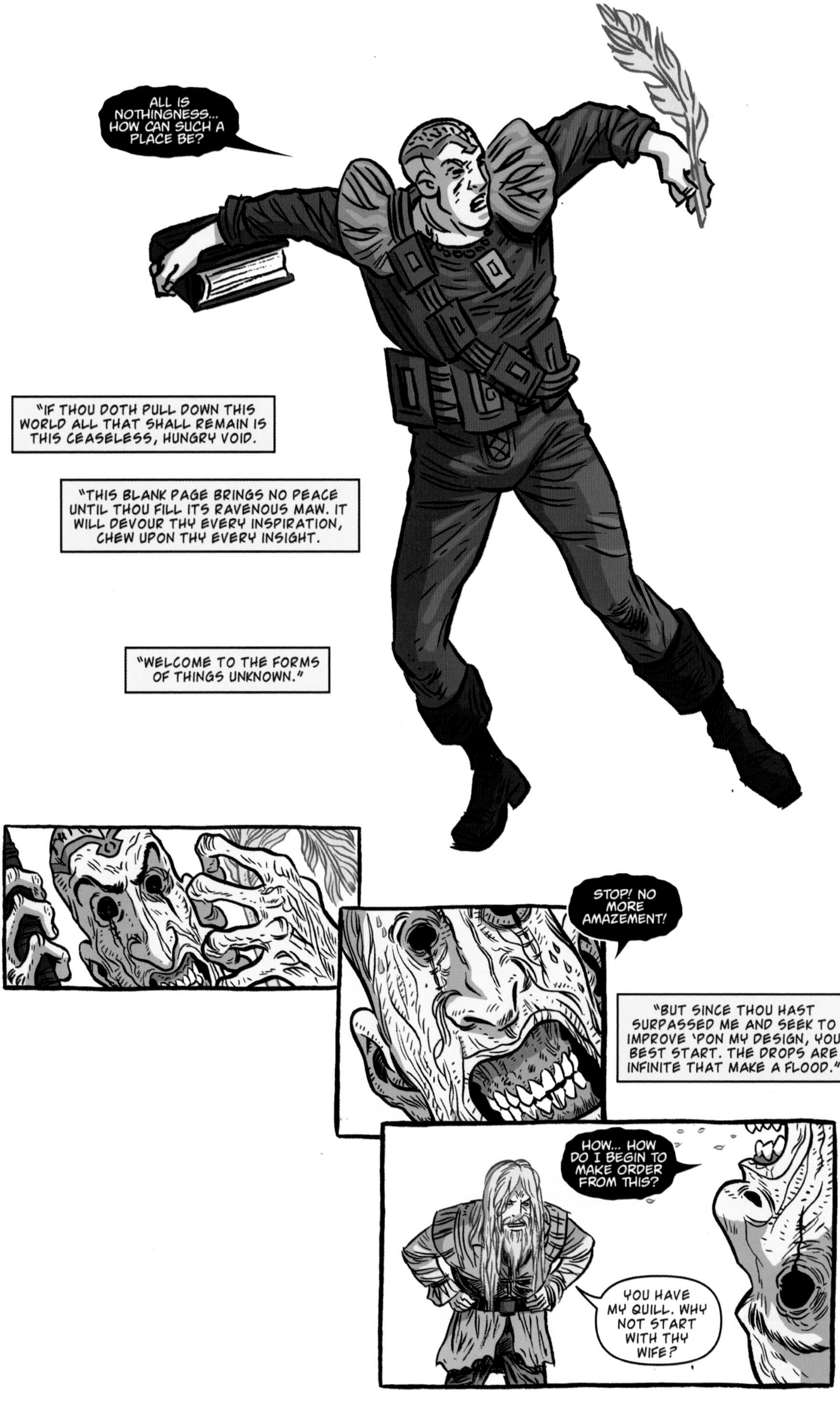
ALL IS NOTHINGNESS... HOW CAN SUCH A PLACE BE?
"IF THOU DOTH PULL DOWN THIS WORLD ALL THAT SHALL REMAIN IS THIS CEASELESS, HUNGRY VOID.
"THIS BLANK PAGE BRINGS NO PEACE UNTIL THOU FILL ITS RAVENOUS MAW. IT WILL DEVOUR THY EVERY INSPIRATION, CHEW UPON THY EVERY INSIGHT.
"WELCOME TO THE FORMS OF THINGS UNKNOWN."
STOP! NO MORE AMAZEMENT!
"BUT SINCE THOU HAST SURPASSED ME AND SEEK TO IMPROVE 'PON MY DESIGN, YOU BEST START. THE DROPS ARE INFINITE THAT MAKE A FLOOD."
HOW... HOW DO I BEGIN TO MAKE ORDER FROM THIS?
YOU HAVE MY QUILL. WHY NOT START WITH THY WIFE?

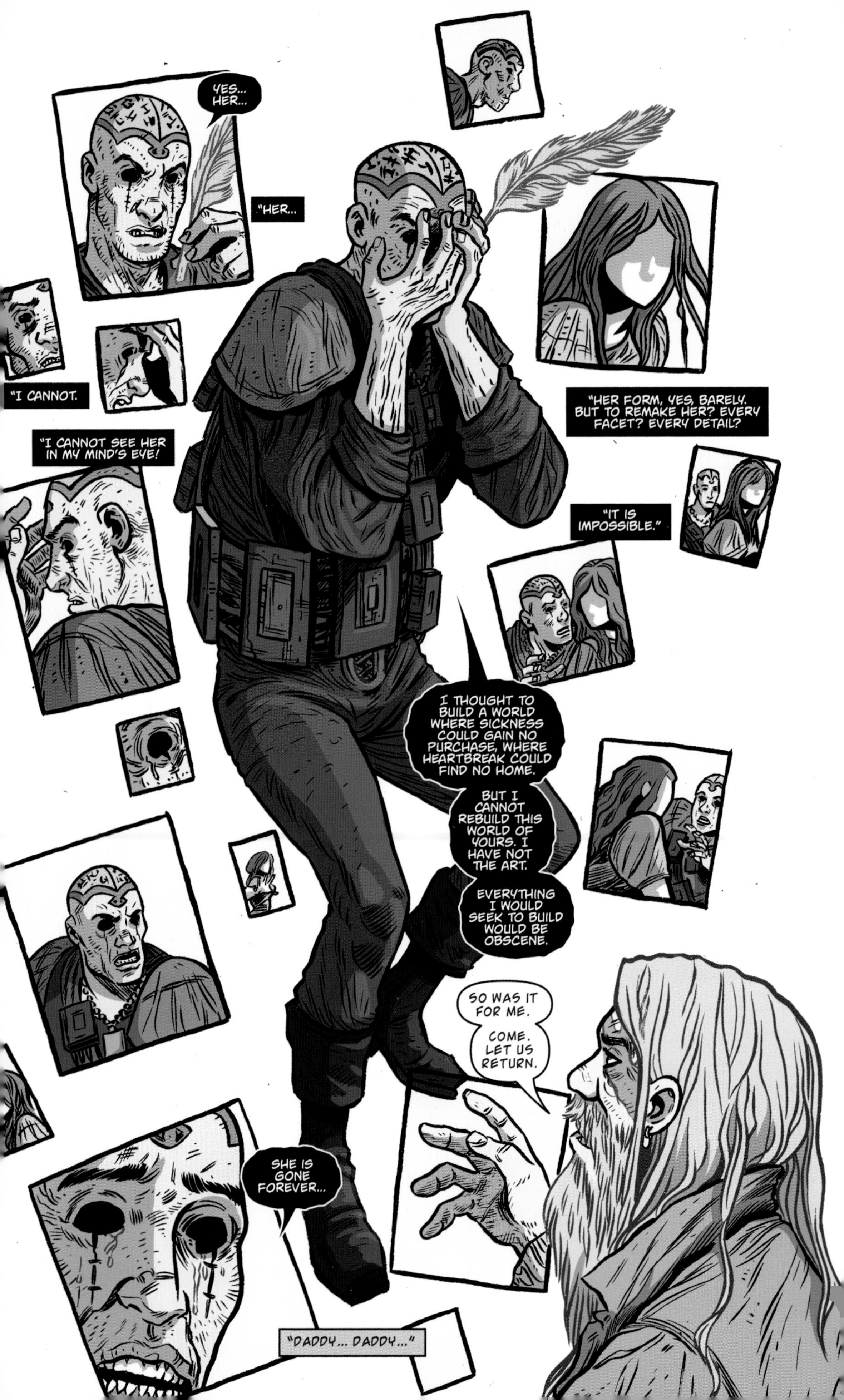
YES... HER...
"HER...
"I CANNOT.
"I CANNOT SEE HER IN MY MIND'S EYE!
"HER FORM, YES, BARELY. BUT TO REMAKE HER? EVERY FACET? EVERY DETAIL?
"IT IS IMPOSSIBLE."
I THOUGHT TO BUILD A WORLD WHERE SICKNESS COULD GAIN NO PURCHASE, WHERE HEARTBREAK COULD FIND NO HOME.
BUT I CANNOT REBUILD THIS WORLD OF YOURS. I HAVE NOT THE ART.
EVERYTHING I WOULD SEEK TO BUILD WOULD BE OBSCENE.
SO WAS IT FOR ME.
COME. LET US RETURN.
SHE IS GONE FOREVER...
"DADDY... DADDY..."

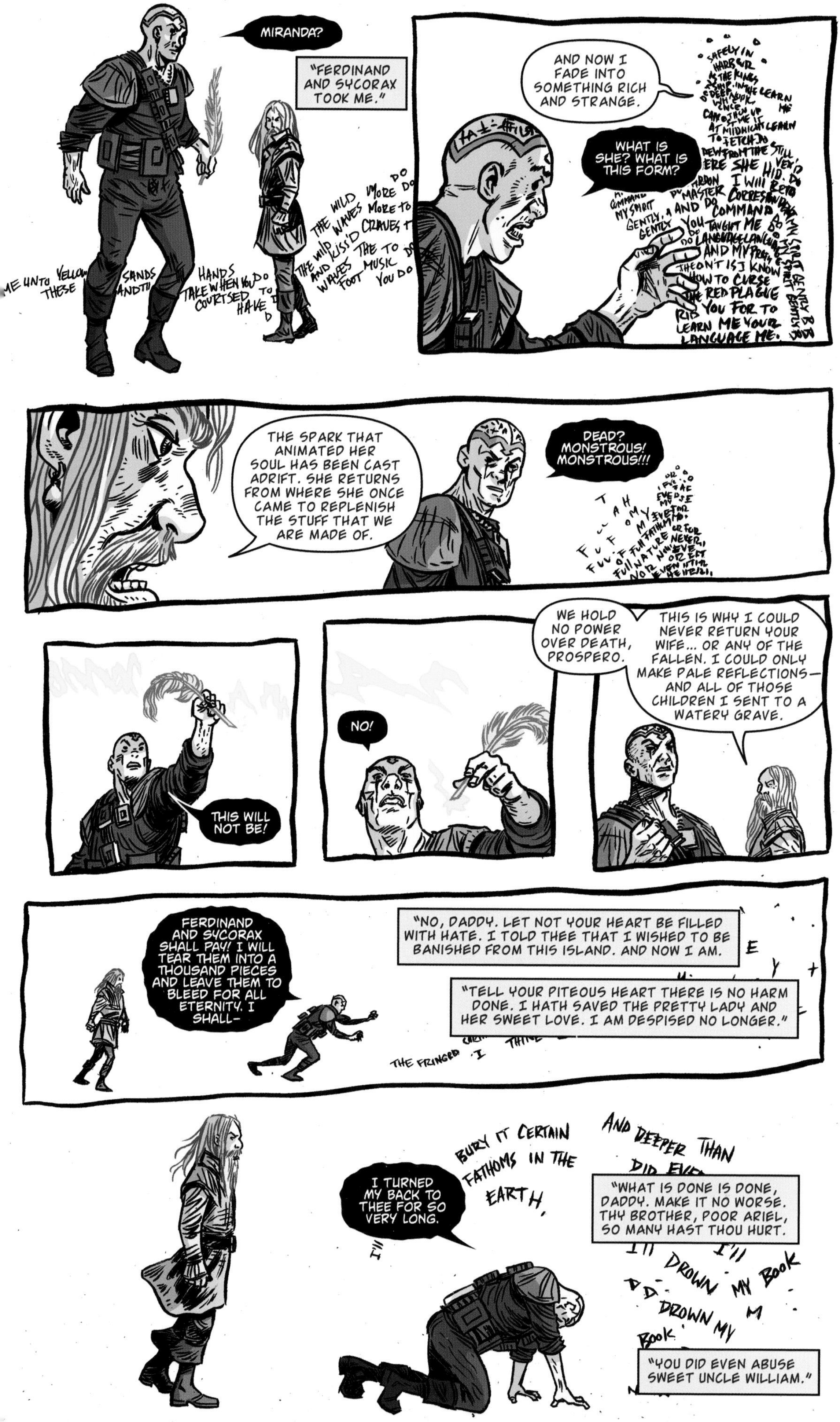
MIRANDA?
"FERDINAND AND SYCORAX TOOK ME."
AND NOW I FADE INTO SOMETHING RICH AND STRANGE.
WHAT IS SHE? WHAT IS THIS FORM?
THE SPARK THAT ANIMATED HER SOUL HAS BEEN CAST ADRIFT. SHE RETURNS FROM WHERE SHE ONCE CAME TO REPLENISH THE STUFF THAT WE ARE MADE OF.
DEAD? MONSTROUS! MONSTROUS!!!
THIS WILL NOT BE!
NO!
WE HOLD NO POWER OVER DEATH, PROSPERO.
THIS IS WHY I COULD NEVER RETURN YOUR WIFE... OR ANY OF THE FALLEN. I COULD ONLY MAKE PALE REFLECTIONS— AND ALL OF THOSE CHILDREN I SENT TO A WATERY GRAVE.
FERDINAND AND SYCORAX SHALL PAY! I WILL TEAR THEM INTO A THOUSAND PIECES AND LEAVE THEM TO BLEED FOR ALL ETERNITY. I SHALL-
"NO, DADDY. LET NOT YOUR HEART BE FILLED WITH HATE. I TOLD THEE THAT I WISHED TO BE BANISHED FROM THIS ISLAND. AND NOW I AM.
"TELL YOUR PITEOUS HEART THERE IS NO HARM DONE. I HATH SAVED THE PRETTY LADY AND HER SWEET LOVE. I AM DESPISED NO LONGER."
I TURNED MY BACK TO THEE FOR SO VERY LONG.
BURY IT CERTAIN FATHOMS IN THE EARTH,
AND DEEPER THAN
"WHAT IS DONE IS DONE, DADDY. MAKE IT NO WORSE. THY BROTHER, POOR ARIEL, SO MANY HAST THOU HURT.
I'LL DROWN MY BOOK
DROWN MY BOOK
"YOU DID EVEN ABUSE SWEET UNCLE WILLIAM."

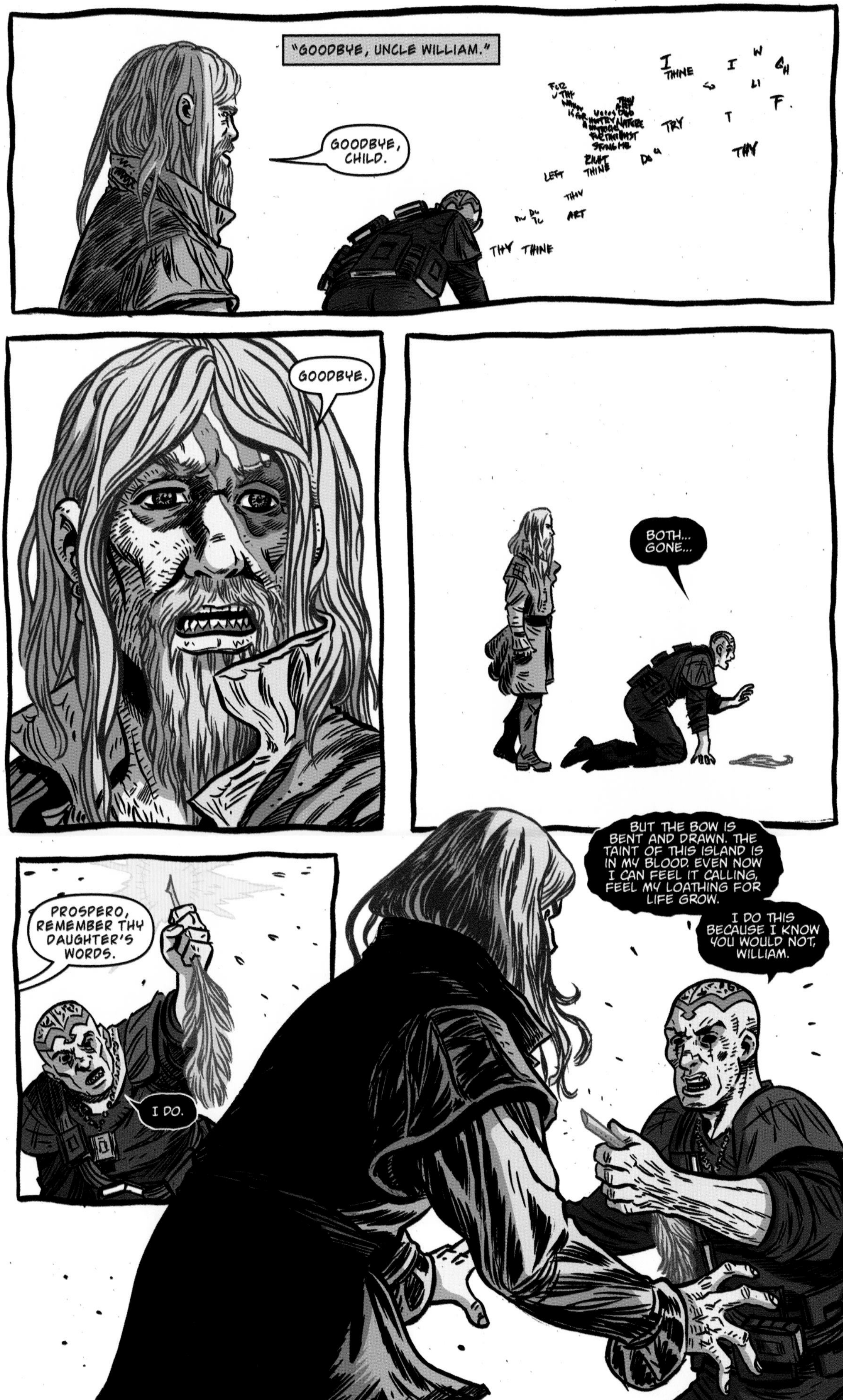
"GOODBYE, UNCLE WILLIAM."
GOODBYE, CHILD.
GOODBYE.
BOTH... GONE...
BUT THE BOW IS BENT AND DRAWN. THE TAINT OF THIS ISLAND IS IN MY BLOOD. EVEN NOW I CAN FEEL IT CALLING, FEEL MY LOATHING FOR LIFE GROW.
I DO THIS BECAUSE I KNOW YOU WOULD NOT, WILLIAM.
PROSPERO, REMEMBER THY DAUGHTER'S WORDS.
I DO.

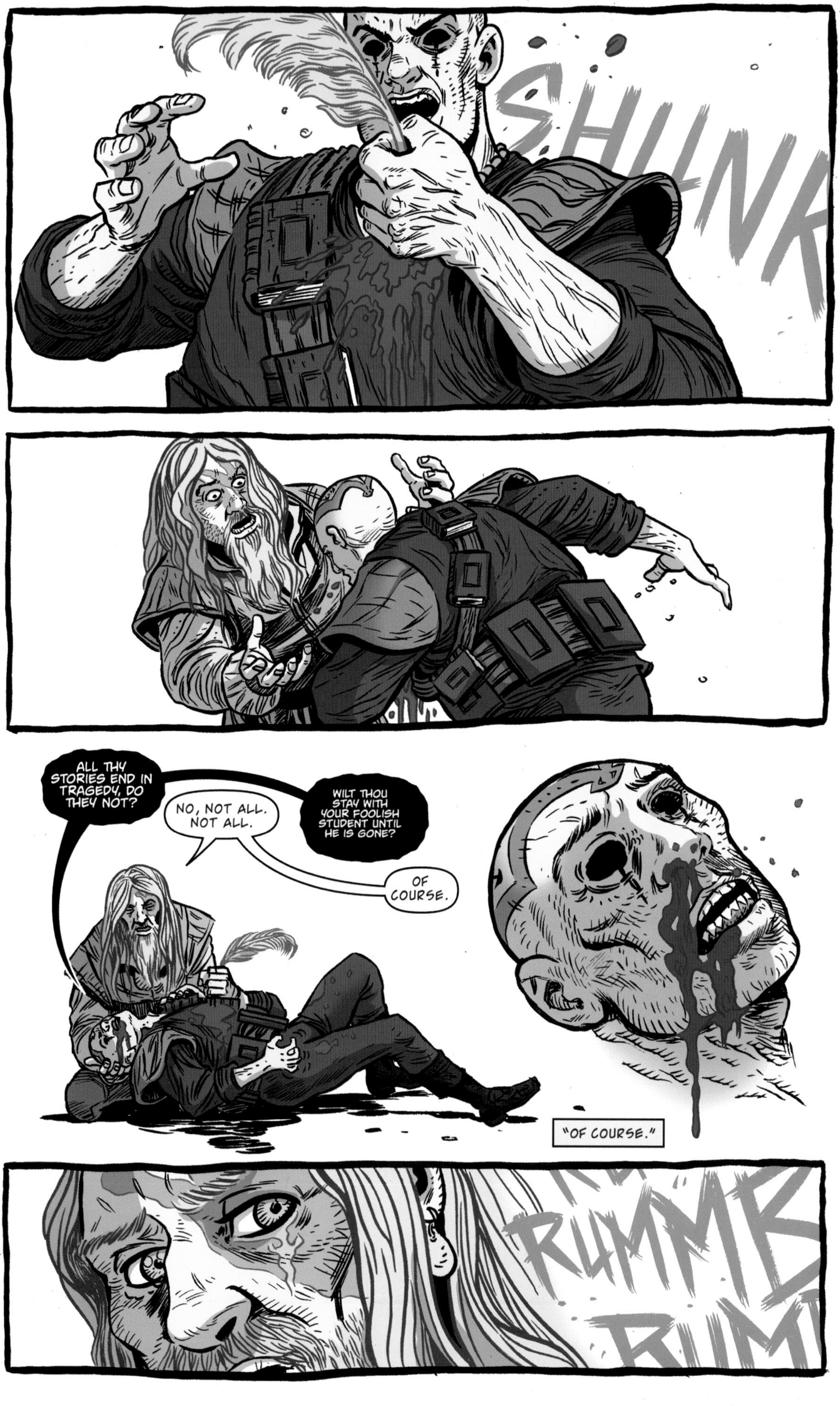
SHUNK
ALL THY STORIES END IN TRAGEDY, DO THEY NOT?
NO, NOT ALL. NOT ALL.
WILT THOU STAY WITH YOUR FOOLISH STUDENT UNTIL HE IS GONE?
OF COURSE.
"OF COURSE."
RUMMB

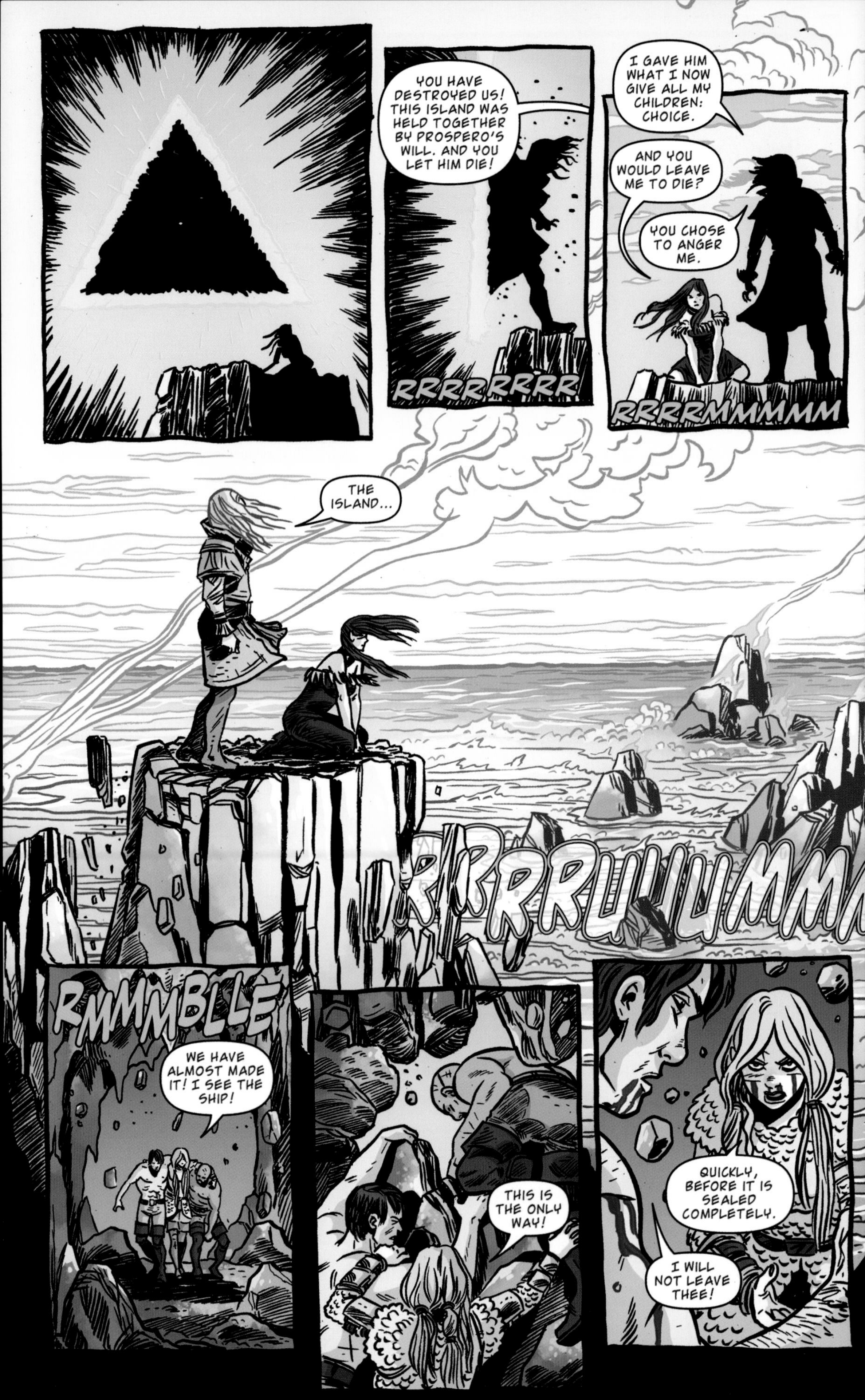
YOU HAVE DESTROYED US! THIS ISLAND WAS HELD TOGETHER BY PROSPERO'S WILL. AND YOU LET HIM DIE!
RRRRRRRR
I GAVE HIM WHAT I NOW GIVE ALL MY CHILDREN: CHOICE.
AND YOU WOULD LEAVE ME TO DIE?
YOU CHOSE TO ANGER ME.
RRRRMMMMM
THE ISLAND...
RRRRUUUMMM
RMMMBLLE
WE HAVE ALMOST MADE IT! I SEE THE SHIP!
THIS IS THE ONLY WAY!
QUICKLY, BEFORE IT IS SEALED COMPLETELY.
I WILL NOT LEAVE THEE!

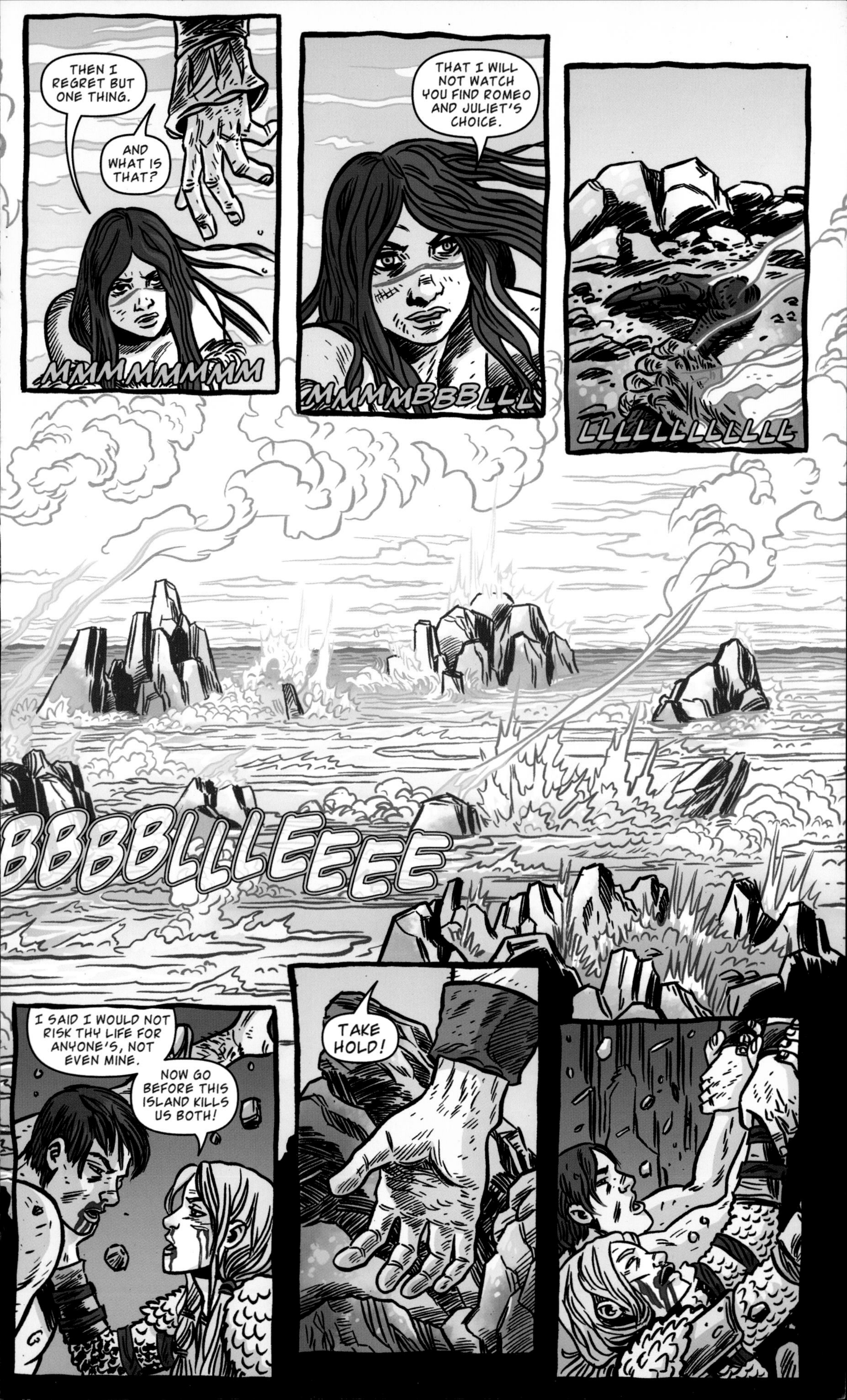
THEN I REGRET BUT ONE THING.
AND WHAT IS THAT?
MMMMMMMMM
THAT I WILL NOT WATCH YOU FIND ROMEO AND JULIET'S CHOICE.
MMMMMBBBLLL
LLLLLLLLLLLL
BBBBLLLLEEEE
I SAID I WOULD NOT RISK THY LIFE FOR ANYONE'S, NOT EVEN MINE.
NOW GO BEFORE THIS ISLAND KILLS US BOTH!
TAKE HOLD!

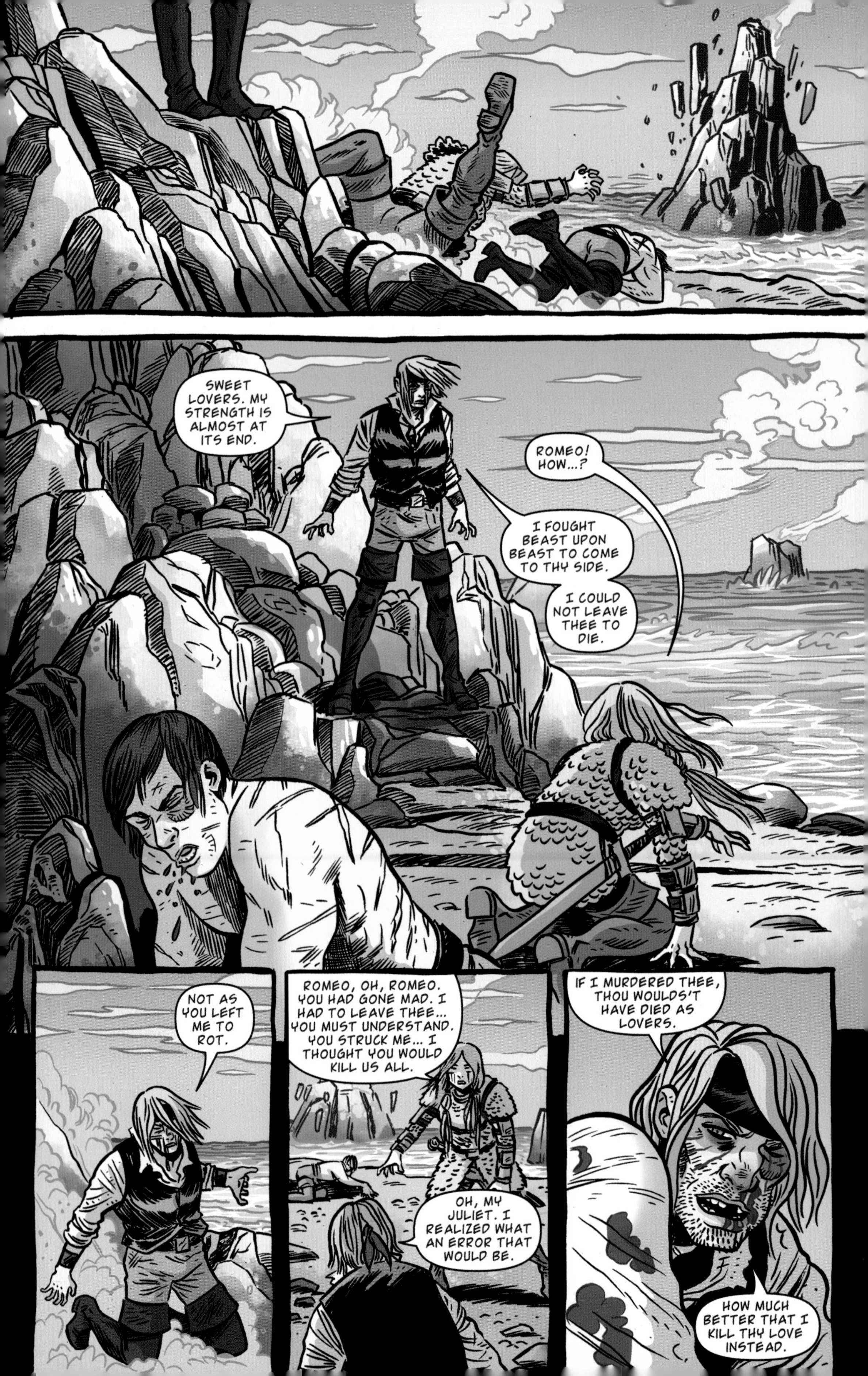
SWEET LOVERS. MY STRENGTH IS ALMOST AT ITS END.
ROMEO! HOW...?
I FOUGHT BEAST UPON BEAST TO COME TO THY SIDE.
I COULD NOT LEAVE THEE TO DIE.
NOT AS YOU LEFT ME TO ROT.
ROMEO, OH, ROMEO. YOU HAD GONE MAD. I HAD TO LEAVE THEE... YOU MUST UNDERSTAND. YOU STRUCK ME... I THOUGHT YOU WOULD KILL US ALL.
OH, MY JULIET. I REALIZED WHAT AN ERROR THAT WOULD BE.
IF I MURDERED THEE, THOU WOULDS'T HAVE DIED AS LOVERS.
HOW MUCH BETTER THAT I KILL THY LOVE INSTEAD.

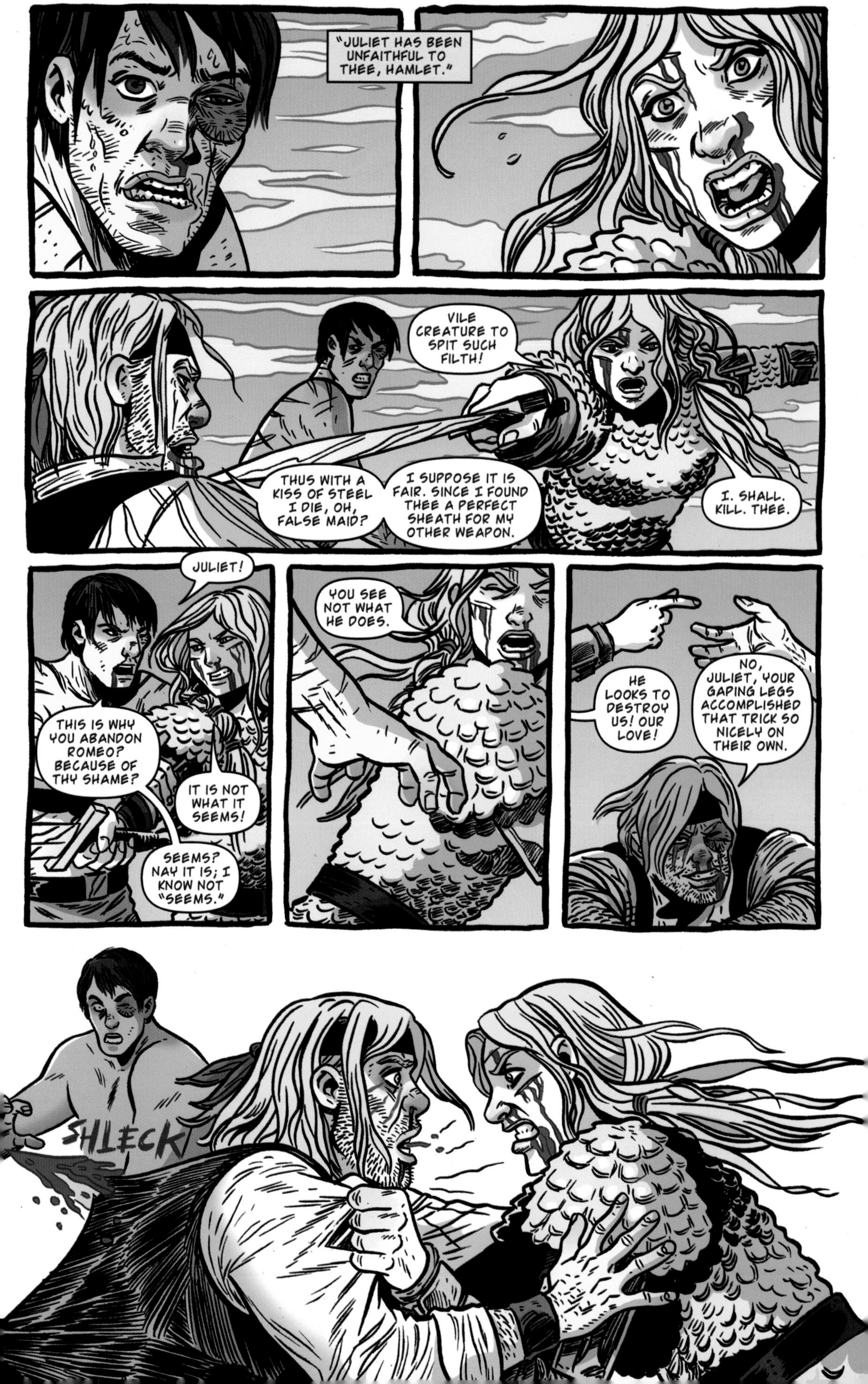
"JULIET HAS BEEN UNFAITHFUL TO THEE, HAMLET."
VILE CREATURE TO SPIT SUCH FILTH!
THUS WITH A KISS OF STEEL I DIE, OH, FALSE MAID?
I SUPPOSE IT IS FAIR. SINCE I FOUND THEE A PERFECT SHEATH FOR MY OTHER WEAPON.
I. SHALL. KILL. THEE.
JULIET!
THIS IS WHY YOU ABANDON ROMEO? BECAUSE OF THY SHAME?
IT IS NOT WHAT IT SEEMS!
SEEMS? NAY IT IS; I KNOW NOT "SEEMS."
YOU SEE NOT WHAT HE DOES.
HE LOOKS TO DESTROY US! OUR LOVE!
NO, JULIET, YOUR GAPING LEGS ACCOMPLISHED THAT TRICK SO NICELY ON THEIR OWN.
SHLECK

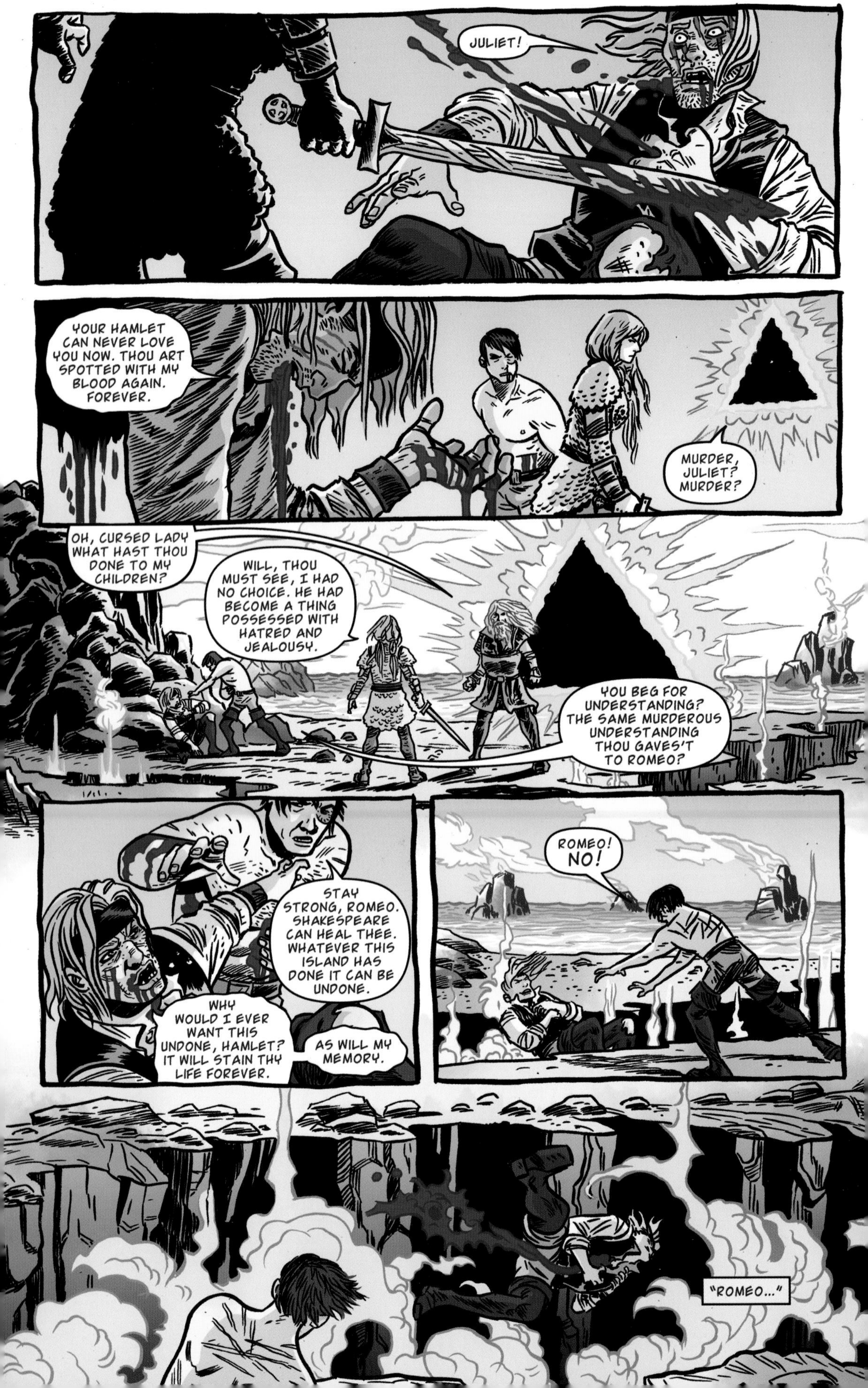
JULIET!
YOUR HAMLET CAN NEVER LOVE YOU NOW. THOU ART SPOTTED WITH MY BLOOD AGAIN. FOREVER.
MURDER, JULIET? MURDER?
OH, CURSED LADY WHAT HAST THOU DONE TO MY CHILDREN?
WILL, THOU MUST SEE, I HAD NO CHOICE. HE HAD BECOME A THING POSSESSED WITH HATRED AND JEALOUSY.
YOU BEG FOR UNDERSTANDING? THE SAME MURDEROUS UNDERSTANDING THOU GAVES'T TO ROMEO?
STAY STRONG, ROMEO. SHAKESPEARE CAN HEAL THEE. WHATEVER THIS ISLAND HAS DONE IT CAN BE UNDONE.
WHY WOULD I EVER WANT THIS UNDONE, HAMLET? IT WILL STAIN THY LIFE FOREVER.
AS WILL MY MEMORY.
ROMEO! NO!
"ROMEO..."

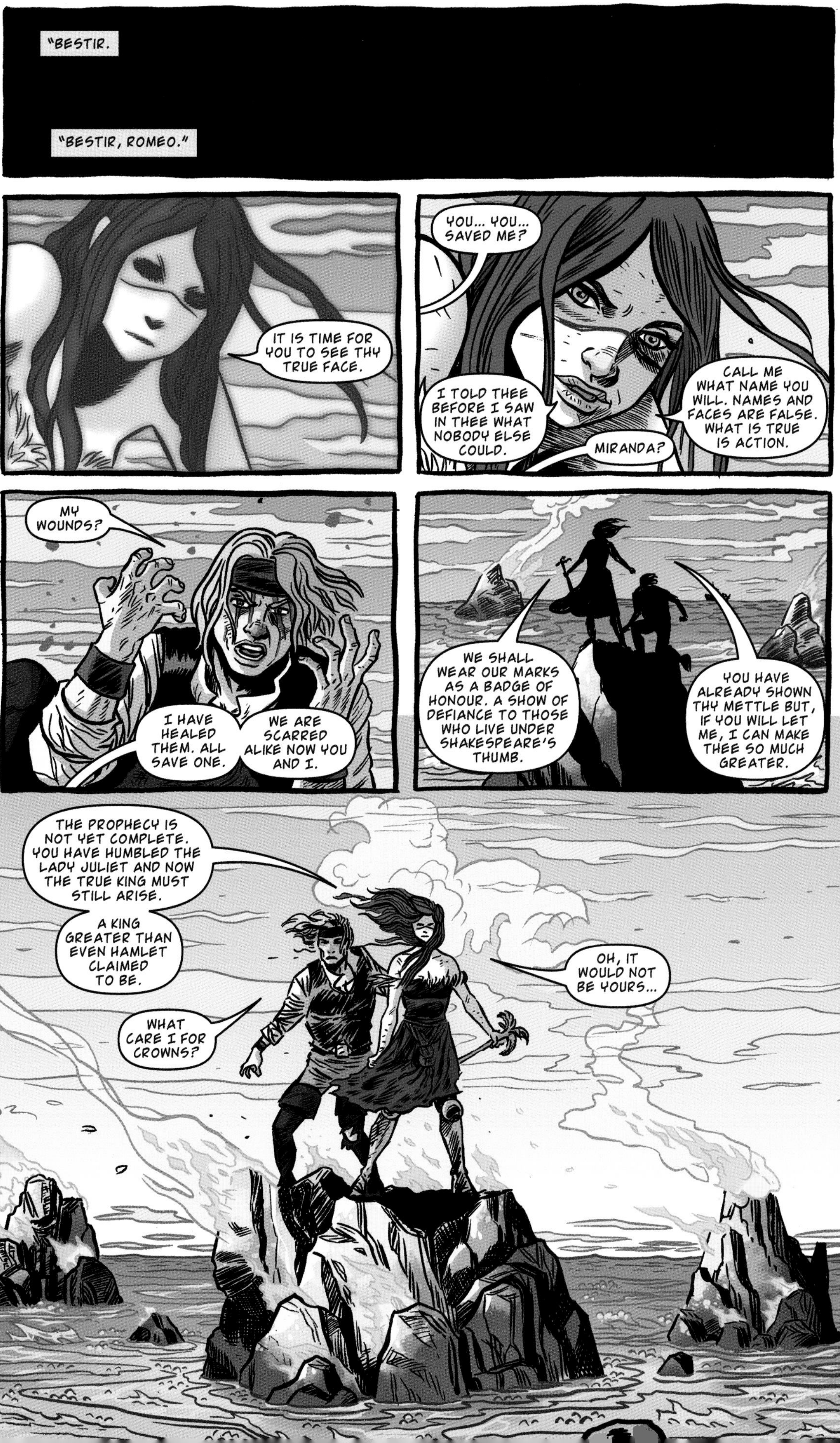
"BESTIR.
"BESTIR, ROMEO."
IT IS TIME FOR YOU TO SEE THY TRUE FACE.
YOU... YOU... SAVED ME?
I TOLD THEE BEFORE I SAW IN THEE WHAT NOBODY ELSE COULD.
MIRANDA?
CALL ME WHAT NAME YOU WILL. NAMES AND FACES ARE FALSE. WHAT IS TRUE IS ACTION.
MY WOUNDS?
I HAVE HEALED THEM. ALL SAVE ONE.
WE ARE SCARRED ALIKE NOW YOU AND I.
WE SHALL WEAR OUR MARKS AS A BADGE OF HONOUR. A SHOW OF DEFIANCE TO THOSE WHO LIVE UNDER SHAKESPEARE'S THUMB.
YOU HAVE ALREADY SHOWN THY METTLE BUT, IF YOU WILL LET ME, I CAN MAKE THEE SO MUCH GREATER.
THE PROPHECY IS NOT YET COMPLETE. YOU HAVE HUMBLED THE LADY JULIET AND NOW THE TRUE KING MUST STILL ARISE.
A KING GREATER THAN EVEN HAMLET CLAIMED TO BE.
WHAT CARE I FOR CROWNS?
OH, IT WOULD NOT BE YOURS...

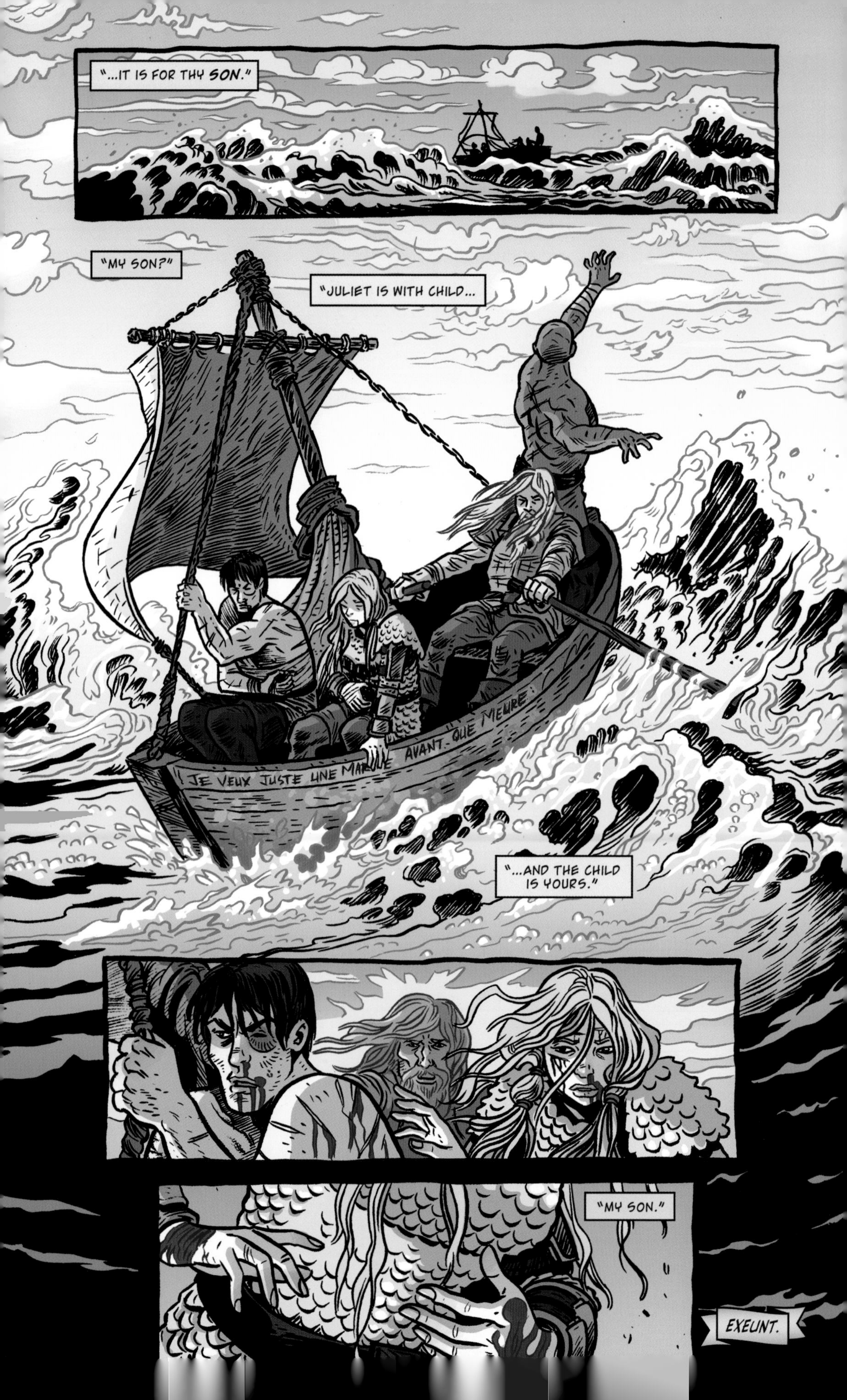
"...IT IS FOR THY SON."
"MY SON?"
"JULIET IS WITH CHILD...
JE VEUX JUSTE UNE MARQUE AVANT QUE MEURE
"...AND THE CHILD IS YOURS."
"MY SON."
EXEUNT.

BONUS
GALLERY

Featuring artwork from
the series as well as the
exclusive story:

"Revenge Shall
Have No Bounds"

WRITTEN BY
Carrie J. Cole

ART & COLORS BY
Vivian Ng

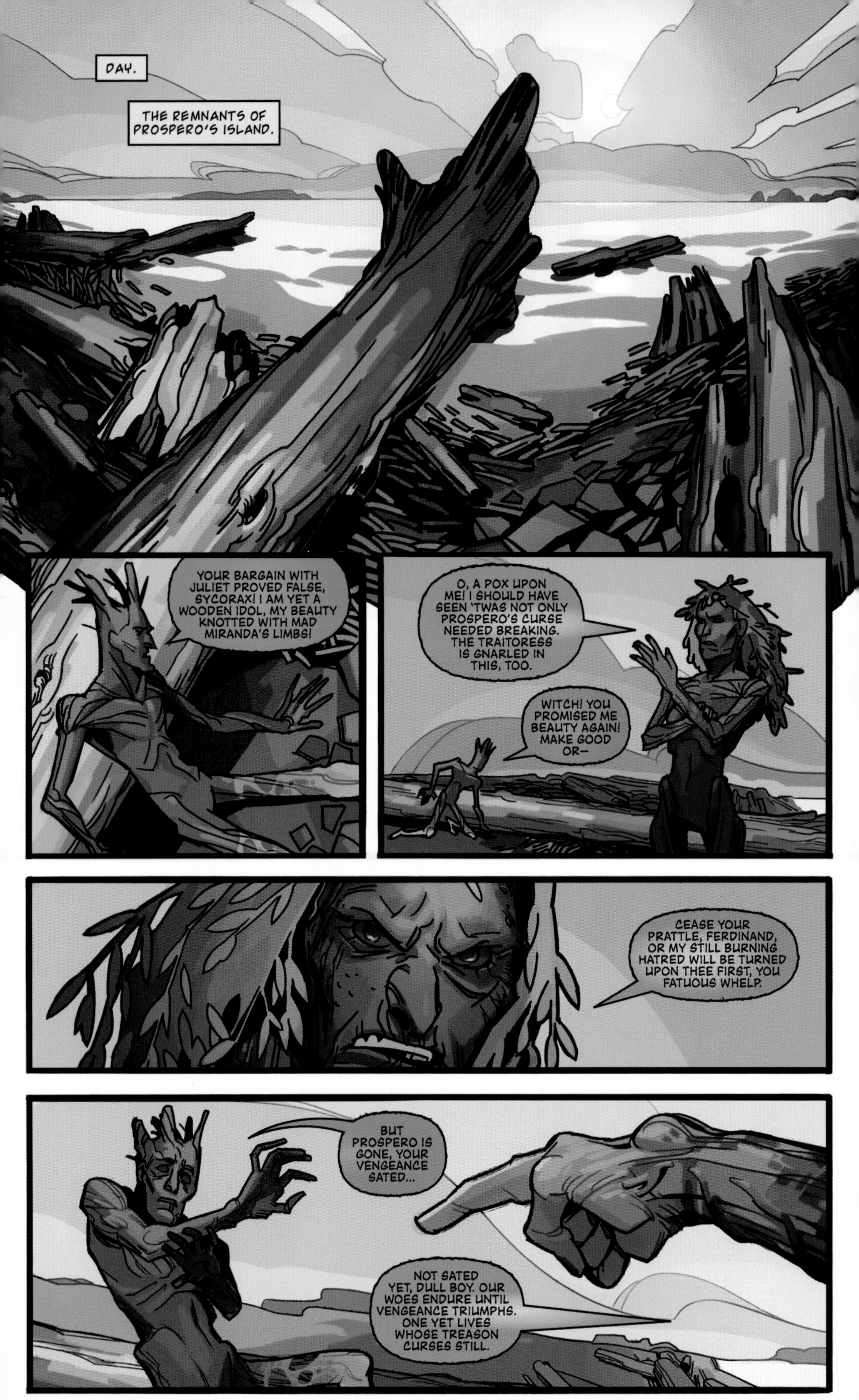
DAY.
THE REMNANTS OF PROSPERO'S ISLAND.
YOUR BARGAIN WITH JULIET PROVED FALSE, SYCORAX! I AM YET A WOODEN IDOL, MY BEAUTY KNOTTED WITH MAD MIRANDA'S LIMBS!
O, A POX UPON ME! I SHOULD HAVE SEEN 'TWAS NOT ONLY PROSPERO'S CURSE NEEDED BREAKING. THE TRAITORESS IS GNARLED IN THIS, TOO.
WITCH! YOU PROMISED ME BEAUTY AGAIN! MAKE GOOD OR—
CEASE YOUR PRATTLE, FERDINAND, OR MY STILL BURNING HATRED WILL BE TURNED UPON THEE FIRST, YOU FATUOUS WHELP.
BUT PROSPERO IS GONE, YOUR VENGEANCE SATED...
NOT SATED YET, DULL BOY. OUR WOES ENDURE UNTIL VENGEANCE TRIUMPHS. ONE YET LIVES WHOSE TREASON CURSES STILL.

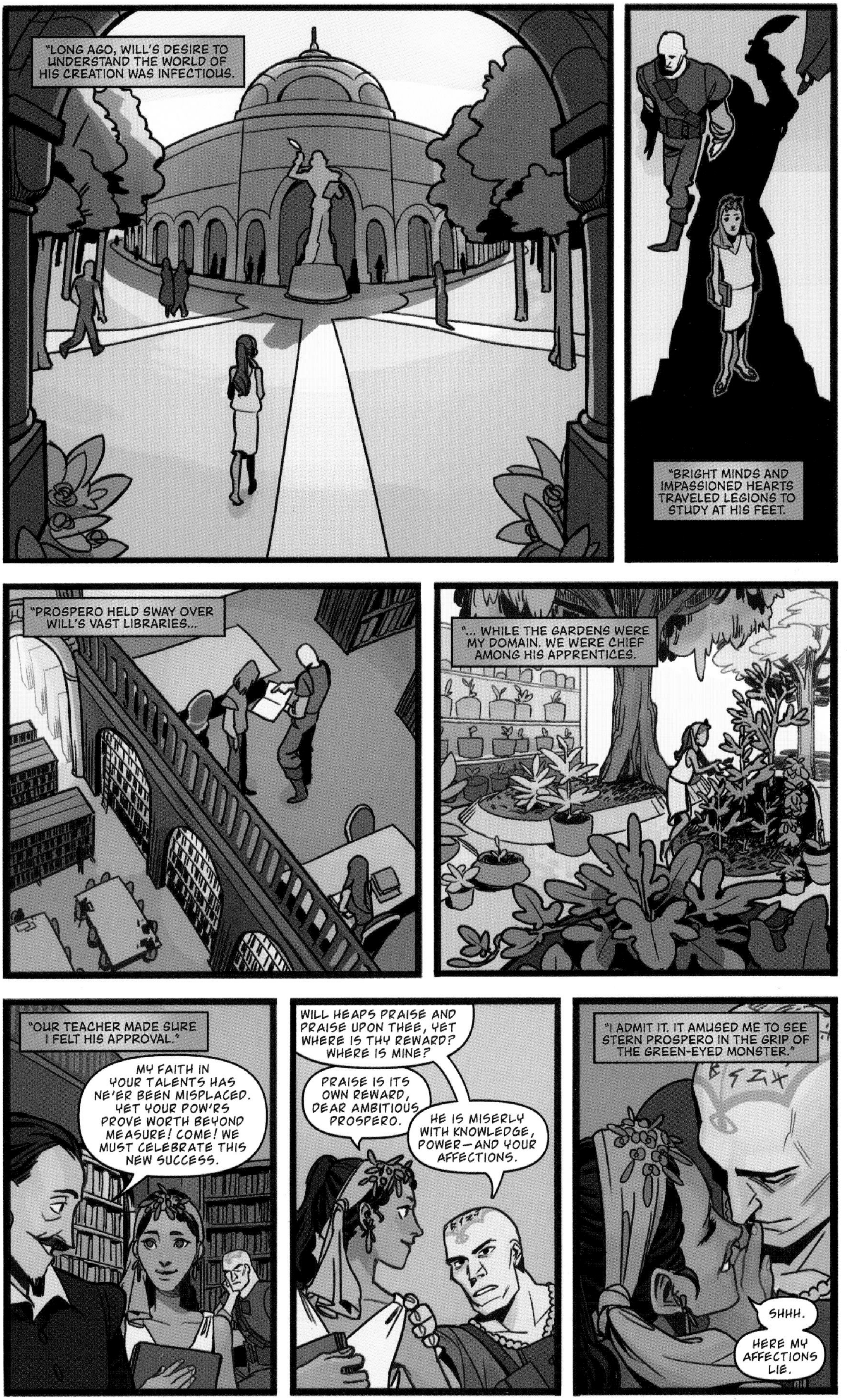
"LONG AGO, WILL'S DESIRE TO UNDERSTAND THE WORLD OF HIS CREATION WAS INFECTIOUS.
"BRIGHT MINDS AND IMPASSIONED HEARTS TRAVELED LEGIONS TO STUDY AT HIS FEET.
"PROSPERO HELD SWAY OVER WILL'S VAST LIBRARIES...
"... WHILE THE GARDENS WERE MY DOMAIN. WE WERE CHIEF AMONG HIS APPRENTICES.
"OUR TEACHER MADE SURE I FELT HIS APPROVAL."
MY FAITH IN YOUR TALENTS HAS NE'ER BEEN MISPLACED. YET YOUR POW'RS PROVE WORTH BEYOND MEASURE! COME! WE MUST CELEBRATE THIS NEW SUCCESS.
WILL HEAPS PRAISE AND PRAISE UPON THEE, YET WHERE IS THY REWARD? WHERE IS MINE?
PRAISE IS ITS OWN REWARD, DEAR AMBITIOUS PROSPERO.
HE IS MISERLY WITH KNOWLEDGE, POWER—AND YOUR AFFECTIONS.
"I ADMIT IT. IT AMUSED ME TO SEE STERN PROSPERO IN THE GRIP OF THE GREEN-EYED MONSTER."
SHHH.
HERE MY AFFECTIONS LIE.

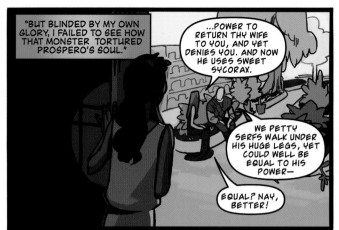

"BUT BLINDED BY MY OWN GLORY, I FAILED TO SEE HOW THAT MONSTER TORTURED PROSPERO'S SOUL."

...POWER TO RETURN THY WIFE TO YOU, AND YET DENIES YOU. AND NOW HE USES SWEET SYCORAX.

WE PETTY SERFS WALK UNDER HIS HUGE LEGS, YET COULD WELL BE EQUAL TO HIS POWER—

EQUAL? NAY, BETTER!

SO WE MUST WREST IT FROM HIM.

WHAT POISON'D TALK IS THIS?

YOU ARE TOO GOOD FOR THIS BASE JEALOUSY, PROSPERO.

I SEEK TO RETURN THIS WORLD TO ITS FORMER GLORY!

IF YOU TRULY FEAR FOR THIS WORLD THEN SPEAK WITH WILL. EVER IS HIS DOOR AND HEART OPEN TO HIS STUDENTS.

AND HOW OPEN ART THOU TO HIM, BEHIND HIS CLOSED DOOR?

I AM HONEST, LORD; AND HONESTY SHALL EVER DRIVE MY ACTIONS.

WILL MUST HEAR OF THIS.

SYCORAX!

YOU SHALL NOT BETRAY ME TWICE!

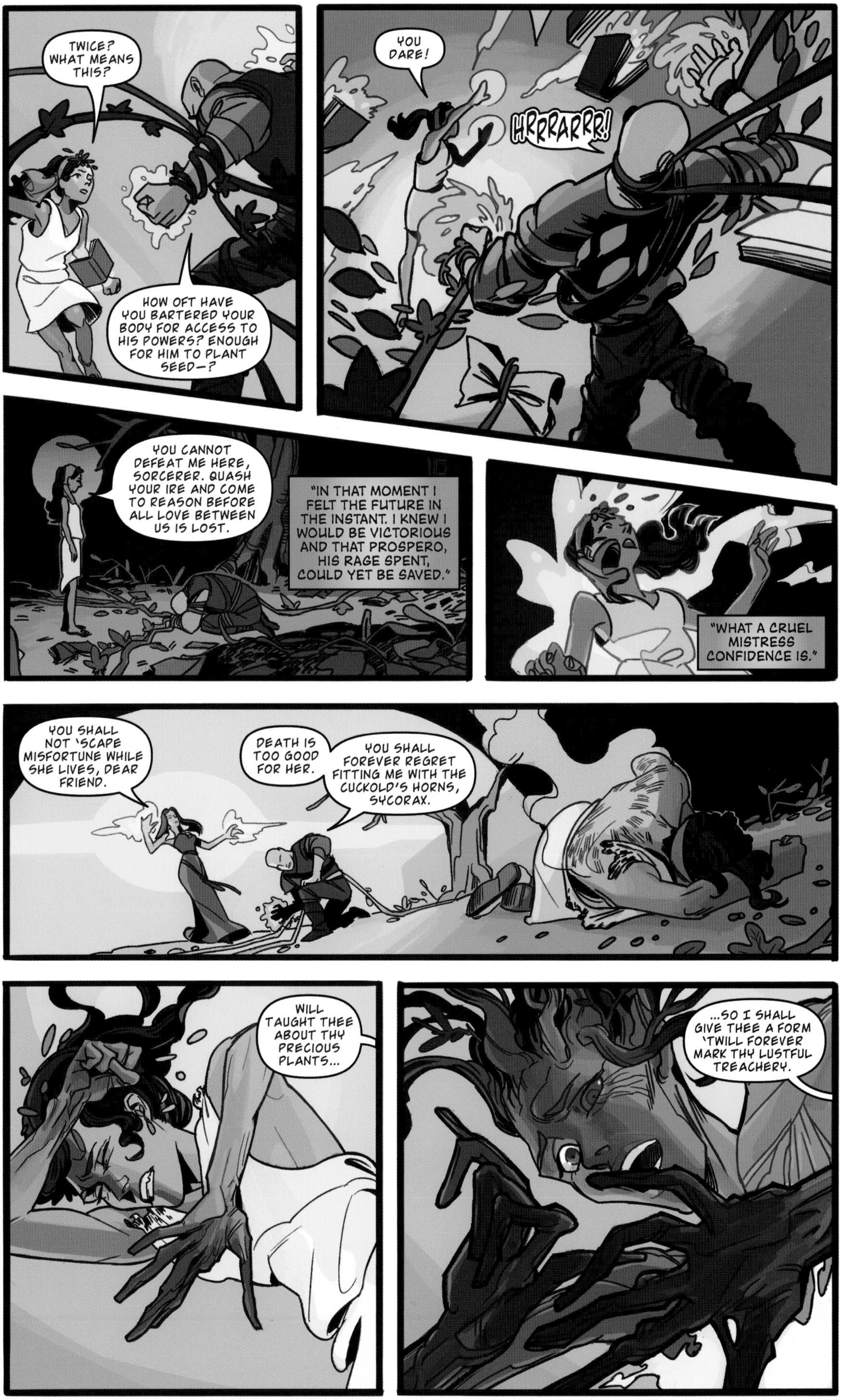

TWICE? WHAT MEANS THIS?
HOW OFT HAVE YOU BARTERED YOUR BODY FOR ACCESS TO HIS POWERS? ENOUGH FOR HIM TO PLANT SEED—?
YOU DARE!
HRRRARRR!
YOU CANNOT DEFEAT ME HERE, SORCERER. QUASH YOUR IRE AND COME TO REASON BEFORE ALL LOVE BETWEEN US IS LOST.
"IN THAT MOMENT I FELT THE FUTURE IN THE INSTANT. I KNEW I WOULD BE VICTORIOUS AND THAT PROSPERO, HIS RAGE SPENT, COULD YET BE SAVED."
"WHAT A CRUEL MISTRESS CONFIDENCE IS."
YOU SHALL NOT 'SCAPE MISFORTUNE WHILE SHE LIVES, DEAR FRIEND.
DEATH IS TOO GOOD FOR HER.
YOU SHALL FOREVER REGRET FITTING ME WITH THE CUCKOLD'S HORNS, SYCORAX.
WILL TAUGHT THEE ABOUT THY PRECIOUS PLANTS...
...SO I SHALL GIVE THEE A FORM 'TWILL FOREVER MARK THY LUSTFUL TREACHERY.

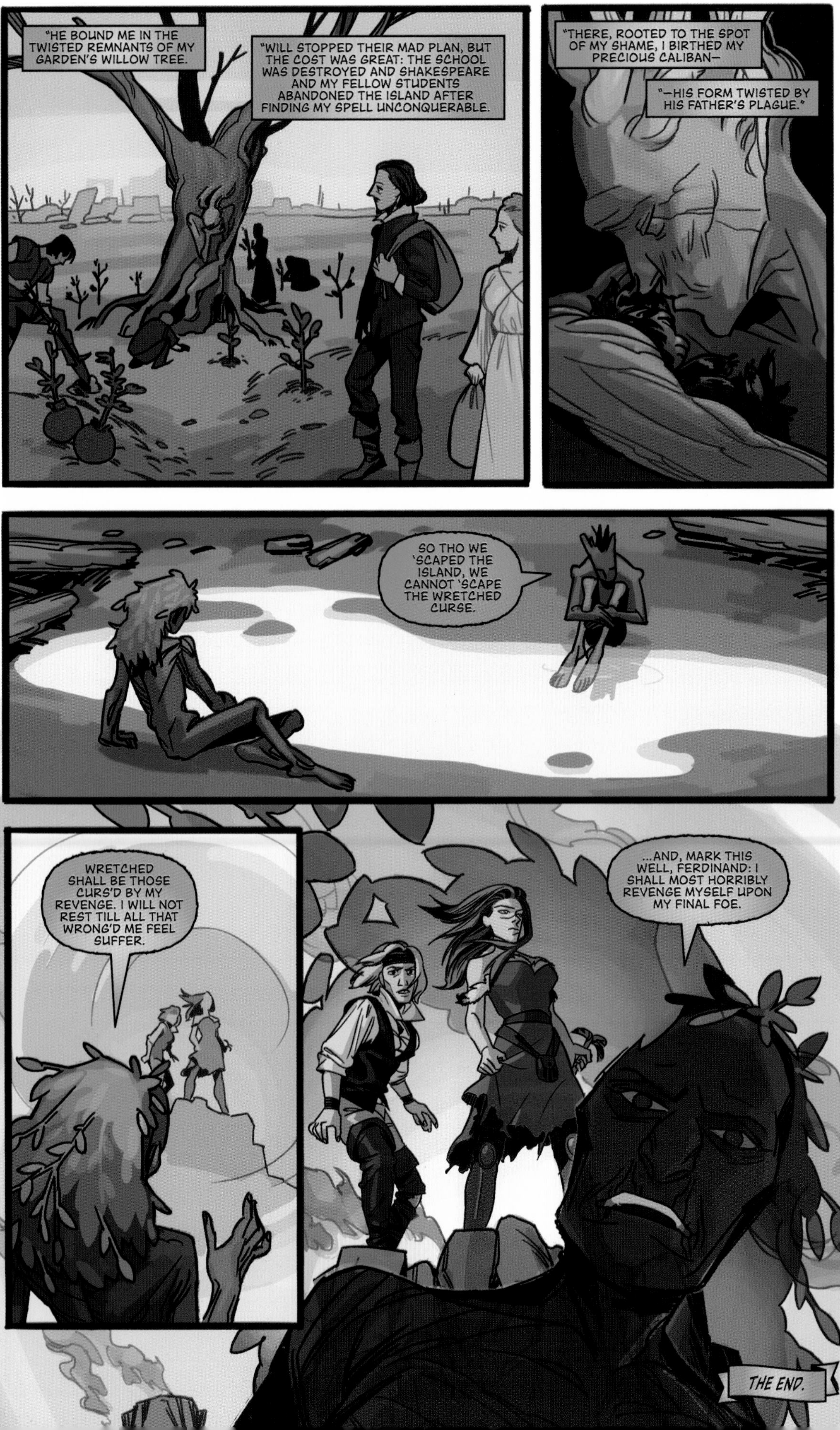
"HE BOUND ME IN THE TWISTED REMNANTS OF MY GARDEN'S WILLOW TREE.
"WILL STOPPED THEIR MAD PLAN, BUT THE COST WAS GREAT: THE SCHOOL WAS DESTROYED AND SHAKESPEARE AND MY FELLOW STUDENTS ABANDONED THE ISLAND AFTER FINDING MY SPELL UNCONQUERABLE.
"THERE, ROOTED TO THE SPOT OF MY SHAME, I BIRTHED MY PRECIOUS CALIBAN—
"—HIS FORM TWISTED BY HIS FATHER'S PLAGUE."
SO THO WE 'SCAPED THE ISLAND, WE CANNOT 'SCAPE THE WRETCHED CURSE.
WRETCHED SHALL BE THOSE CURS'D BY MY REVENGE. I WILL NOT REST TILL ALL THAT WRONG'D ME FEEL SUFFER.
...AND, MARK THIS WELL, FERDINAND: I SHALL MOST HORRIBLY REVENGE MYSELF UPON MY FINAL FOE.
THE END.

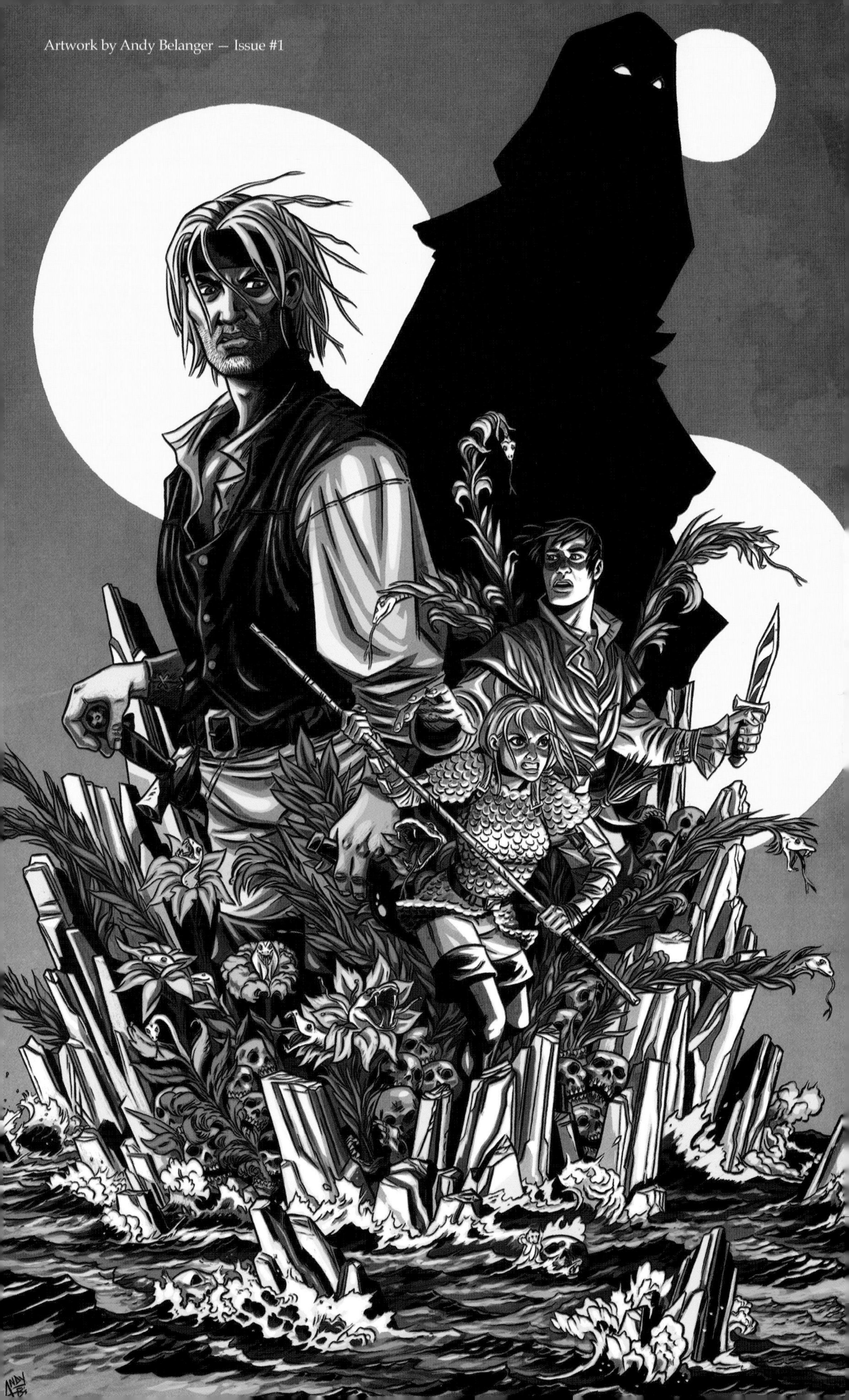

Artwork by Andy Belanger — Issue #1

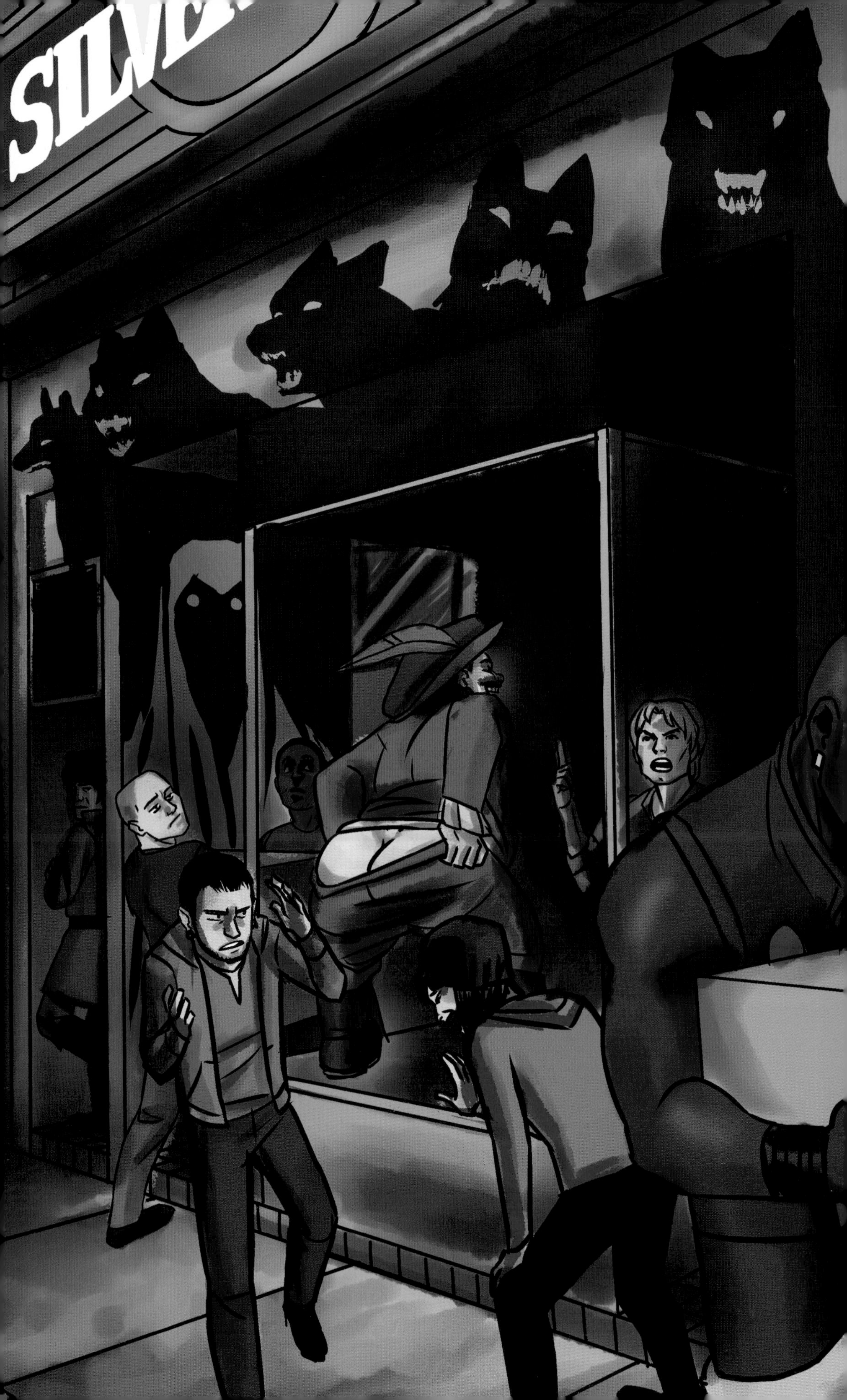
SILV

Artwork by Maya Nord – Silver Snail Exclusive cover – Issue #1

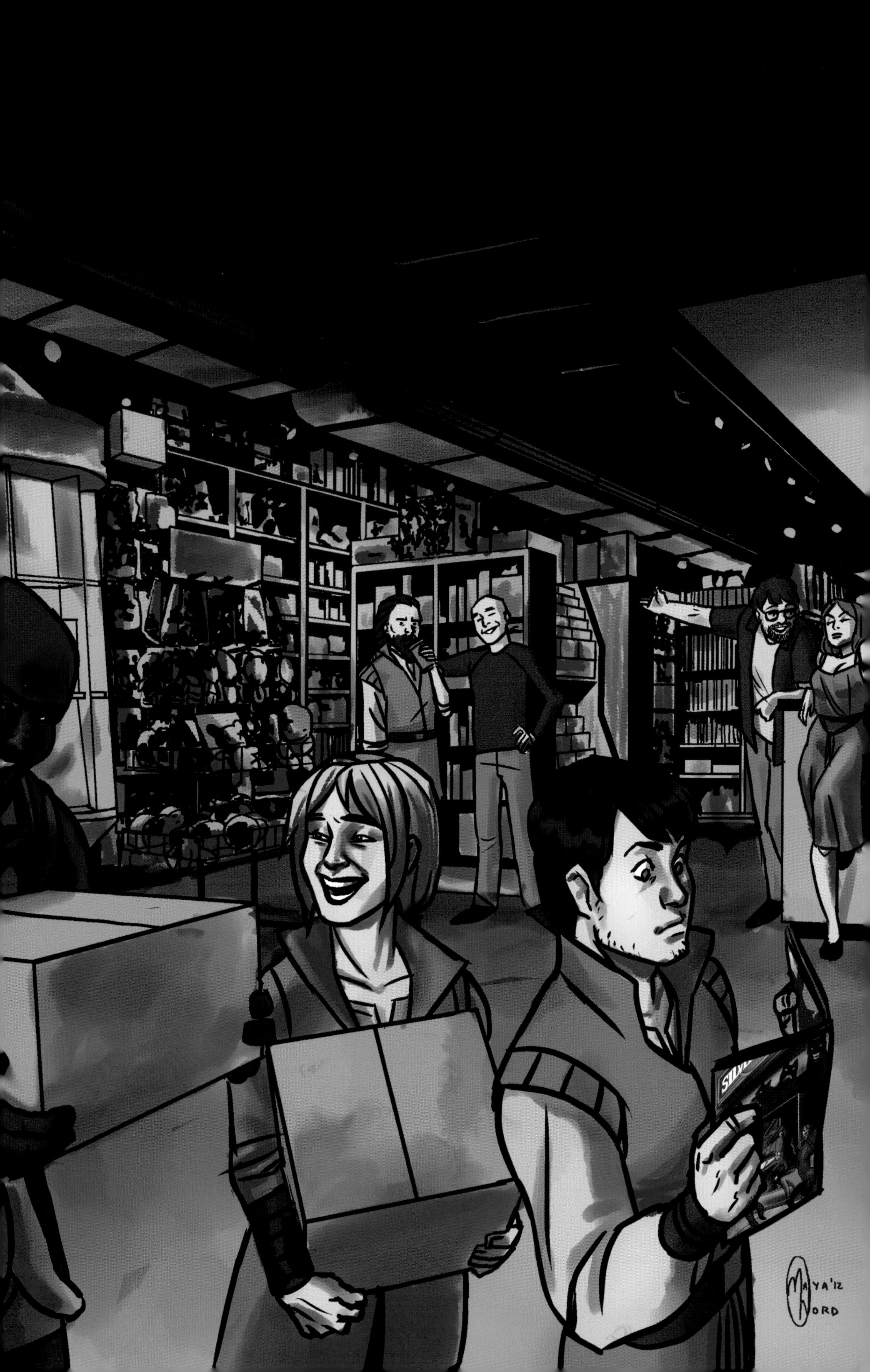
Maya'12 Nord

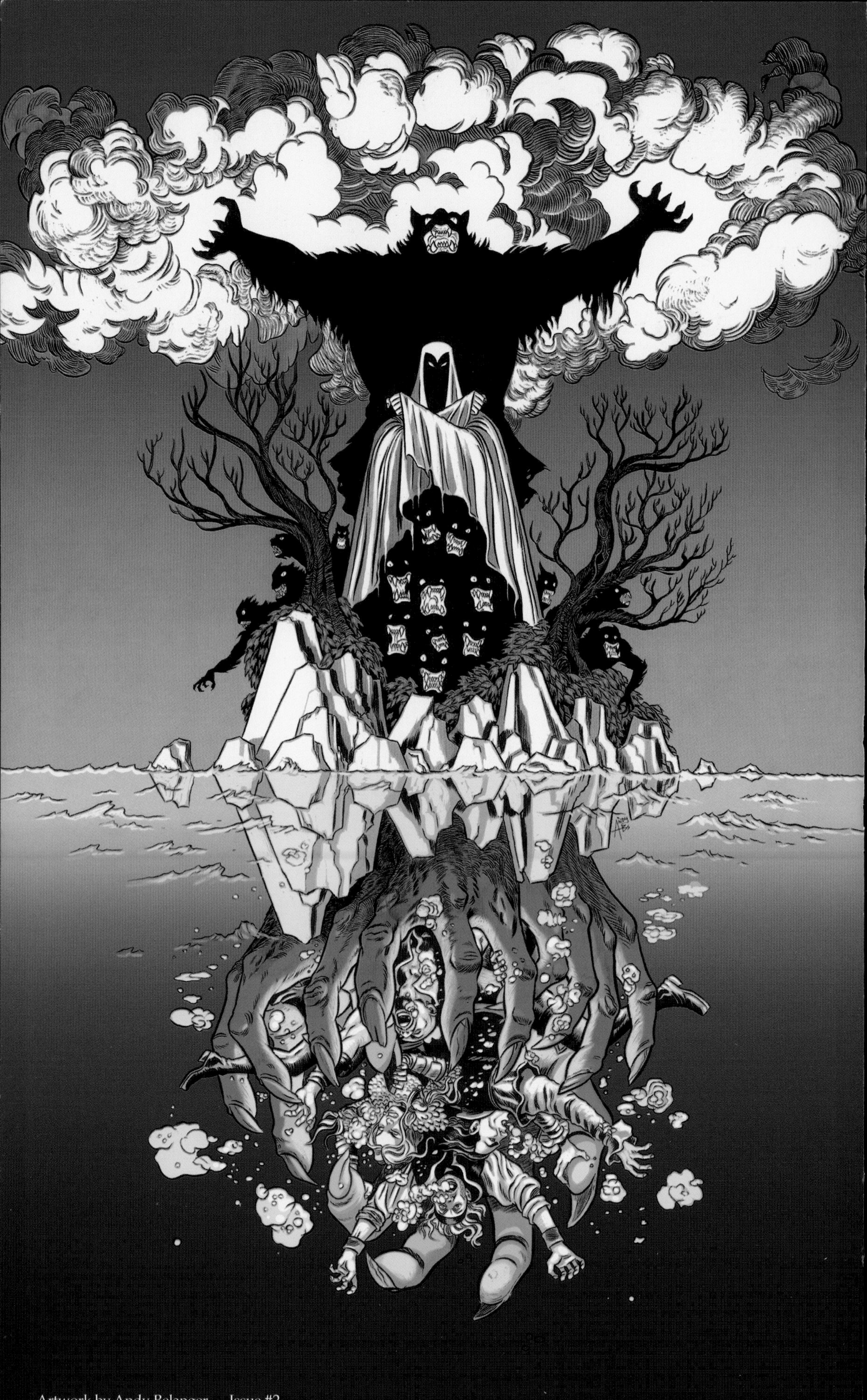

Artwork by Andy Belanger — Issue #2

Artwork by Andy Belanger – Issue #3

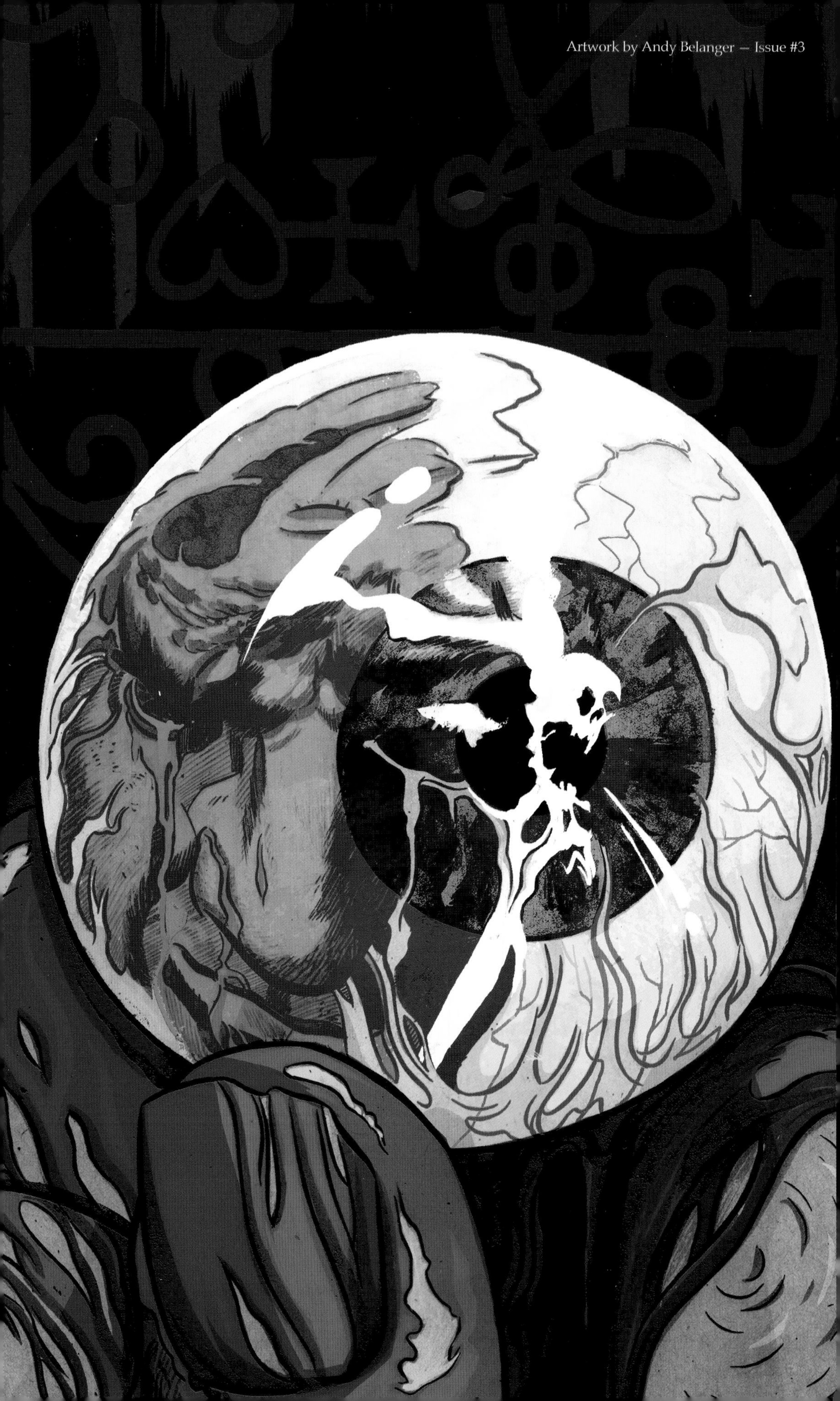

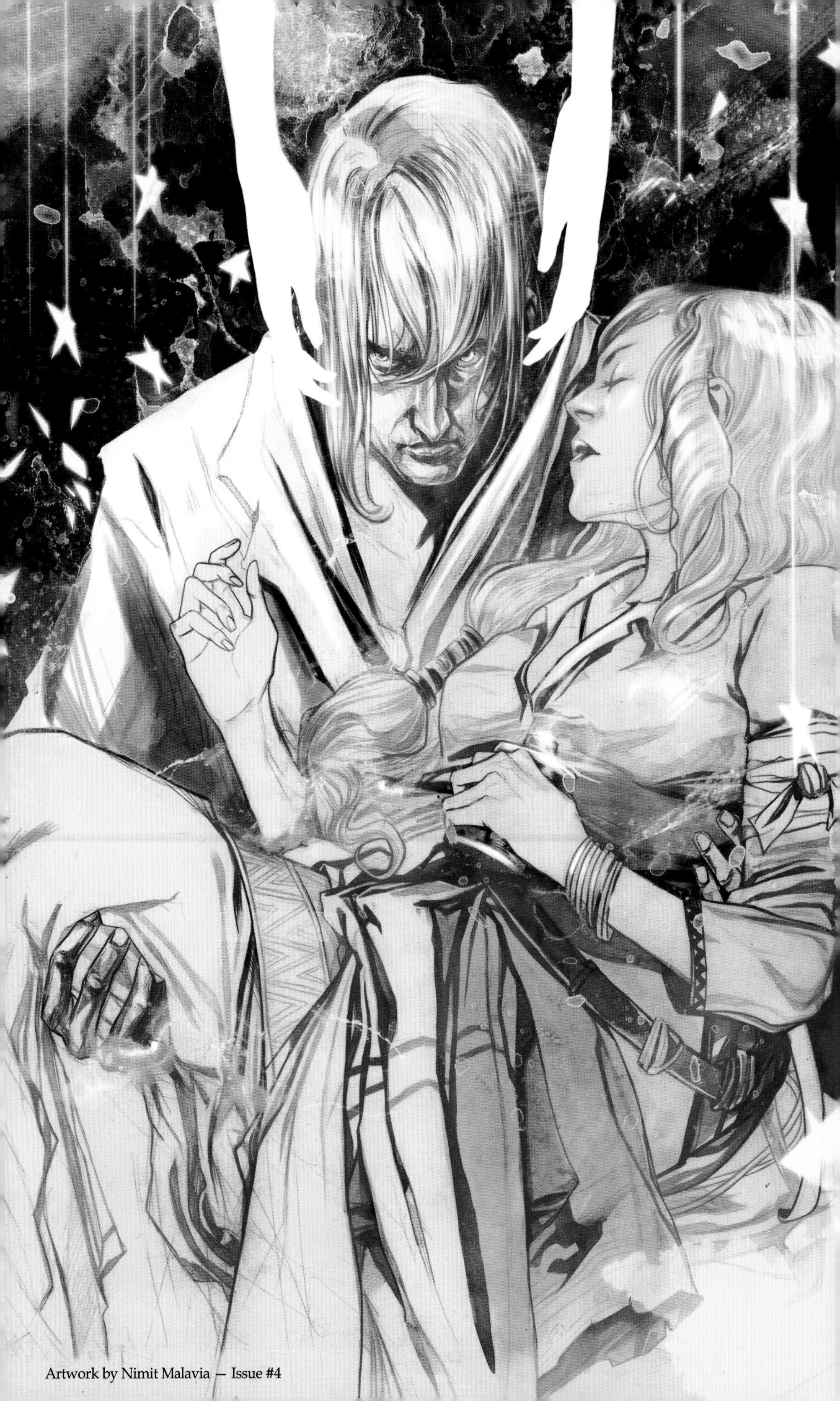

Artwork by Nimit Malavia — Issue #4

Artwork by Simon Davis — Issue #5

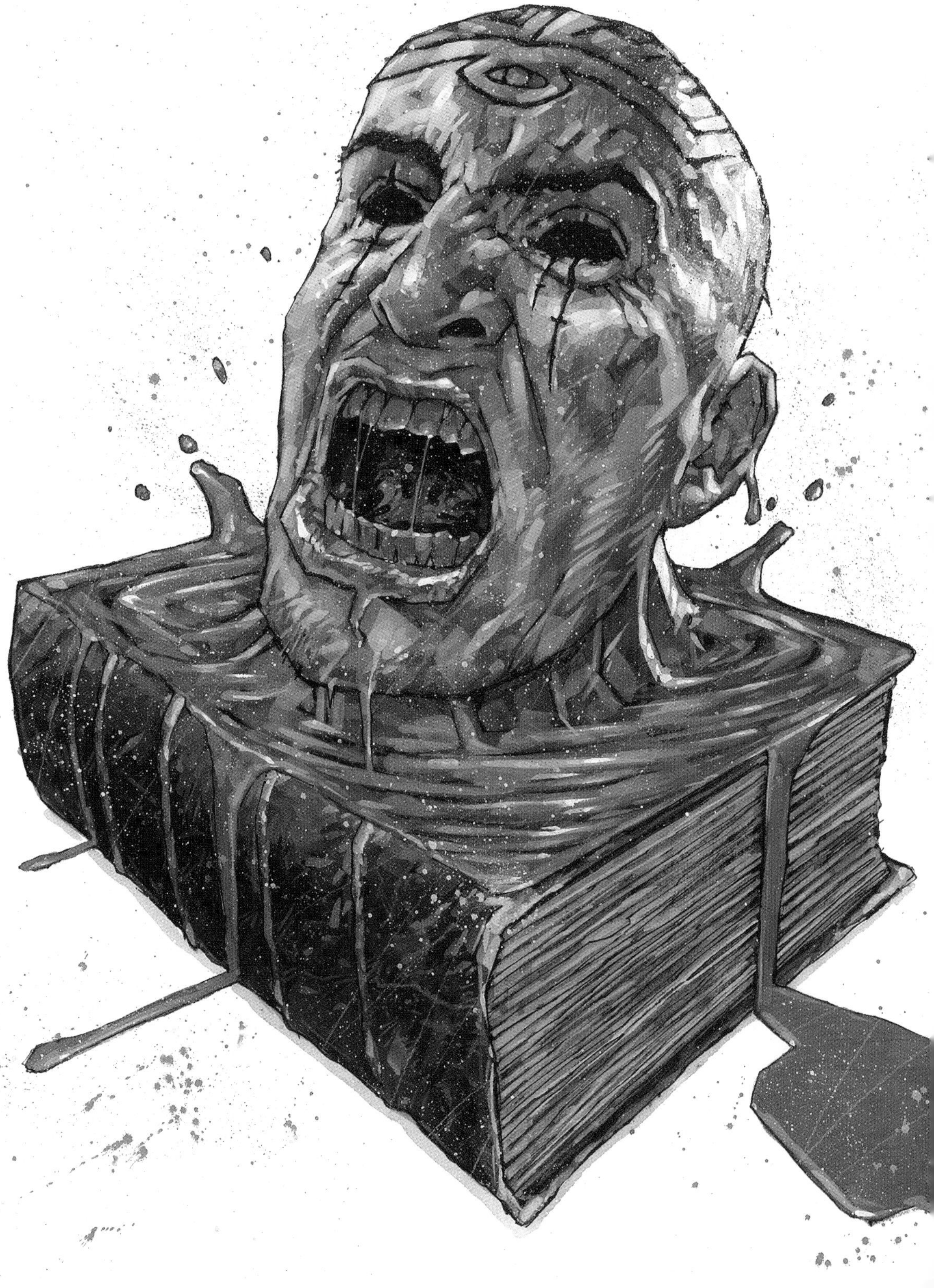

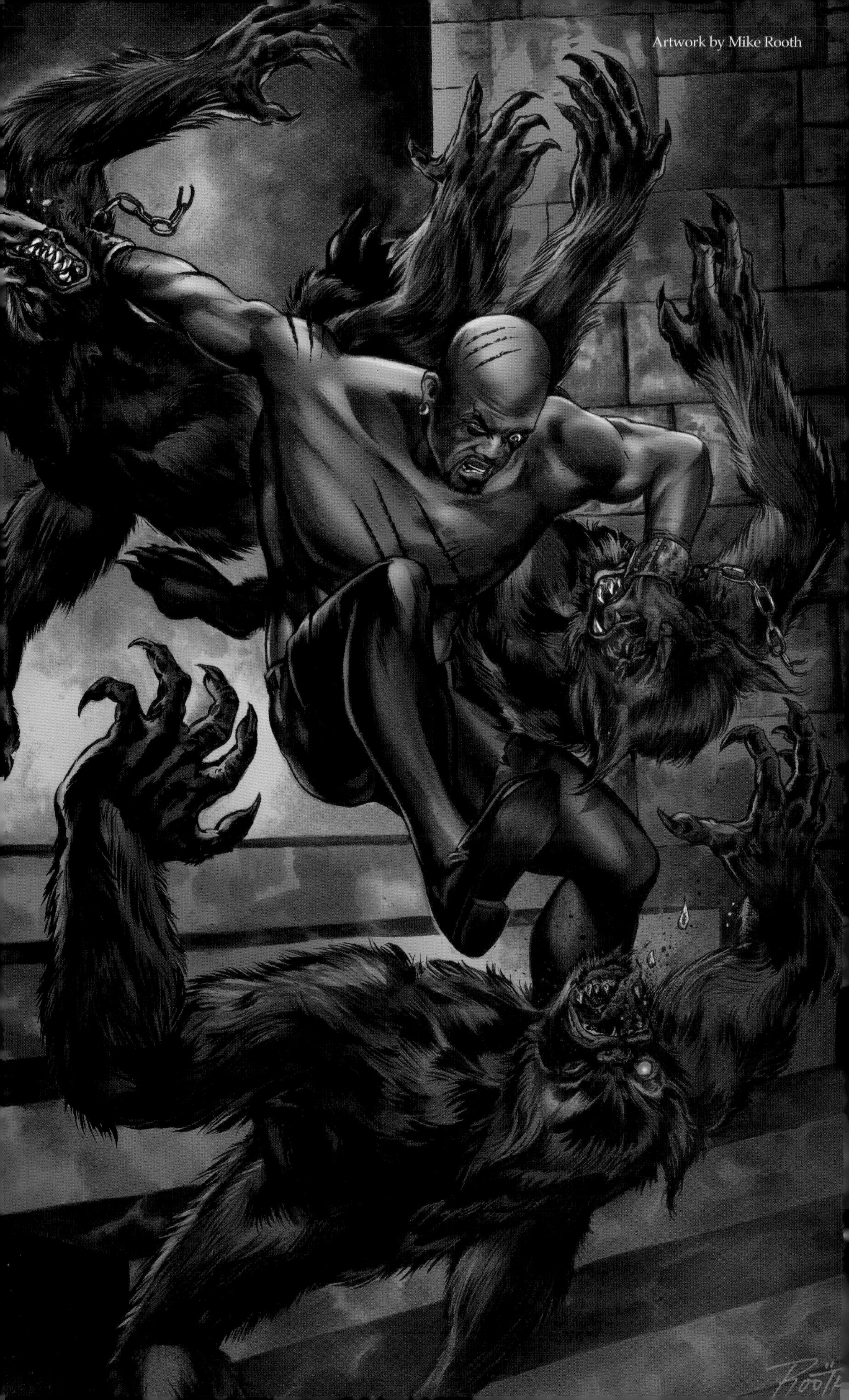

Artwork by Mike Rooth

GIBSON QUARTER!

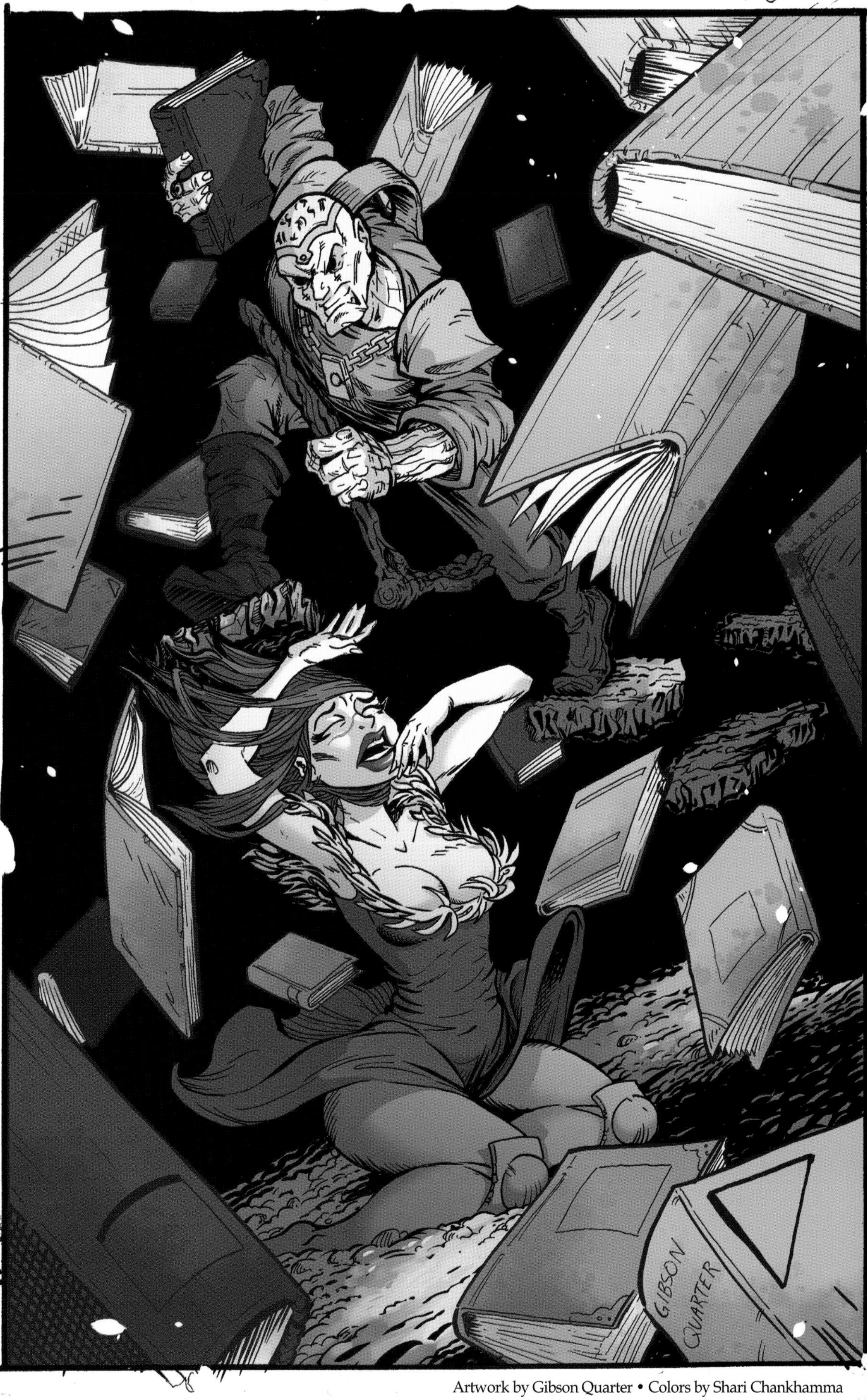
GIBSON QUARTER

Artwork by Gibson Quarter • Colors by Shari Chankhamma

CHARACTER SKETCHES BY

Andy Belanger

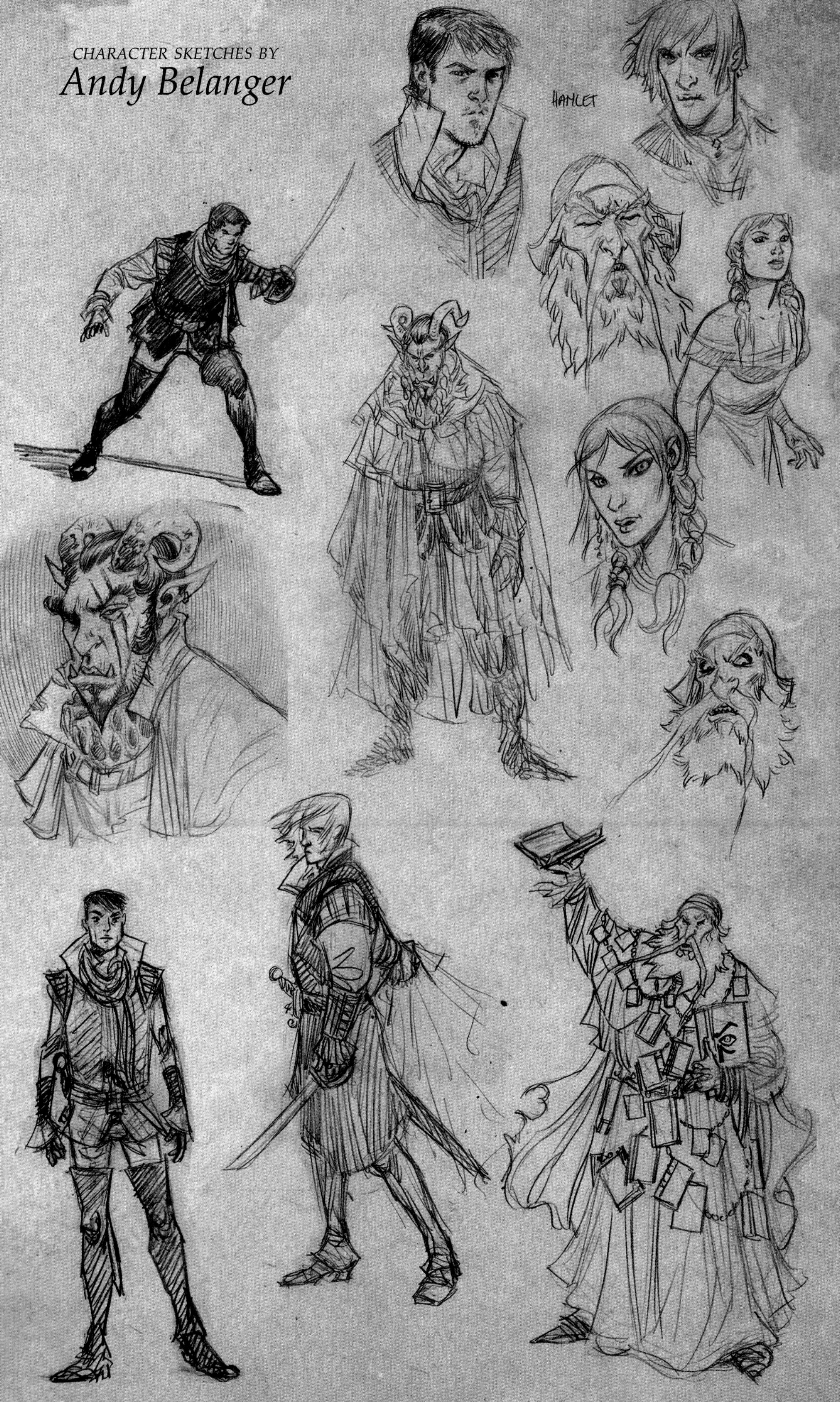
HAMLET

CREATOR BIOS

ANTHONY DEL COL (CO-CREATOR / CO-WRITER)

Prior to embarking on this epic quest to bash the Bard, Toronto-based Anthony successfully completed journeys in the film (producer of two independent feature films), music (served as a manager for international pop star Nelly Furtado), and television landscapes.

CONOR MCCREERY (CO-CREATOR / CO-WRITER)

Conor has spent most of his career in film, television, and journalism. He's covered everything from the NBA, to stock-market apocalypses, with a little dash of celebrity gossip for (questionable) taste. *Kill Shakespeare* is his first comic. He lives in Toronto with his wife Crystal and daughter Peregrine.

ANDY B. (ARTIST AND COVERS)

Andy is a comic artist and commercial illustrator working out of the Montreal-based Studio Lounak. He has worked on D.C.'s *Swamp Thing* as well as other projects with Marvel, Wildstorm, and Boom!. He is the creator of Zuda Comics' *Bottle of Awesome* and also self-publishes the awesomely gonzo medieval horror comic *Black Church*.

SHARI CHANKHAMMA (COLOURS)

Shari hails from Thailand. She previously worked on creator-owned titles such as *The Sisters' Luck, The Clarence Principle, Pavlov's Dream,* and short stories in various anthologies. When there's spare time, she enjoys wasting it on casual games and romance novels.

SIMON DAVIS (COVERS)

Born in the Bard's hometown of Stratford-Upon-Avon it was Simon's karmic destiny to work on *Kill Shakespeare*. The London-based artist mainly illustrates for the UK anthology title *2000 AD (Sinister Dexter, Stone Island, Ampney Crucis Investigates* and numerous covers). In the US, he has provided covers for *The Crow, DarkAge Spawn,* and *Cy-Gor*. Alongside his comic work, Simon is also an award-winning portrait painter and a member of the Royal Portrait Society.

NIMIT MALAVIA (COVERS)

Nimit Malavia is a freelance illustrator from Toronto, Canada. Clients include 20th Century Fox, DC/Vertigo Comics, Marvel Comics, Shopify, IDW Publishing, Chomu Press, *Canadian Wildlife Magazine, The National Post,* and *The Globe and Mail.* His work has been exhibited in galleries across North America and Europe, including Gallery Nucleus, Spoke Art Gallery, Bold Hype Gallery, Thinkspace Gallery, AQUA Art Fair in Art Basel, LeBasse Projects, Gallery 1988, London Miles Gallery, and Show & Tell Gallery. Find him at www.nimitmalavia.com.